# FRANKLIN COUNTY

## VIRGINIA

# A HISTORY

by

## MARSHALL WINGFIELD

CLEARFIELD

Originally published
Berryville, Virginia, 1964

Reprinted for
Clearfield Company, Inc. by
Genealogical Publishing Co., Inc.
Baltimore, Maryland
1996, 2003

International Standard Book Number: 0-8063-4617-5

*Made in the United States of America*

CONTENTS

# ACKNOWLEDGMENTS

Grateful acknowledgment for assistance and for encouragement is made to J. E. Jamison, W. P. Campbell and F. A. Dillon; to Boutwell Dunlap; and to Mrs. Eliza Pinckard Pearson and Mrs. Elizabeth Brodie Lester.

Also to T. W. Carper, Edwin Greer, Mrs. Blanche Garrett Gillispie, J. N. Montgomery, Jr., Harold W. Ramsey, A. G. Fralin, and B. A. Davis. Also to Mr. and Mrs. J. B. Allman, Dr. and Mrs. O. T. Kittinger, Arthur Davis, Carroll C. Brodie, Arthur Bernard, Dr. W. T. Chitwood, Mrs. Mary Carper Willis, Mrs. Lucy Nelson Price, Mrs. J. R. Foster, D. Henry Davis, N. B. Hutcherson, Judge Abram H. Hopkins, Mrs. Viola Love Dudley, W. C. Brown and C. C. Lee. Also to the following ministers: W. L. King, W. C. Clark, J. T. Cassell, G. McLaren Brydon, W. G. Bates, B. M. Beckham, G. T. Kesler, B. E. Kesler, J. A. Naff, R. B. Montgomery, C. J. Hollandsworth, Roy Smith, Clifford Ramsey, J. E. Poteet, G. E. Powell, J. W. Wade, L. G. Tinnell, Edward Frantz, G. W. Amos and J. B. Lavinder.

Also to Mrs. Annie Price Ker, Miss Mary R. Cockran, Dr. E. G. Swem, Dr. H. R. McIlwaine, Col. Walter Lee Hopkins, T. F. Montgomery, Prof. William T. Laprade, R. Page Laprade, E. D. Naff, B. C. Goode, R. E. L. Fralin, Mrs. C. Wildman Hubbard, P. W. Lynch, Mrs. Mary R. B. Mullins, Claud B. Nolen, Miss Mary Cooper, Mrs. J. W. Farrell, Miss Sarah Dinwiddie, Mrs. Cassie Bernard Cooper, Mrs. Sallie Cook Booker, R. L. Milliron, Wilson Mills, Mrs. Maude H. Beckham, Prof. A. E. Akers, Mrs. Temple Hall Brown, H. E. Boone, Mrs. W. H. Buckner, Miss Ida Gilliam Gilchrist, Mrs. Essie Wade Smith, Prof. C. J. Payne, Miss E. Ruth Pyrtle, Mrs. Minnie B. Smith, Mrs. Virginia Dudley Walker, A. W. Robbins and Pedro T. Slone. Also to Dr. L. G. Pedigo, Dr. R. R. Lee, Judge A. L. Duncan, Dr. S. S. Guerrant, John W. Hancock and to many others.

Also to my nephew, Herman Craig.

And, finally, to my wife, Marie Gregson Wingfield, a musician and an artist, who mastered the typewriter so as to be able to reduce to typescript my thousand and one pencil notes.

MARSHALL WINGFIELD

# FOREWORD

A generation ago, Dr. Marshall Wingfield completed the writing of the history of his native Franklin County.

However, not enough advance subscriptions could be secured to make its publication a financial success, and the manuscript, upon which Dr. Wingfield had worked for more than a decade, was laid away with regret.

Thereafter, Dr. Wingfield published The Marriage Bonds of Franklin County (1939), and An Old Virginia Court, Being a Transcript of the Records of the First Court of Franklin County, Virginia, 1786-1789. With Biographies of the Justices and Stories of Famous Cases (1948).

Then, several years after Dr. Wingfield's death, Chesapeake Book Company of Berryville, Virginia, undertook the task of publishing the manuscript, and in 1964, the genealogical portions of the manuscript appeared under the title of Pioneer Families of Franklin County, Virginia.

I wish this volume and Pioneer Families of Franklin County, Virginia to be memorials to Dr. Wingfield.

MARIE GREGSON WINGFIELD

## DR. MARSHALL WINGFIELD

Born in Franklin County, Virginia, February 19, 1893, Marshall Wingfield, D.D., Litt. D., was the oldest of the twelve children of Tazewell Tarleton and Mary (Motley) Wingfield. His widow, Marie Gregson, is a daughter of the late James C. and Gertrude (Hoagland) Gregson of Cincinnati. Her twin sister, Anita Gregson, retired in 1960, after thirty-six years as a Presbyterian missionary in India and Pakistan. Mrs. Wingfield is an ordained minister. She lives at 233 South Watkins Street, Memphis.

Dr. Wingfield's formal education was often interrupted by illness, yet he completed the usual studies, and gained recognition in the most scholarly circles. Tutored, during a long illness, by his physician, Dr. R. N. Younger, he matriculated, in 1910 in Johnson Bible College near Knoxville, Tennessee.

Illness struck Dr. Wingfield again at the end of 1912, and a stay in New Mexico was prescribed, but even there his studies were continued by unusual help from the New Mexico Military Institute in Roswell. After recovery, and an interim ministry, he entered Texas Christian University's Brite College of the Bible for his seminary studies.

Refresher courses in Dr. Wingfield's earlier years included four summers in Union Theological Seminary, New York, four spring sessions in Vanderbilt University, and two summers in the University of Chicago. The degree of Doctor of Divinity was conferred upon Dr. Wingfield by Lincoln Memorial University of Tennessee in 1947, and the degree of Doctor of Literature was conferred on him by Erskine College of South Carolina in 1951. As critic-judge for Pacific Forensic Conference, Dr. Wingfield served in debates at the University of Idaho and Washington State College, 1927-30; he was trustee of Southern Union College, 1953-7; and he has given baccalaureate sermons and commencement addresses in many colleges and universities.

Ordained a minister of the Christian Church, November 10, 1912; pastorates in Virginia, Idaho and Mississippi; First Congregational Church of Memphis, 1937 to retirement in 1958; delegate, World Christian Endeavor Convention, London 1926; president, State Convention Christian Churches in Mississippi, 1936; interchange preacher between England and United States 1926, 1927 and 1930; co-founder, Institute of Religious Education at University of Idaho, 1929; director, Seminary Foundation of Vanderbilt University, 1946-9; moderator, Kentucky-Tennessee Conference of Congregational Churches, 1939-40; corporate member, American Board of Commissioners for Foreign Missions, 1940-2; president, Memphis Ministers Association (All denominations), 1943-4; delegate, Federal Council of Churches' Study Conferences on Just and Durable Peace, Delaware, Ohio, 1942, and Cleveland, 1945; visited United States military installations with priests and rabbis, speaking for inter-group understanding, 1945; delegate, Congregational General Councils, 1940 and 1952, and to 6th International Congregational Council, 1949; preacher for inter-denominational union church services in Boston six weeks of summer, 1947; president, Memphis Council of Churches, 1946-7, and 1953-9; inaugurated and conducted radio (WMPS) program of religious news: delegate, Constituting Convention National Council of Churches, Cleveland, Ohio, 1950; preacher for the American Church in Paris, April 1951; supply minister in Portland and Hawaii, 1958; and interim pastor, First Congregational Church, Portland, Oregon, 1959. Most interesting assignment; preaching for the Nez Perce Indians of Idaho, through an interpreter, August 16, 1936.

Dr. Wingfield was author of the following books:

A History of Caroline County, Virginia (1924)

Forces of Destiny (1932)

Translating Christmas and Other Poems (1933)

Nostalgia and Other Poems (1937)

Hills of Home (1938)

The Marriage Bonds of Franklin County, Virginia (1939)

The Deathless Preacher (1942)

Literary Memphis (1942)

The Shrine in a Temple (1943)

Boston Sermons (1947)

An Old Virginia Court (1948)

The Life and Letters of General A. P. Stewart (1954)

Strangers First (1958)

Leila Scott's Century (1960)

The Gentle Pilgrim (1962)

The Singing Spirit (1963)

Pioneer Families of Franklin County, Virginia (1964)

Dr. Wingfield co-authored or made a contribution to the Following books:

History of Henry County, Virginia (with J.P.A. Hill) (1925)

American Poetry Anthology (1927)

Windows and Wings (1928)

Harmony of Voice Methods (1931)

Washington Sermons (1932)

Christmas Lyrics (1936)

American States Anthology (1936)

Year Book of Contemporary Poetry (1936)

American Voices (1936)

American Lyric Poetry (1936)

The Crown Anthology of Verse (1937)

The World's Fair Anthology of Verse (1938)

Strength for Service (1942)

Worship Highways (1943)

A list of Dr. Wingfield's writings, prepared in 1951, when Erskine College conferred upon him the degree of Doctor of Literature, recorded nearly one hundred other items, including monographs, magazine articles and introductions to the books of other authors. Other literary activities included the initiation, on February 22, 1941, of a radio (WMC) program, "The Voice of Books", and the review of a book every week. Dr. Wingfield also served as mid-South correspondent of the The Christian Century, 1940-59, and of the Religious News Service 1943-60.

Dr. Wingfield's address on George Washington was published in volume of thirty-four prize-winning sermons by the George Washington Bicentennial Commission in 1932. He gave the dedicatory address, June 3, 1941, when Beauvoir was set apart as a Southern Shrine; he was lecturer for the World Affairs Forum, University of Tennessee, 1942; he received the Pro Bono Publico award for promoting inter-group understanding in Memphis, 1944; he gave the address in Biloxi, Mississippi, dedicating the Jefferson Davis Highway, June 3, 1945; his lecture "Atomic Fission Tomorrow" given before the Daughters of the Confederacy in Arkansas was read into the Congressional Record, December 13, 1945; a Memphis thoroughfare was named Wingfield Road in his honor, 1946; he was appointed member of the Second National UNESCO Conference in Cleveland 1949, and his address at this conference was published in Liberty Quarterly, Vol. 44, No. 3, 1949; his address, May 23, 1949, dedicating Booker T. Washington's birthplace as a Virginia shrine, was published in Vital Speeches of the Day, June 15, 1949; his lecture on R. E. Lee, Memphis, January 19, 1953, was published in Vital Speeches of the Day, February 15, 1953; he was given a city-wide testimonial dinner in 1952 in recognition of his ministry of reconciliation in Memphis; he was a member of President's Committee for Traffic Safety; and he was a delegate to the Southern Regional Traffic Safety Conference, 1958 .

On the service of his grandfather, Pinckney Greene
Wingfield, Tenth Virginia Cavalry, C.S.A., Dr. Wingfield joined
the Sons of Confederate Veterans at an early date, serving as
camp commander and as State commander in both Mississippi and
Tennessee, as chaplain-in-chief, as historian-in-chief, and as
commander-in-chief. He was a Sponsor for the restoration of
Stratford, 1935; and he was awarded the Distinguished Service
Medal by the S.C.V., 1938. He was commissioned a member of
staff of J.N. McCord, Governor of Tennessee, 1945 (a.d.c. with
rank of Colonel); he was on the staff of Gen. J. W. Moore, 1950
(a.d.c. with rank of Colonel); and he was on the staff of Gen.
J. F. Howell, with rank of Colonel. His Memorial Day address
delivered in the Amphitheatre of Arlington National Cemetary,
1947, was read into the Congressional Record June 24, 1964; he
was speaker in Elmira, N.Y., June 6, 1946, at the first locally
sponsored meeting ever held in the North honoring Confederate
dead; and his addresses in 1948, 1950 and 1951, to the cadets
of the Flight Training Course, Naval Air Station, Pensacola, were
published, with introduction by Adm. J. W. Reeves. He was chaplain of the Civil Air Patrol of United States Air Force, 1956,
with rank of Lieutenant Colonel. He received the annual citizen-
ship award from Post 684, Veterans of Foreign Wars, April 4,
1956.

## Social Service Connections

Co-founder, Gailor Hall Home for Boys in 1939, and
board chairman, 1941-7; co-founder and first secretary, Memphis
Interracial Commission May 5, 1940; member, national panel of
American Arbitration Association since 1942; life member boards
of the Y.M.C.A., and of the Salvation Army in Memphis; member,
Community Fund Council; director, Memphis branch of the American
Cancer Society; founder, Memphis Round Table, 1944; member,
Memphis Council of Social Workers, and president, 1944-5;
organizer and first chairman, Memphis unit, American Christian
Palestine Committee, March 1947.

## Fraternities

Member of the Alpha Epsilon Chapter, Kappa Alpha, Memphis; frequent convicium speaker and author of the Lee section
in the current Pledge Manuel; and holder of all Masonic degrees
in both Scottish and York Rites, including the honorary Thirty-
third degree and Red Cross of Constantine. Wise Master, Calvary
Chapter, Knights Rose Croix 1950-1; Master, Memphis Masonic
Veterans Association, 1950; chaplain, Al Chymia Temple, A.A.O.

N.M.S., 1938-48; chaplain, Imperial Council of the Shrine, 1955; and chaplain, Grand Lodge (F. & A.M.) of Tennessee, 1955. As proxy of Grand Master R.L. Allen, who was ill, Dr. Wingfield laid the cornerstone of the temple of McLemore Avenue Lodge, No. 715, on December 30, 1954.

## Historical Interests

President, Monroe County (Miss.) Historical Society, 1931-6, president, West Tennessee Historical Society since 1937; member, Tennessee Historical Commission since 1939, and of its executive committee since 1941; Ninth District (Tenn.) representative in Southwest Territory Commission, 1940; and member, Tennessee Civil War Centennial Commission, 1959.

## Travels

Led study groups through Europe in 1926, 1927, 1930, and a study group through Alaska in 1928; and member of the American Christian Palestine Commission's study group which traveled in and reported on conditions in the Middle East in 1951.

## Clubs

The Tennessee; The Egyptians, president 1955-6; The Cross-cut, president 1941 and 1955; The Executives; Sertoma, president 1945-6; Gavel; and Agricultural.

## Other Biographical Sketches

All editions of Who's Who in America since 1938; Who's Who in the Churches (1929); Who's Who in the Clergy (1935); Biographical Encyclopedia of America (1940); Biographical Encyclopedia of the World (1940); Religious Leaders of America (1941); American Authors and Books, 1640-1940 (1943); The Southerner (1945); World Biography (1948); and Who's Who in the South and Southwest (1952). Listed as an authority on R. E. Lee in Who Knows and What, (1949).

Dr. Wingfield died on May 7, 1961.

# Chapter 1

## PRE-SETTLEMENT ERA

The area with which this history deals has been known to white men for nearly three centuries. J. F. D. Smyth in his "A Tour of the United States of America" says that in the 1780's many buffaloes roamed the hills of what is now Franklin County. The early settlers made their roads in the trails these animals used in crossing the hills between their feeding-grounds and watering-places. One such path is named in connection with Chestnut Creek in Franklin. A gap in the Blue Ridge in Franklin County was called Buffalo Gap. There were also "buffalo beds", "buffalo camps", "buffalo rowls" (rolls), "buffalo fords" and "buffalo licks". These licks are mentioned in connection with Pigg River and Chestnut Creek in Franklin. The licks were where the earth was impregnated with salt, and were usually natural treeless openings, covered with grass. They were frequented by deer, elk and other animals.

Bears were numerous, and surveyors frequently refer to trees which were felled in connection with catching them. The surveyors refer to "bear-gardens", "beaver-ponds", "elk-shoals", "goose-ponds" and "wolf-dens". Wolves were so numerous that Franklin paid a bounty on them as late as 1800. Wild turkeys were plentiful, and gave their name to such places as Turkey Bottom on Pigg River and Turkey Cock Mountain in Franklin.

John Lederer explored in 1670 the area now embraced in Franklin County.

Louis Michel explored the same area in 1702. He states that the Indians would fire the woods in a large circle and so drive the game to a small center where it could be easily killed. This firing so cleared the woods of brush that one could ride through the forest without difficulty.

Colonel William Byrd came to this area in 1728, as a member of the Commission which surveyed the line between Virginia and North Carolina. In his "History of the Dividing Line", he tells of a stream which they named the Dan River. He refers to the mountains to the northwest which seemed like blue clouds piled one above the other. Bears were feeding on wild grapes. Wild geese were arriving from the north. He shows that the War Trail of the Iroquois must have crossed what is now Franklin County. Over this the Indians traveled when they came down to make war with southern tribes. Byrd, too, says the woods had little brush because of the Indians' fire-hunting. He refers to the bear, deer and wild turkeys on which the surveying party feasted. Streams were named in honor of the two surveyors, William Mayo and Alexander Irwin. Irwin River now bears the name Smith River. Banister River was named for John Banister, a member of the Byrd party.

A second trip to this area was made by Colonel Byrd in 1733, during which time he visited a pioneer named Aaron Pinston on Tewahominy River, now called Aaron's Creek. Byrd refers to a buffalo which the party killed on this expedition. He also tells of a protected area where a sweet grass grew, and a kind of pea that remained green all winter. These grew so luxuriously that horses kept themselves.

The country described by Lederer, Michel and Byrd was for many years the paradise of the "long hunters". There were few settlers in the Franklin area prior to 1750. The rapid settlement of the mid-eighteenth century drove the game further into the wilderness, and the "long hunters" pushed on toward what is now Kentucky and Tennessee. They usually left home when crops were gathered and returned for planting time in the spring. They traveled in small groups so as not to excite the hostility of the Indians who coveted the game and pelts for themselves. Each "long hunter" was equipped with guns, traps, repairing tools, ammunition and two horses. A good hunter would take from a thousand to five thousand dollars worth of pelts in a season.

Many traces of Indian occupancy have been discovered within the county. The author of this volume, when a lad, had a half gallon fruit jar nearly full of arrow heads he had picked up in the corn and tobacco fields.

2

# Chapter 2

## ORIGIN AND ESTABLISHMENT

As early as 1779, the inhabitants of Bedford County living on the south side of the Staunton River began to petition the Virginia Legislature for a new county. In a petition dated May 24, 1779, it is set forth that a new county on the south side of the river should be formed because of the difficulty of crossing the water courses in order to reach the court house; and, further, because "many of the inhabitants of Bedford live fifty miles from the county seat". Thomas Watts, Henry Guttry, William Christopher, Peter Wood, Peter Holland, Aquila Greer and fifty-six others signed the original petition.

On the same day that the inhabitants of Bedford on the south side of the Staunton River. Petitioned for a new county, Barnabas Arthur, Jacob Irion, Lewis Irion, Benjamin Johnson, William Owen, Francis Corby and five hundred and twenty-seven other Freeholders protested against the division of the county "lest the people incur such expense for new county buildings as will constitute a burden too heavy to be borne".

On May 24, 1779, the inhabitants of Henry County joined those inhabitants of Bedford who lived on the south side of Staunton River in asking for a new county. This petition asked for a division of Henry County, "By running a line from the head of Shooting Creek to the head of Turkey Cock Creek, thence to intersect the dividing line between Henry and Pittsylvania, thence along that dividing line to the mouth of Blackwater River, which part of Henry contains about three hundred freeholders. Further, your petitioners pray that that part of Bedford which lieth on the south side of the Staunton River may be cut off and added to them, which proposal your petitioners are informed is much desired by those inhabitants of Bedford who reside on the south side of the Staunton". There are nearly five hundred signatures to this petition.

On May 28, 1779, a petition signed by Will Tunstall, John Salmon, E. Lyne, Mordecai Hord, Henry Lyne, William Gardner and Waters Dunn remonstrated against dividing the county, and asked that "Edmund Winston, Paul Carrington, John Wilson and Benjamin Lankford, esquires, Gentlemen having no connections, no property or concerns in this county, may be called upon to be examined concerning the premises".

On November 2, 1779, another petition was presented to the General Assembly by nearly three hundred citizens of Henry

3

County asking for a division of the county along lines similar to those named in the petition of May 24, 1779.

On November 9, 1779, Thomas Arthur, Thomas Doggett, William Wright, William Walton, John Underwood, William Slone and ninety-four others, living in Bedford on the south side of Staunton River, and having to go from thirty to fifty miles to reach the court house, petitioned the Legislature to add their section of the county to a part of Henry, and form a new county.

On May 23, 1780, William Martin, Brittan Scruggs, John Harris, John Starkey, Aquilla Greer, John Craghead and twenty-five others petitioned the General Assembly for a new county on the south side of the Staunton River. The petitioners declared that they have to go from thirty to sixty miles to reach the court house; that they are liable to be imposed upon by tax assessors; and, besides, that they have great difficulty in bringing grain to points indicated by law, of which there are only one or two in each county. On the same day this petition was presented, there was presented a counter petition signed by Jesse Burton, Henry Tate, Christopher Lynch, Joseph Blankenship, William Perrey, Harry Wiley and fifty-one other "freeholders" protesting against such a division. These opponents of a new county were joined by twenty-seven of their neighbors who signed a duplicate petition.

The matter of forming a new county was permitted to rest in both Bedford and Henry Counties for over a year, when the Bedford inhabitants, on November 20, 1781, took up the matter with renewed vigor. They declared that Bedford was seventy miles long and thirty-five miles wide, hence many had to travel an unreasonable distance to reach the court house, that tax assessors could not get around to perform their duties, and that the militia numbered 1700. The original petition was signed by William Armstrong, James Sharp, James King, Robert Dooley, John McClanihan and thirty-two others. There were thirteen duplicates of this petition containing 805 names. The counter petition, bearing the same date, in protest and reply, stated that the opponents of a new county, James Callaway, Charles Callaway, William Callaway, W. Read, Bourne Price and Francis Thorp, have had the county surveyed and find it smaller than the petitioners estimated, that the court house was in the center of the county, and that the militia had been divided in two battalions.

Henry County, so far as Henry legislative petitions show, let the matter of a new county rest from November 2, 1779, to June 8, 1782. On the latter date a petition was presented with approximately three hundred signatures declaring the new county would contain twelve hundred tithables. The ever present remonstrance bore the same date as the petition for the new county, and contained about three hundred signatures. On this date,

4

June 8, 1782, the inhabitants of Bedford living on the south side
of the Staunton River, again petitioned for a new county along
Blackwater and Staunton, with three hundred and twenty militia
and six hundred tithables.  The original was signed by Thomas
Arthur, John Starkey, Jesse Dillon, William Markum, John Banks,
James Markum and 316 others.

    The matter was not permitted to rest long, for in the
fall of 1782, both Henry and Bedford presented petitions.  Both
bore the same date, November 23.  The Bedford petition was signed
by Issac Rentfro, Thomas Green, Charles Roston, Robert Wickens,
Thomas Huston, John McGinnis and 300 others, and set forth that
the new county will contain 1000 tithables, leaving Bedford with
1576.  The Henry County petition had 285 signatures, and was
attached to a remarkable pen drawn map showing the proposed lines.
It indicated that the proposed division would leave Henry County
with 1500 tithables.  Bedford presented another petition later
in the year signed by Chattin Doggett, Moses Greer, John Gibson,
Edward Wilson, William Miller, Samuel Langdon and fifty-seven
others.  There were, of course, the ever present counter-petitions
with about an equal number of signatures.

    According to the petitions on file in the State Library
Archives, Bedford let the matter rest from the fall of 1782 until
October 27, 1785, but on November 4, 1783, Henry County forwarded
to the General Assembly a petition for a new county containing
over a thousand signatures.  There was a remonstrance from Henry
County dated June 4, 1783, and signed by 135 citizens, but I was
unable to find any petition for a new county of about that date.
Perhaps it was a belated remonstrance against the petition of the
previous November.  Henry County advocates of a new county rested
from November 4, 1783, to December 4, 1784, at which time they
presented another petition containing 280 signatures.  There seems
to have been no remonstrance against this petition.

    Both Bedford and Henry made the last effort for a new
county in the fall of 1785.  At that time Thomas Arthur, Moses
Greer, George Doggett, Patrick Lingoe, William Miller, William
Pollard and 337 other Bedford citizens dwelling on the south
side of Staunton River repeated the arguments in which they had
persisted since May 1779.  At the same time Henry County forwarded to the General Assembly two petitions for a new county.
One of them asked that the part of Bedford on the south side of
the Staunton River, and the part of Henry on the north side of the
river, be taken to form a new county.  This petition contained
264 signatures.  The other, asking the same thing, is on a roll
of paper nearly ten feet long and containing about fifteen
hundred signatures.  Accompanying this overwhelming petition is
an equally remarkable pen drawing of the county.  There seems to
have been no remonstrances against these petitions.

5

The next reference found in the legislative petitions concerning this matter is in a document from Henry County dated November 8, 1786, and which states that at the last session of the General Assembly an Act was passed dividing Henry and Bedford counties, and forming Franklin County from the territory, which division left the Henry County court house so near the north side of the county as to make it inconvenient for the majority of the citizens to attend, therefore the petitions prayed for a court house at a more central point. The persistence of the Bedford and Henry citizens had won.

Franklin County was enlarged in 1848 by an Act of the General Assembly, passed March 13, 1848.

# Chapter 3

## PIONEER LIFE

The dwellings of Franklin pioneers were usually near living springs. I use the word "near" in a comparative sense, for these springs were from 200 to 500 yards distant and often at the foot of a steep hill or cliff from 100 to 300 feet below the level of the houses. Up these steep paths water was carried in buckets, largely by the women and children of the household.

In my early childhood a few men installed what was commonly called a "telegraph". By it the buckets were sent to the springs by gravity over a wire and drawn back by winding a cord around a wheel. This equipment was very rare. I often wonder why Franklinites let the ancients surpass them in building cisterns and digging wells. When the soot in the chimneys caught on fire, and the roaring hearth-fire had to be extinguished, the hurried carrying of water from these springs was a trying ordeal. These hearth fires were usually more cheerful in appearance than comfortable in fact. Rugs were almost unknown and the winds came through crevices in the floors and under doors so it was difficult for one to get warm all over at the same time.

The first Franklin County houses were one or two room log cabins, facing the south. They had a "compass mark" in the door which served as a substitute for a clock. When the sun reached a certain mark it was time for the housewife to blow the ram's horn or cow's horn for the noon meal dinner. These houses were two or three log squares covered with split clapboards held in place by weighted poles. Wooden pins were used to fasten the timbers. To bore augur holes and make wooden pegs to drive in them was tedious work, but not much more so than the blacksmith's process of making the "shop nail" which was the forerunner of the "cut nail" which was the forerunner of the "wire nail" of modern times. When the log house was erected the crevices between the logs were "pointed" with a mortar made of white sand and lime. This material, when properly smoothed with a trowel, made a very pleasing exterior. By pointing was meant to daub or plaster. Point was considered a more elegant term than daub, and a more correct term than plaster. The former was limited to stopping the crevices in a tobacco barn, and the latter meant to cover the whole wall of a building with mortar.

The floors were laid of puncheons, which were the halves of split logs. They did not require so much labor as the making of planks by the pit-saw method. All one had to do was to split

7

a small, straight chestnut log and then smooth the split side with a broad-ax. Under most of these houses was a sort of cellar where fruits and vegatables were stored for the winter. During the long evenings a puncheon was often lifted for bringing up apples or potatoes for roasting on the hearth. Banjo and fiddle supplied such music as these rustic households enjoyed. The winter evenings were far from cheerless.

The chimneys were built of native stones and had fireplaces large enough to take logs four or five feet in length. The settlers slept with their feet to the fire to prevent rheumatism. I have heard my elders say that many of the chimneys were called "stick and dirt chimneys", and were made of sticks of wood daubed within and without with red clay mud. When such a chimney caught on fire it was difficult to bring enough water from the spring to quench it. As a rule, it was pushed down to keep it from firing the house.

There was generally only one window in these pioneer cabins. It was in the corner, near the fireplace, and was closed at night by a shutter. When the use of glass became prevalent in Franklin these windows were frequently enlarged but their number was seldom increased. In addition to the light supplied by the hearthfire, there was common use of grease-burners, pine-knots (called lightwood) and tallow candles. Butchering season not only provided meat, it furnished tallow for candle-making. Every household had its candle molds, candle sticks and candle snuffers. I have seen all of these in use in my own boyhood.

The furniture was hand made and crude. The table furniture consisted of a few pewter dishes, plates, and spoons, but mostly of wooden bowls, trenchers, and noggins. If there were scarce, gourds and hard shelled squashes made up the deficiency. All iron pots, vessels, knives and forks, as well as salt and iron were brought in over the Wilderness Trail and much of this equipment was brought in on pack horses.

Most Franklin County families at the turn of the century owned numerous home made articles of furniture, such as chairs, stools, baby cribs, sideboards, wash stands, writing desks and tables. I remember best the old home made corded bedsteads. The side-rails and end-pieces were about six inches square, shouldered at the ends so as to fit into mortices in the large corner posts. Both side-rails and end-pieces were bored with an auger of about an inch in diameter. These holes were approximately six inches apart. Through these holes were threaded a long hemp rope, called a bedcord. There was a distinct technique of threading. Certain holes had to receive the rope first and others in the proper order. After the rope had been inserted in all the holes the tightening process began. For this particular process a "cording-jack" was used. This was made by cutting off a locust sapling about two feet below the fork. It was necessary that the two prongs of the fork be close together rather than of wide V shape. Through the jack, about eighteen inches below the fork, an auger hole was bored. Into this a two foot pin of wood or iron pipe was inserted. The slack bedcord was caught between the prongs of the fork and the fork was twisted by means of the pin. When the cording process was finished the hemp rope not only held the bed together, it supplied a very desirable substitute for the modern bedspring. Trundle beds were made to push under these corded beds and for the same reason that the pioneers made his drop leaf table, namely to conserve space in his crowded cabin.

Most of the pioneers wore knee boots in winter, and nearly every home had a boot-jack. The method of making one of these household necessities was simple: one found a board two feet long, six inches wide and an inch thick. In one end of it he sawed a V after which a three inch block was tacked on, just beyond the point of the V, and the instrument was ready. The jack was placed on the floor with the block down. The user stood on the jack with one foot, and hooked the heel of the boot on the other foot in the fork of the jack and pulled.

The art of basket-making from white oak "splits" reached its highest perfection in Franklin County. Every householder had several of these "feed" baskets which he used for many purposes. Even the name basket oak became attached to the type of oak from which "splits" were made. Chairs were "bottomed" from the same material. Basket-making and chair-bottoming are not yet lost arts in Franklin. While in Rocky Mount in 1934 completing the manuscript of this volume the author bought a particularly fine specimen of the basket makers craft. The maker, a man named Hall, was an artist with white oak "splits".

Pioneer farm machinery was made at home or in the nearby blacksmith shop. Horse collars were made of platted corn husks. Fences were made of rails split from chestnut logs with maul, iron wedges and wooden wedges called "gluts". Pens and toothpicks were made of goose or turkey quills. Wool, flax and cotton were spun into thread and woven into cloth on the farms where they grew. Sumac berries and madder supplied the red dyes; cedar berries the slate color; oak bark and logwood the black; green walnut hulls the brown. Nor did these exhaust the bark, root and berry dyes. The cloth was cut and made into clothing by hand. The pelts of bear, deer, racoon supplemented the products of the spinning wheel and hand loom. Stockings were home knit. The usual form of invitation from one woman to another was "Come over and bring your knitting".

9

The first wagons in Franklin were crude wooden-spindled affairs. The tar which was used to lubricate their spindles was made by burning rich pine in kilns. Farming was conducted by the signs of the zodiac and the phases of the moon rather than by scientific standards. The rows in a field were often "laid off" up and down hill, with the result that the land soon washed away. Hogs fattened on "the mast" which was of two kinds, sweet and bitter. The former consisted of chestnuts, hazelnuts and white oak acorns; the latter of black oak and chestnut oak acorns. Hogs were penned, if possible, and fed on corn two or three weeks prior to butchering "to remove the wild game flavor from the meat". Wheat was cut with reap hooks and threshed by flails. Fan-mills for separating the wheat from the chaff were brought into Franklin about 1825. There were very many ingenious artisans among the Franklin County pioneers. I have seen bread trays, churns, piggins, hogsheads, barrels, runlets, keelers, tubs, and buckets that revealed real artists in wood work. The old coffin maker was an "institution" in pioneer days. He would go to the home where a death had occurred and make the coffin on the premises in ample time for the burial. Wild cherry and black walnut were the most popular coffin materials. Many Franklinites had their coffins made of these materials while yet alive and exhibited them to their friends with especial pride.

Many of the pioneers wore moccasins, often made for them by the Indians, but the later settlers wore the mocassin's successor called a "shoe pack". The leather was home-tanned. The pelts were soaked in strong wet ashes to remove the hair. Later, regular tanneries were established in Franklin. These used oak bark in the tanning process. The tanner generally required one half of the finished leather for his services. There are many names in Franklin suggestive of these old tanyards.

Every pioneer household made its own soap. The ingredients were lye and grease. All old bones and meat scraps were saved throughout the year for soap making. The lye was obtained from the wood ashes which accumulated in the huge fireplaces. These were stored and kept dry until soap making season in spring. An ash hopper for leaching lye was made by driving four posts into the ground in the form of a square, about four feet apart. On top of these posts, poles or slats were fastened, making a square frame. Then a log which had been "adzed" into a trough was placed on the ground in the center of this frame with one end slightly raised so as to give drainage. Boards were then set in the trough, the frame supporting them at the top, making a V shaped hopper. When the ashes had been placed in the hopper water was poured over them. When it filtered through it was a coffee-colored liquid. The lye was then put in a huge iron pot and boiled down to a very strong solution. Its strength was tested by dipping a feather in it. If it ate up all the feather except the quill it was ready to receive the soap-grease, meat scraps and bones. The mixture was then boiled down to the consistency of thick paste. When it cooled and hardened, it was cut into cakes and stored away to serve for nearly all purposes. If a softer soap was desirable for removing the "gum" from the hands of those who worked with green tobacco then the mixture was boiled for a shorter period after which it was stored in crocks or fat-gourds. This method of soap making was still in vogue in my boyhood. I recall how the ash hopper, with its leached out ashes, often served me as a pulpit. I cannot remember a time when I did not expect to be a minister. As a lad of seven or eight I would gather my own sisters and the children of our tenants, black and which, around the ash hopper and "preach" to them. After delivering the "sermon" I would come down from the "pulpit" and distribute some cold biscuit and water which had been colored and sweetened with sorghum as the holy communion.

The Franklin pioneer invariably had a "cane patch" from which the table syrup was made. Sugar being difficult to obtain, this syrup or sorghum was often used instead. Sometimes the householder had both, in which case he would ask his guest if he would have "short sweetening" or "long sweetening". By the first he meant sugar, by the second, molasses. The first settlers cut the cane in short pieces and boiled the juice out of it. Then they devised a wooden cane mill which pressed most of the juice from the stalks. Afterward came the cast iron mill which was in vogue in my own boyhood. The earliest settlers also discovered they could make an acceptable syrup by boiling ripe persimmons.

In the fertile soil of a fence corner the householder planted his gourd seed. The vines would use the fence as a trellis. I have seen gourds hanging from rail fences that would easily have held two or three gallons. They were called fat gourds. When dry the seeds and pulp were removed through a hole cut near the point where the gourd began to taper off into a handle. A hole was then bored in the handle so that the nature-produced vessel might be suspended by a string from the wall and used as a container for soft-soap, lard, sugar, coffee, herbs and other kitchen necessities. During my boyhood more refined containers were coming into use for coffee, sugar and lard, but the fat gourds were used widely for storing meat scraps and rinds which were to be used for soap making. There were several small varieties of gourd with long, slender handles which made them especially useful as drinking gourds. At nearly every wayside spring one of these could be found suspended from a limb by a string or wire which had been tied through the handle.

The food was of the plainest. Hog and hominy was the proverbial dish. Johnny cake and corn pone were the bread used for the most part. Milk and mush was the standard dish for supper. When milk was scarce, hominy supplied the place of mush. Mush was frequently eaten with sweetened water, bear's oil, or the gravy of fried meat. Truck and garden patches were much in evidence, and the vegatables were usually cooked with venison or bear meat.

Salt was of great concern to the first settlers. It was brought in on pack horses. The common price of a bushel of salt was a cow and calf.

Coffee was not used until after the Revolution. When tea was introduced, it was a puzzle to prepare it. One old lady is reputed to have said she drank the broth and her husband ate the greens, and both were disappointed.

There were many articles of food which had survived from pioneer days and were in common use in my boyhood. The ash cake and the johnny cake come to mind at the moment. The former was so named because it was baked in the hot embers of the open fire-place. The latter name was a corruption of journey cake, so called because it was a type of bread which was cooked in large quantities prior to a long journey. I have eaten both and found them palatable. There were no cooking stoves in Franklin in the days when stoves were common in the cities. Indeed there were few cooking stoves in our end of the county during my boyhood. Bread was baked in ovens, and in bakers which were placed over glowing coals raked out upon the hearth. These vessels had lids with turned-up rims so as to hold the live coals which were heaped on top to increase the heat. The ovens, skillets and many other utensils had legs to keep them from actual contact with the live coals. The vessels which did not have such legs were set on a three-legged iron stool called a trivvet. Pots were often placed on top of the logs in the fireplace. If the wood rolled down, the forelog burned in two, or the firedogs turned over, the dinner was partly lost. To prevent such mishaps the crane and potrack were invented. With these devices fastened in the chimney, the suspended pots could be easily raised or lowered or turned off or on the fire. Other utensils for open hearth cooking were firedogs, tongs, poker, fire shovel and pothooks. The last named were for lifting skillet lids, ovens and other eared utensils.

The apple butter making season came in the fall, just before the sorghum making season. The cooking of both was carried on out of doors on rock ovens especially constructed for that purpose.

12

With the common use of the stove there arose the complaint from many that the food so cooked was inferior in flavor to the food cooked on the open hearth. A similar contention arose when a few Franklinites began to operate grist mills by steam power. The majority contended that water ground meal was better and owners of water powered mills began to have the phrase "water ground" stamped on their meal and flour bags.

Franklin County in pioneer days was a hunter's paradise. In my boyhood there was still enough game to make a day in the woods interesting. The "big game" such as buffalo, deer, bear and wolves had been killed off by my grandfather's generation, but there were foxes, squirrels, racoons, opossums and wild turkeys in abundance. There were few modern fire arms in Franklin during my youth. The old flint and steel guns had passed, but muzzle-loading rifles and shot guns were still in general use. I can well remember the rainy days when my father, shut off from farm work, would melt and pour lead in molds thus making bullets for his "Long Tom" rifle. He kept his powder in a ram's horn similar to the one which our cook, "Aunt" Lucy, blew for a dinner horn. The percussion caps he carried in a small tin box in the shot bag. Squirrels, rabbit and partridge meat were often on our table, though father regarded such small game as almost beneath the dignity of a real huntsman. He had not shot deer as my grandfather had, but he gloried in the number of wild turkeys he had killed. He would frequently find where a flock ranged, build a "blind" in the area, dig a straight trench in front of the "blind" bait the trench with grain until the turkeys came regularly to it. Then he would take his place in the "blind" before dawn and wait for his quarry. When all heads were picking grain the discharge of the old "muzzle-loader" down the trench would wipe out the whole flock. I recall that he brought in seven turkeys one morning as the trophies of such an ambuscade. The modern hunter would call that unsportsmanlike, but my father was not hunting turkeys for sport.

Fox, racoon and mink pelts could be seen hanging in any country store of Franklin during my boyhood. My own traps often contributed to the stock of the last named animal. I bought my first long-trousered suit of clothes with the pelt of a mink that gave me a severe bite through the thum, as I attempted to remove it from the gum trap just as I removed rabbits.

I trapped scores of rabbits every fall and winter, using the old gum traps, or boxes made of four boards six inches wide and three feet long. My father and his neighbors kept hounds with which we chased racoons at night and foxes in the daytime. The former were very destructive of the corn that grew in the bottoms, and the latter equally destructive of young turkeys, chickens and pigs.

13

Tough a mountain county, the citizens of Franklin observed many of the customs and indulged in many of the sports common to their Scotch-Irish ancestors, and common also to the inhabitants of Tidewater Virginia.

One of the most popular sports in Franklin's pioneer life was the tournament. The marshals and knights generally bore the names of the communities from which they came. They wore spectacular regalia and mounted on their well decorated horses made an imposing spectacle. Each carried a long lance with which to catch the rings that were suspended along the course. When the orator of the occasion had delivered his charge to the knights, and all else was in readiness, the Marshal would call for the Knight of Snow Creek, the Knight of Hale's Ford, the Knight of Blackwater, the Knight of Rocky Mount, and all the others in their proper order. In response, each would try to outdo the other in spearing the greatest number of rings at the greatest speed. The winner had the privilege of crowning the lady of his choice as the queen of the community whose name he bore. The tournament was usually followed by a ball, the grand march of which was led by the winning knight and the lady whom he had crowned queen.

The stage coach was the only method of public travel in the early days of the county. The sturdy team of four, the lumbering stage coach, the hard-bitten driver, the luggage (largely old cow hide trunks with the hair on the outside), the mail bags, the curious crowds gathered at the taverns to witness the arrival and departure of the stages, the crack of the whip, and the dash over rough roads through mud and mire, to the point of relay where a new driver and fresh horses were speedily hitched - - - these form a part of the picture of the county's pioneer days.

Stages ran to Big Lick (now Roanoke), to Lynchburg and to Danville. Their arrival was announced by the coachman's horn.

William Moore who married Polly Fisher at the beginning of the 19th century, drove one of these coaches. His daughter, Amanda Moore Blankenship Nunley, better known for a half century as "Granny" Nunley, was born in 1812. Her mother died when she was five years old, and she was "bound out" to John Hartman who lived near Roanoke. Here she lived until she married Pleasant Blankenship, in 1840, and moved to Hale's Ford. While her husband was away in the Mexican War, she moved to a place three miles west of Boone Mill. She often related her difficulties in making a living after her husband's death in 1851, and of how she worked throughout a whole wheat harvest for $12 with which she bought a cow and a calf. She married Andrew J. Nunley in 1853. By her first husband she had Darinda, Alex, and Dillie: by her second, Sallie, Nannie, Lydia, Mary, and Callie. She walked some distance

14

to a barn on the morning of April 27, 1916, and died a little
later on the same day, at the age of 104 years, leaving many
descendants. She retained her faculties until her death and
often hoed in her garden when she was past the century mark.
Her stories of the happenings in the early days of the county
were thrilling. She recalled the days when deer, bears, wolves,
and panthers were often seen, and told of having run from a bear
which was killed by John Hartman. In her childhood there were
no doctors and no stores within many miles of her home. The only
medicines were the herbs, which grew in the gardens. The limited
wheat crop was cut with reap hooks and threshed with flails.
Clothing was home made from home-grown flax, cotton and wool.
Buckskins were plentiful, and were used for making breeches and
moccasins. She was grown before she saw a conventional shoe.
There was no postal service that reached within miles of her
home. Pewter dishes, wooden bowls, and wooden spoons were generally used.

John S. Wise, in his "The End of An Era" wrote: "the
miles of travel into Franklin seemed much more than merely measured
distance, for they carried us into a new class of population, as
distinct from that which we had left behind as if an ocean instead
of a mountain range separated the two communities. Soon the broad
pastures and fields of grain had disappeared. In their places
were rough hillside lots, with patches of buckwheat or tobacco.
Instead of the stately brick houses standing in groves on handsome knolls, all that we saw of human habitations were log
houses far apart upon the mountain sides, or in the hollows far
below us. No longer were pastures visible, with well-bred cattle
standing in pooly places, shaded by sugar maples, bathing their
flanks at noontide. No more did we greet smart equipages drawn
by blooded horses. No more the happy darkey greeting us with
smiles.

"Up, up, up, - - - until the mountain side fell far below
our track; down, down, down, - - - until our wheels ground into,
and our horses scattered about their feet, the broken slate of a
roaring stream. Now, following the sycamores along its bank,
with here a patch of arable land and its mountain cabin, whence
a woman, smoking a pipe, and innumerable tow-headed children,
hanging about her skirts, eyes us silently; and there another
roadside cabin with hollyhocks and sunflowers and bee-hives in
the yard, the sound of a spinning wheel from within, a sleeping
cat in the window, and a cur dog on the doorstep; here a carry-log
with patient team drawn aside upon the narrow road to let us pass,
the strapping teamster in his shirt sleeves, with trousers stuck
into his cowhide boots, leaning against his load so intent in
scrutiny of us that he barely notices our salutation; here a
bearded man, clad in homespun and a broad slouched hat, riding

leisurely along on his broad-backed, quiet horse, carrying the inevitable saddlebags of the mountaineer; here a woman on horseback, with long sun-bonnet, and coarse cotton riding-skirt, and bag slung at the saddle bow, and small boy with dangling bare feet, riding behind her; here a spout-spring by the roadside, where the living water of the mountain side leaped joyously from a hollow gum-tree long grown green in service; now mounting upward again until all that is visible is the winding road, with the blue sky above it, and the massed tree-tops below, and the curling smoke of some mountain distillery, with nothing to break the stillness but the heavy hammering of the log-cock upon some dead limb, or the drumming of the ruffed grouse far away. So, on and on we toiled, until we reached the open country beyond the mountains, and late in the evening our steaming horses drew up at our new home, which was strange and different from any we had ever had before."

Everything in Franklin was crude in my boyhood, expecially the dentistry. A traveling dentist by the name of Keene came through the county each year and extracted and filled teeth. Between his visits if a tooth needed extracting the job was done by our neighborhood "tooth puller". He was a Negro named Mintus Cook. All classes, white and black alike, used his services. He was a member of the Democratic party. Consequently he always voted.

Frequently a tooth was removed by even cruder means than "Uncle" Mintus' forceps. I well remember the method. I was in the tobacco field one day with "Uncle" Charlie Gravely. I had an aching molar and told "Uncle" Charlie something had to be done about it. He said he had removed many aching teeth and would remove mine. He tied his plow horse at the end of the tobacco row, walked to a tobacco barn where some tools were stored, and soon returned with a nail almost as big as a railroad spike and a wicked-looking monkey wrench. He told me to open my mouth and show him the offending tooth. I did so. Whereupon he set one end of the nail against the tooth and gave the other a sharp blow with the wrench. The tooth was removed with much less pain than I have suffered since at the hands of modern dentists in splendidly equipped offices.

## Chapter 4

## ROCKY MOUNT AND OTHER TOWNS AND VILLAGES

When Franklin County became a political unit in 1786, the village of Rocky Mount was already in existence. Being nearly in the center of the new county, it was selected from the beginning as the county seat. Construction of a courthouse and other public buildings began in 1786. The first courthouse was built of logs and served the county until 1830.

An entry in the Clerk's office states that in 1830, a commission was appointed "to have a new courthouse built on the site of the present buildings". Accordingly, the old log structure was razed and the second courthouse was erected in 1830-31. A new prison house was erected about the same time, and in connection therewith, the county's first regular prison bounds were laid out to provide for the more humane treatment of prisoners. There is of record in the Clerk's office the following entry in connection with this provision: "Surveyed, July 14, 1830, by order of the worshipful court of Franklin County, nine acres of land for the prison bounds of the county aforesaid. Beginning at a point at the southeast corner of the public lot to a stake near Robert T. Wood's house, to a post at Matthew W. Jackson's upper gate, to a black oak at the west side of Calhoun's Store and through Dr. Taliaferro's garden to a post at the south side of said garden to the old jail." Signed, Samuel H. Woods, Deputy Surveyor.

A map of the "bounds" appears in the records, showing that the line started at a corner on Main Street, and ran in a northerly direction three blocks on Main; thence in an easterly direction two and one-half blocks; thence in a southerly direction three blocks to the beginning, embracing the lot on which the present courthouse stands.

The object of the 'prison bounds" was to provide prisoners convicted of minor offenses with means of exercise and fresh air. If a prisoner disregarded the rules, and went beyond the prescribed limit, the privilege was forfeited.

For many years there were two towns within the area now included in the corporate limits of Rocky Mount. A deed from Thomas Hill and James Callaway, dated October 8, 1805, is of record in the Clerk's office at Rocky Mount conveying to William A. Burwell, John Noftsinger, Benjamin Cook, W. H. Shelton, William Greer, Josiah Woods, Shelton Taylor, Robert Innes and

Moses Greer, Trustees of the town of Mt. Pleasant, "at Franklin courthouse for five shillings, current money, one certain lot or parcel of land containing twenty-five acres, lying and being in the county of Franklin, adjoining that on which the courthouse and other public buildings now stand".

Rocky Mount and Mt. Pleasant were then independent villages. Each had its own town government. The two villages were separated in most places by nothing more than a street or alley. There was much antagonism between the residents of the two villages and social ostracism was mutually practiced. Tradition has it that the establishment of the two towns in such proximity was the result of personal feelings between two families prominent in the county at that time.

The second courthouse served the county from 1831 to 1910, when it was razed to make room for the present architectural monstrosity. The circuit court is in session now but twice annually, despite the fact that the first Monday of every month is called "court day" by most Franklin citizens. The explanation is as follows: Before the county court was abolished, regular sessions were held in Rocky Mount on the first Monday in each month. It was the occasion of a large gathering of people from all parts of the county. Since the passing of this court, the date and occasion are still observed, and hundreds of people continue to assemble at the county seat on this date as was the custom for more than a century. These "court days" for the most part bear names which indicate the chief interest of the season. There is "horse trading court" in March, "seed potato court" in April, "shoat court" in May, "watermelon court" in August, and "tax court" in December.

The "Gazetteer of Virginia", published in 1836, has the following on Rocky Mount: "The town has three stores, two taverns, two tailors, two blacksmiths, a saddler, a cabinet maker, a boot and shoe manufacturer, a printing office, which issues a weekly paper, and a tan yard. In the vicinity there is an iron furnace and forge employing one hundred men, and manufacturing about one hundred and sixty tons bar iron and castings annually. Population, (exclusive of furnace operations) one hundred and seventy-five, of whom there are three attorneys and one physician".

Henry Howe in his "Historical Collections of Virginia", published in 1845, devoted only fifteen lines to Franklin County and Rocky Mount, the latter half reading as follows: "Rocky Mount, lies 179 miles S. W. of Richmond: it derives its name from an abrupt precipice in the vicinity. The town contains

18

about 30 dwellings, and near it is an extensive iron furnace. Union Hall is a smaller post-village, at the intersection of the road from Pittsylvania courthouse to Rocky Mount".

No railroad, steamboat, omnibus or din of trade invaded the quiet of Rocky Mount. The chief link connecting with the outside world was the tri-weekly stage, a long, ponderous, yellow wagon. The body sat low on the axles, as a preventative against upsets. The driver's seat was inside. Sometimes there were terrible accidents. Horses taking fright on some hilltop would run away, wrecking the vehicle and maiming the passengers. The perils of stage travel were the theme of oft-repeated stories around the winter evening's fire.

Court days were seasons of general convocation. With few occasions for visiting, Franklin peiple availed themselves of these opportunities for attending to business matters. Then customers were dunned, bills paid, and auctioneers sold cheap horses with high praise of their matchless qualities. The Sheriff brought down his hammer on the household goods of some poor unfortunate. His busy deputy called the names of jurors or witnesses from the courthouse steps. Farmers poured doleful plaints into each other's ears over backward seasons, droughts, short crops, and low prices. Gossip was the order of the day. News carried off at the close of such days, was referred to for weeks afterwards as "heard at court".

Election days were also great days. Candidates, in their Sunday clothes, were conspicuous. On the hustings they poured out their well-conned speeches, making the farmers shake their sides over their oft-told jokes. Others were polished, classical, eloquent. Eager eyes were turned upon each voter, as, according to the custom, the sheriff grasped his hand, called aloud his name, and demanded, "Whom do you vote for?" When the setting sun gave the signal for closing the polls, the victors celebrated their triumph, and the vanquished solaced their defeat with the liquid for which Franklin has ever been famous.

"General Muster" was the day of days. From early dawn the crowds began to gather. The courthouse square was the property for the time of thrifty farmers from Blackwater and Snow Creek, whose tables were laden with potatoes, apples, chestnuts, cider and other goodies they had brought to sell or barter. Troopers, with stub-tailed coats and leather helmets with horse-tail pendants, dashed about on their spirited mounts. Drums rattled, and fifes shrieked. Captains and subordinates roared "Fall into ranks!", "Dress by the right!", "Mark time!". Then the Colonel appeared in his plumed chapeau, as did the adjutant; and the surgeon.

The order, "Forward, march!" was heard, and the "warriors" moved through the village to the muster ground on a neighboring hill. Half of the troopers were in the full panoply of horse-tail helmets, short coats with bullet buttons. The others were arrayed as seemed best in their own eyes. Some horses jogged along as if going to church, others were standing on their hind legs, and still others were trotting sidewise. The infantry performed fewer evolutions, but they were, in their own way, as glorious as the troopers. There were all varieties of uniform, black coats, blue coats, green coats, linsey-woolsey coats, long coats, round jackets and hunting shorts. There were shot guns, squirrel riffles, old muskets and rusty swords. The maneuvers were miscellaneous and original. The men would stand at rest, lie on the grass, play practical jokes, march, counter-march, and form hollow squares that were far from square. After having displayed their power and prowess to the satisfaction of all, the heroes would undertake individual adventures. As a result of their private "charges" many found it difficult to mount or sit horses when the time came for turning their face homeward. Wild whoops would echo in and around Rocky Mount long after nightfall, when the majority of the celebrants had returned to their homes.

The author personally remembers when Rocky Mount was not lighted by electricity, and when the residents procured water from cisterns, springs and wells. Spring Street derived its name from several of these springs. Claiborne Avenue perpetuates the name of N. H. Claiborne. The old Angle and Shoaf homes were the first houses erected on Claiborne Avenue. Maple Avenue, so named for its predominant trees, was once a part of Main Street, and ran past the old brick house of the Greers, and by the former Methodist Parsonage and on into Court Street. The City Auditorium occupies the site of a livery stable that was in operation when the author first began to visit the town. The house erected by Col. Caleb Tate, and afterward the residence of the late Judge J. P. Lee, was once an academy, presided over by Miss Hattie Doniphan of Lynchburg. A tobacco factory belonging to John S. Hale (nicknamed "Pad") once occupied the site of the present Hotel Rocky Mount. There were two other tobacco factories in Rocky Mount belonging to George and Tazewell Helm. The house recently occupied by Mrs. H. E. Moseley served for many years as a building for T. A. Walker's Private School.

John S. Wise, illustrious son of a noted Virginia Governor, gives a vivid description of Rocky Mount as an eye-witness of its life during the War Between the States. (His brother, Henry Wise, was then a pastor at Rocky Mount.) Wise wrote, in part, as follows: "Rocky Mount, our place of refuge, was a typical Virginia mountain village. Even at this present time, when it has its railroad and telegraph, one in search of seclusion from the outside world might safely select it for his purpose. Month after month, year after year, roll by without other things to vary its monotony than the horse-trading, or public speakings, or private brawls of court days, or an occasional religious 'revival'.

"My brother Henry, being a clergyman and non-combatant, was in charge of our family in Franklin. After driving our horses across country, and conducting our slaves to their new abode, I again went East for some household effects, and he and I, returning together to Big Lick, were there seized upon by some friends, detained for several days, and finally dispatched to our journey's end in the private vehicle of a Mr. Tinsley. His home stood near the river bank, in a handsome inclosure, surrounded by fields of harvested wheat, where the very heart of the city of Roanoke is now located.

"Our visit to these good folk was charming, and from time to time, when wearied of our mountain isolation, we would return to their lovely valley to mingle anew with such congenial friends.

"To the east and south of them was the Blue Ridge, and beyond it our home. From the railroad station the stage road ran for a mile or two through the valley, then crossed the Roanoke River, by a ford, at the base of the mountains, then plunged into the rugged range. Winding up hill and down vale it went on, through pass and gorge and over tumbling mountain-stream, until it emerged into the rough foot-hill country east of the Blue Ridge, in which was our new home.

"Our house,* was large, among the newest and most modern in the village, prettily located on the outskirts, on the highest knoll in the place, and commanded a fine view of the little valley and Bald Knob and the mountains through which we had come. The stage road after passing our house, entered the main street of the village, which was a rocky lane upon a sharp decline, with stores and houses scattered on either side, terminating at an inclosure where stood the courthouse, clerk's office and the county jail. Halfway down the street was the tavern, an antiquated structure, with a porch extending along its entire front, its brick pillars supporting a second story overhanging the porch. This porch, which was almost on a level with the street, was provided with an ample supply of benches and cane-bottom chairs. At one end of it, suspended in a frame, was the

---

* Later owned by Judge John P. Lee.

tavern bell, whose almost continual clang was signal for grooms
to take or fetch horses, or summons to meals.

"The tavern porch was the rallying-point of the town;
hither all news came, here all news was discussed; hence all news
was disseminated. From this spot the daily stage departed in the
morning. Here villagers and country folk assembled in the day
and waited in the evening; and to this spot came the stage in the
evening, bearing the mail, the war news, and such citizens as had
been absent, visitors who drifted in, or soldiers returning sick,
wounded, or on furlough.

"Supreme interest centered ever about the arrival or
departure of the stage. In the foggy morning it appeared with
its strong four-in-hand team, and took its place majestically in
front of the old tavern. The porters rocked it as they dumped the
baggage into the boot; the red-faced driver came forth from the
breakfast-room with great self-importance. With his broad palm
he wiped away the greasy remnants of his meal, lit his brier-
root pipe, drew on his buckskin gloves, settled his slouched hat
over his eyes, clambered to his seat upon the box, gathered his
reins and whip, and cast a glance toward the post-office across
the way; an aged man and a meek-eyed woman in simple garb slipped
quietly into the rear seats, going perhaps on some sad mission
under summons to a far-off hospital at the front; a dainty miss,
with bonnet-box and bunch of flowers, kissed papa and mama and
took her place within, full of joyous anticipation, doubtless,
for even in war times girls loved to visit each other; a fat
commissary, returning from his search in the back country for
supplies, came forth, reeking with rum and tobacco, and swung up
awkwardly to the seat beside the driver. Tom, Dick and Harry,
the new recruits bound for the front, proud in their new and
misfit uniforms, seized mother, wife, sister, or sweetheart in
their arms, kissed them, bade them have no fear, and scrambled
lightly to the top. The lame and tardy postmaster hobbled forth
at last, and threw his mailpouch up to the dashboard. The coachman gave his warning cry of 'All Aboard', the hostlers drew off
the blankets, the long whip cracked its merry signal; with discord
in each footfall at the start and concord as they caught the step,
the horses pulled away; and the lumbering stage went grinding up
the stony street, its horn singing its morning carol to those who
were awake. As they disappeared over the hilltop, a last merry
cry of parting came back from the bright boys on the stage-top,
and the last they saw of home was the waving tokens of love from
those they left behind. As the day advanced, the tavern porch
again took on an air of life.

"Everygody traveled on horseback. By midday the country
folk began to stream in. Up and down the street a gradually

increasing line of saddle-horses were 'hitched'. Women, old and young, arrived, all of conventional dress, and with horses singularly alike. Their bonnets were the long-slatted poke-bonnets; their riding skirts, of coarse cotton. Alighting at the horse-blocks, they untied and slipped off the skirts and tied them to their saddle-bows, revealing their plain homespun dress. Their horses were broad-backed, short on the leg, carried their heads on a level with their shoulders, and moved with noses advanced like camels. They had no gaits but a swift walk, a gentle fox-trot, or a slow, ambling pace. When they had 'hitched the critturs', these women went poking about the stores, or the tavern kitchen, or the private houses, with chickens or butter, or other farmyard produce, seldom speaking further than asking one to buy; and when their sales were effected and little purchases made, they went away as silently as they had come.

"The men came by themselves. Their principal occupation seemed to be horse-trading. At times, the neighboring stables, and even the street itself, were filled with men leading their animals about, and engaged in the liveliest of trading. A considerable proportion of the population belonged to a religous sect known as Dunkards. In appearance, they were solemn and ascetic. The men wore long, flowing beards, and their homespun dress was of formal cut. Their doctrinal tenets were opposed to slavery and to war. Whenever political or military discussions arose, they promptly withdrew. They were very strict temperance men, and decent, orderly, law-abiding citizens, but horse-traders! It must have been a part of their religious faith! A Dunkard was never so happy as when he was horse-trading!

"There were others to whom temperance was not so sacred as to the Dunkard. By three or four o'clock, the tavern bar was liberally patronized. The recruiting office had its full quota of young fellows inquiring about the terms of enlistment. The tavern porch was filled with people discussing war news, and the quartermaster down the street had more horses offered to him than he was authorized to buy. At such times, a favorite entertainment was to draw General Early out upon his views of men and events, for the edification of the tavern-porch assemblage. The arrival of the stage not infrequently interrupted the General's vigorous lecture. For half an hour or more before the event, the expectant throng would increase, and, as those who 'brace' themselves for the crisis were there, as everyone else, conversation grew louder and agitation greater as the time approached. Then the stage would heave in sight in the gloaming, and come rattling down the rough street, the horseshoes knocking fire from the flints. Before the smoking and jaded beasts had fairly stopped, loud inquiries would be made on all hands, of driver and passengers, for war news. Somebody would throw down the latest newspaper; somebody else would mount a chair and read aloud; and, just as the news was encouraging or depressing, there would be cheering or silence. Then would come the rush for the mail to the post-office across the way.

"The passengers, also, were a source of engrossing interest. There was a young man* with an empty sleeve. A year ago he had left the place, and passed safely through all the earlier battles; but at Malvern Hill a grapeshot mutilated his left arm. Amputation followed, and now, after a long time in hospital, here he was, home again, pale and bleached, with an honorable discharge in his pocket, and maimed for life. And there, collapsed upon the rear seat, more dead than alive, too weak to move save with the assistance of friends, was a poor, wan fellow, whom nobody knew at first. How pitiful he seemed, as they helped him forth; his eyes sunken yet restless, his weak arms clinging about their necks, his limbs scarce able to support his weight, his frame racked by paroxysms of violent coughing! 'Who is it?' passed from mouth to mouth. 'Good God!' exclaimed some one at the whispered reply, 'it can't be! That is not Jimmie Thomson. What! Not old man Hugh Thomson's son, down on Pigg River? Why, man alive, I knew the boy well. He was one of the likeliest boys in this whole county. Surely, that ar skelton can's be him!' But it was. The exposure of camp life had done for poor Jimmie what bullets had failed to do.

"There, perched gayly in the air, and tumbling down upon the heads of the bystanders with joyous greeting, was the sauciest, healthiest youngster* * in the village, some home on his first furlough in a twelve month, wearing on his collar the bars of a lieutenant (conferred for gallantry at Seven Pines), in place of the corporal's chevrons on his sleeve when he marched away. Camp life had made no inroads on his health. The sun and rain had only given him a healthy bronze. His digestion would have assimilated paveing-stones. The bullets had gone wide of him. And his little world, the dearest on earth to him,-- the little world which had laughted and cried over the stories of his capers and his courage in the field, -- stood there surprised and delighted, with smiling faces and open arms, to welcome him home, their own village boy, their saucy, gallant fighting chap, their hero -- home again, if only for a week!

---

* George H. T. Greer, whose gallantry is mentioned in Major Stiles' book "Four Years Under Marse Robert".

** Beverly Carper, who mysteriously disappeared after the war and was never heard of again.

"Each day opened and passed and closed, with its excitements. It was all very narrow and primitive, the out-of-the-way world of this obscure village in an unknown region. Yet in it were the same old hopes and fears and joys and tears, hearteases and heartaches, loves and hates, and all the moods and tenses of human nature, to be found in the most populous and cosmopolitan hives of humanity."

An Act to Incorporate the Town of Rocky Mount became effective February 17, 1873.

"The boundaries of the town shall be one-half a mile from the courthouse building in said town, extending east, west, north and south, and embracing the area contained therein, so as to make said area one mile square."

"The following named persons shall constitute the board of trustees, to-wit: Giles W. B. Hale, Hughes Dillard, Thomas B. Greer, John J. Saunders, William E. Andrews, Hugh Nelson, and Robert A. Scott."

"The trustees shall have power to select from their own body a presiding officer, who shall act as mayor of the town, and appoint a town sergeant and such other officers as they may think necessary, together with a police force for the proper government of the town."

G. W. B. Hale was the first mayor, and served for many years without salary.

The first physician in Rocky Mount was Dr. Richard M. Taliaferro, who also served the village as Notary Public.

The first brick building in the county seat was the structure on Court Street behind the courthouse. It was originally used as the County Clerk's office. Many expatriated Franklinites seem to think of their native county as a land of beautiful mansions, extensive plantations and numerous slaves. But, despite their romanticising, it was for a century largely a land of log cabins, unlike Tidewater Virginia. The first dwellings in the county seat of decent proportions were the buildings occupied in after years by Judge Hugh Nelson and Judge John P. Lee. There were some houses in the county above the cabin type but they were few and far between.

The first concrete sidewalk was laid in 1909, in front of the courthouse and extending the length of the block. Prior to 1909, the sidewalk was of brick or stone.

Boone Mill, a progressive town of approximately five hundred population, derived its name from an old mill built many years ago, owned and operated by Abraham Boone, of the family of Daniel Boone. Albert E. Boone of Zanesville, Ohio, wrote at the beginning of this century as follows: "My grandfather built Boone Mill, Franklin County, Virginia, some thirteen miles south of Roanoke. His name was Abraham Boone. My father's name is David Boone, who resides at Troy, Ohio. My grandfather and his family left old Virginia in 1824, going to the Miami Valley, near Dayton, Ohio, where I was born in 1845."

An Act for establishing several towns was passed on November 10, 1792, reading as follows: "That forty acres of land in the county of Franklin, the property of Moses Grier, shall be, and they are hereby vested in John Early, Jacob Boon, John Northsinger, Daniel Barnhart, Samuel Thompson, William Wright, jun., William Turnbull, and Swinfield Hill, gentlemen, trustees, to be by them, or a majority of them, laid off into lots of half an acre each, with convenient streets, and established a town by the name of Wisenburgh. And that thirty-two acres of land lying in the County of Franklin, the property of Daniel Layman and Stephen Peters, as the same are already laid off into lots and streets, be, and they are hereby established a town by the name of Germantown, and Swinfield Hill, George Turnbull, Jacob Hark-rider, Daniel Pearry, Jubal Early, John Fergarson, and Tobias Miller, gentlemen, constituted and appointed trustees thereof."

These two places existed as villages for a short time, then ceased to be. John Hook's effort to establish a town on Merriman's Run, about 1800, did not result in a settlement of even village proportions.

The village of Ferrum had its beginning in 1889.when the Norfolk and Western Railway was built through Franklin. The name, derived from the Latin word for iron, originated with the railroad surveyors who became interested in an iron mine within a few hundred yards of where the station now stands. This mine was worked for some time and produced a good grade of ore. Being the most accessible shipping point for that large area extending westward to the top of the Blue Ridge and to the eastern part of Floyd County, Ferrum became one of the most important stations on the Roanoke and Winston-Salem Division of the railroad. The shipments consisted largely of lumber, crossties and tanbark.

Among the first residents of the village were: J. E. Angle, W. H. Buckner, Dr. W. C. Cousins, I. W. Ferguson, William Feazell, Elkanah Keys, A. L. Lemons, George A. Menefee, H. E. Menefee, D. A. Nicholason, W. H. Nolen, J. H. Young, R. M. Young and W. L. Thornton.

# Chapter 5
## LIFE ON THE FARM

With the exception of the land along the rivers and creeks, Franklin County is hilly and stony, and yields discouragingly small harvests in proportion to the labor required to cultivate it. Much of the soil is thin, and when plowed, it washes away in a few years, leaving stones and clay. But it is well watered with many living springs, brooks, creeks and rivers. The people have been healthful and the population has increased as rapidly as the soil has failed. Every year the difficulties of making a living from the soil have multiplied. There was never much market for anything but tobacco and whiskey. There were few manufactories in the county until after the opening of the twentieth century.

Yet, despite the difficulties of wresting an existence from the soil, I am convinced that the average native of Franklin is happier on the soil than anywhere else in the world.

In the early years of the twentieth century (with which this chapter deals) the man who owned a large farm and had tenants on it was just about as poor as the tenants themselves. That is, unless the farm consisted largely of bottom land. It was an extra good farm if half the acreage was tillable. Sometimes a hill farm would run down to the creeks, and thus afford a narrow strip of a few acres of fertile soil. These strips were never large enough, however, to justify the use of modern machinery. Yet when a man had a farm with a few acres of fertile bottom land for a corn crop, his position was admired or envied by his less fortunate neighbors. And all of the land, whether bottoms or eroding uplands, was considered precious. The neighborhood quarrels I remember best were those that had their rise in disputed land lines. Such feuds would last for years, and out of them would eventually grow divided churches and antagonistic political and social circles. These people loved the land.

Nearly every family kept cattle, sheep, pigs and poultry. Yet there never seemed to be a surplus. There was often an over-supply of puppies and kittens, but a few trips to the creek with guano bags weighted with rocks, brought the proper adjustment between supply and demand. The oak and chestnut trees were so laden with nuts that one did not have to feed his hogs. A blight has long since killed the chestnut trees, but the oaks continue to bear, though the fence law now keeps the hogs from the acorns. There were no fence laws at the turn of the century.

27

Nor were there any wire fences. Rail-making, in the Abraham
Lincoln manner, was a part of every year's labor. The rails
were made chiefly of chestnut trees, and many of the fences,
built fifty years ago, are still standing.

The hogs and cattle of various owners ran together.
The only way one could establish ownership was by certain marks
cut in the ears of the animals. I well remember the mark of my
father's pigs and cattle. It was "a slip in the left ear and a
hole in the right". An unmarked pig was the property of the
man who caught it. Hogs frequently became so wild that they
ceased to return to the feeding lot at all, and had to be killed
in the woods. If a man killed one of his neighbor's pigs by
mistake, he dressed it and carried it to the owner. Each man
knew his neighbor's mark. In many instances these marks were
of record at the court house. A litter of eight pigs belonging
to my paternal grandfather went wild. He told me that I might
have them if I would catch them. Though meat was cheap, I
decided the job would be worth while. So I found their "range"
and began to bait them with corn. Soon they began to come early
each morning, directly from their bed, for the bait. Then I
built a square rail pen with one corner raised high enough for
the shoats to go under. I put the corn in this pen for a day or
two and found that they got it. Then I baited the pen before
day, tied a plow-line to the post that held the corner up, and
secreted myself. Soon the eight were within the pen enjoying
breakfast. I gave a mighty pull, out came the post, and down
came the pen. I got eight dollars for the eight pigs, and felt
as rich as Croesus.

When we wanted beef, pork and mutton, we got them from
our own pastures, and when we wanted eggs, guineas, ducks, geese,
turkeys and chickens we got them from our own poultry yard. The
minks, weasels, hawks, owls, dogs, foxes and snakes made frequent
raids, but the barnyard population increased in spite of these
marauders.

Father bought green coffee in burlap bags for our own
family, and for the tenants. Mother roasted it on the kitchen
stove. Coffee-roasting days were great days for me.

In the springtime it was thought healthful to drink
sassafras and spicewood tea. The former which was palatable,
was made from the roots of the sassafras, and the latter from
twigs of the spicewood bush. Persimmon beer was a favorite
drink with us in the late fall. After frost, persimmons were
gathered and put in a hogshead which had been well floored with
wheat straw. The straw served as a strainer. Later, we learned
that it was also well to put layers of the straw between layers

28

of the persimmons. We also discovered that by adding dried
apples, or dried apple parings, an even better drink resulted.
No sugar was required. After the barrel had been well filled with
fruit, warm water was added. It was left about two weeks to
ferment. Years have passed, but memory still insists this was
the finest drink ever brewed.

At the beginning of the century many Franklin County
families had cards and spinning wheels, and a few of them had
hand looms. Children went to sleep at night to the whirring
and clacking. Clothing and stockings were made from the homespun
yarn. Sewing machines were rare. Most of the clothing was made
with a plain needle. A girl's reputation, and desirability as
a wife, depended to a great extent upon her ability to spin, knit,
weave and sew. In carding, a woman held a card, somewhat like an
oblong, wire-bristled hair brush, in each hand and by raking the
teeth together cleansed the wool of all foreign particles, and
made it into rolls about a half or three quarters of an inch in
diameter. Worn out cards were often used as curry combs and
sometimes as hair brushes. Flax-hackles were also to be found in
many homes during my youth, though flax growing had largely
ceased. These hackles were made by setting sharp steel spikes,
eight inches long very close together in a wooden field about
eight by twelve inches. An old flax-hackle was among my childhood toys. I used it as a harrow on my imaginary farm.

I can remember the first wheat drill that was brought to
Franklin County; I saw also the first automobile owned in the
county; and I distinctly remember the first telephone wire that
was erected. I recall how fearful the farmers were that it might
conduct lightning and kill travelers who happened to be on the
highway during a thunder storm. Mowing machines and binders were
introduced in the county shortly after the turn of the century.
The first "traction engine" in the county created as much excitement when it pulled a threshing machine down the "big road" as if
a circus were passing by. This particular threshing outfit was
limited to wheat crops along the main road. The horse-drawn
outfits continued to thresh most of the wheat for a long time
after the coming of the tractor, for most of the wheat was off
the "big road". I saw the inauguration of rural free delivery
which brought us daily mail. I saw the acquisition of breech-
loading guns relegate the old muzzle-loaders to the attics. I
saw game become scarce in Franklin. The rural blacksmith shops
were the busiest places in the community at the turn of the
century. They were still doing a flourishing business when I bade
good-bye to the farm. They have now disappeared.

In the first years of the twentieth century nearly every
Franklin county farmer grew enough wheat to supply bread for his

29

own family. As a rule, the land from which corn and tobacco had been harvested was seeded to wheat, rye and oats in the late fall. If corn land was being seeded, the dry corn stalks, from which the ears and fodder had been gathered, had to be cut, piled and burned, so the land might be properly plowed and harrowed. This stalk-cutting was considered light work. The children did much of it, and they were usually kept from school until the work was done. I have chopped down these dead stalks until my arms, back, and shoulders ached. The hoe seemed to grow heavier as the day progressed, and by night it felt as if it were made of lead. At the end of the day there were often blisters in my hands which had been made by the friction of the hoe handle. Frequently, I went home too tired to eat, and so climbed the stairs and went supperless to bed. But the stalks had to be cut before I could go to school again. Only that fact could have driven me to such labor. The smaller children followed the stalk-cutters and picked up the stalks and piled them for burning. When my body began to ache from the weariness of endless hoe strokes, I would covet the job of piling stalks. But as it was "a child's job", I stuck to the hoe rather than sacrifice my dignity. I remember that I was cutting stalks, and Steve and May Prunty, little step-children of a Negro tenant, were piling them, when word was brought that I had a little brother at the house. I dropped my hoe and ran home with all the possible speed. I had four sisters at the time, but no living brother, hence my interest. It was on October 24, 1902. I was not quite ten years old which will indicate how very young the stalk pilers were.

If tobacco land was being seeded to wheat, farm children still had a job. The tobacco was usually cut in late August and early September. The wheat was not sown until November. In the interim, suckers would come up from the tobacco stubbles and grow as tall as a man. These stubbles had to be plowed up, and the suckers had to be pulled from them beforehand. Green tobacco leaves a sticky, black gum on the hands of those who handle it, so this sucker-pulling was a dirty, disagreeable job. I still wonder at the vast amount of unnecessary work done by Franklin County farmers. They were ingenious in discovering so much of it. And they were equally ingenious in devising the hardest possible method of doing the unnecessary. But this is not the whole story of preparing tobacco land for fall seeding.

When the stubbles were plowed up, the mass of fine roots held together so much soil that each stubble sod was almost as large as a peck measure. These huge masses of roots and soil had to be separated. It might have been done with a harrow. But that would not have accorded with the policy of doing things the hardest way. So hoes were again brought into service. The dirt was literally beat out of these sods. "Knocking stubbles" this task was called. It was even more laborious than cutting corn-stalks, and not half so needful. When I recall how many days this hard and unnecessary drudgery kept me out of school, I still tingle with keen resentment.

During my grandfather's boyhood, much wheat in Franklin County was cut with a crooked knife called a reap-hook. It was the most primitive as well as the slowest method of harvesting. The harvested grain was then threshed with flails. During my boyhood, wheat was cut with cradles and threshed with horse-powered threshing machines. At harvest time, the owner would invite his neighbors to come and bring their cradles. He would then procure a jug of brandy or whiskey for the occasion, and his wife, aided by neighboring women, would prepare a big dinner or supper. When the neighbors came, they set out for the fields with the jug. It was considered a necessary refreshment between "rounds". The cradlers paused to rest, whet their blades, and refresh themselves when they had cut around the field two or three times. Each "cradler" had a "binder" who followed and bound the straw in bundles using wisps of the same for bands. If the "binder" failed to keep within reasonable distance of his "cradler", he was penalized (theoretically) by not having the jug passed to him. The older men put the sheaves in shocks. Sometimes "cradlers" and "binders" joined in the shocking after the field had been cut, or even before, if rain threatened. The average wheat crop consisted of from ten to fifteen acres and could usually be harvested in half a day.

If this cooperative "working" succeeded in cutting one man's crop in the forenoon, the big dinner was then eaten, and the harvesters proceeded to another farm for more "cradling", and a big supper in the evening. In this way each farmer got his wheat cut before it ripened so dry as to shatter and waste in the cutting process. In retrospection it seems to me that the men who had no wheat crops had everything to lose by such an arrangement; yet I recall they were always on hand, attracted perhaps by the jugs and the marvelous meals. "Cradling" was no job for a weakling. If one was weak-chested in the least, he could not "cradle" at all. In addition to being great physical exertion, the harvesting of wheat was done during the hottest days of summer.

Wheat threshing was also a cooperative enterprise. After the shocks had seasoned for a while in the fields, they were hauled to the threshing yard. This yard was usually near the stables and cattle sheds. There the bundles were built into large stacks to await threshing day, which was frequently two months after harvest. Threshing outfits were scarce and some-times one of them would serve over a hundred farmers in a single season. The owner of the outfit took "toll" for his threshing, instead of cash. The usual rate was three bushels for placing the outfit on the threshing yard, and one bushel for each twenty bushels threshed. The outfit consisted of a threshing box, a power machine, and a dozen or more horses. In moving from farm to farm, the horses were evenly divided, and hitched to the two pieces to haul them over the unspeakable roads. When the equipment was set up, all of the horses were hitched to the power machine and driven around in a circle to generate power for the threshing box. As a lad, I thought it would be romantic to travel with a threshing outfit and see the world. There was no nobler profession to my youthful mind than that of the man who stood on the platform of the power machine, cracking his long whip and crying, "Get on Tobe", "Come on Nell", "Get up Bill". I saw the old horse power machine supplanted by a cumbersome steam engine, and though it took more horses than ever to pull the engine and thresh box from place to place, for me the glory of threshing-day had departed.

Probably the gayest of all the cooperative "workings" were the corn shuckings. They did not sap so much physical energy, and there was ample vitality for the games and dances that followed. When the corn was gathered, it was hauled to the shucking yard, in front of the corn crib. There it was put into rail pens to protect it from rain until the wheat sowing season was over. The neighbors then came in for the shucking, which usually began in the afternoon, and lasted well into the night. If there was no moonlight, resinous pine knots, commonly called lightwood, were wired to posts and ignited. Kerosene lanterns were also used. Many farmers had their corn thrown into the cribs as it was husked, but my father had it tossed near the crib door to be "cribbed" on the morrow. In this way he got the long corn separated from the nubbins. There was a partition which divided the crib into a large and a small room. Back of the partition the long corn was stored. In front and near the door, was stored the nubbins which were fed to horses, mules, cattle, hogs and fowls. When the unhusked corn was in two or more pens of equal size, the huskers would divide into equal groups and "shuck a race". This was not always advantageous to the owner. In the eagerness to win, many would toss ears into the shucked pile without thoroughly husking them. This prolonged the cribbing process next day. Occasionally a "sport", or red ear, was found, which was a signal for passing around the ever-present whiskey jug. The older men would tell that when they were young a red ear gave the finder the privilege of taking it to the "party" held after shucking, and presenting it to the lady of his choice in exchange for a kiss. But this custom had passed before my day. I suppose the custom which prevailed in my day was more acceptable, or it would not have supplanted the older one.

The quiltings, which were the feminine accompaniments
of most "workings", were at their best when held in connection
with the corn shuckings. When there were two spare rooms and a
sufficient number of women present, two quilts were often "framed"
and quilted on the same day. Six or eight women were assigned to
each quilt, and its completion meant a good day's work. The "tops"
were made of vari-colored remnants of dress goods. There were
cut in small pieces and sewed together in squares of beautiful
design. These squares were often stitched together in the quilt
so as to form a still larger pattern. The lining was usually
unbleached cotton cloth, called "domestic", which the housewife
had dyed with green walnut hulls, or some other home made dye.
The padding between top and lining, which gave weight and warmth
to the quilt, was cotton "batting" which had been carded by hand.
The making of a quilt was a long, tedious process. A blanket,
equally warm, could have been bought in the city for one or two
dollars, but the women, like the men, seemed to do as many unnecessary things as possible in their housekeeping. And, like
the men, they did the necessary things in the hardest possible
way. Women who did their own washing, would often carry dozens
of huge pails of water from the spring to the house for laundry
purposes. They might have taken the soiled clothes and the
laundry equipment to the spring. As a rule, the men of the household prepared the fuel for wash day. The rest of the task fell
to the women.

The farmer with an average size family, and with one
or two tenant families on his farm, would butcher from a dozen
to a score of hogs each season. "Hog killing time" was always
in the coldest period of winter. When the day was set, nothing
could change it except rising temperature. Snow, sleet and hail
were not allowed to interfere. An excavation was made to receive
a huge box or hogshead, so that the top of the same would not
be too high above the ground. This was the scalding vat. Dry
wood was stacked high between upright post, and as the pile grew,
it was filled with stones weighing from ten to twenty pounds.
These were to heat the water in the scalding vat. Before dawn
on butchering day the pile was ignited. The light from it shining
through the window often made my bedroom brighter than any kerosene lamp could have made it. I knew then that the hour had
arrived which I had dreaded for days. The squealing of the pigs,
as they were being killed, upset my nerves for weeks afterward,
and caused me to dream horrible dreams. One of my earliest
ambitions was to spend hog killing day at school, or at my grandfather's home a mile away. The dream was seldom realized. There
were too many things a boy could do on butchering day.

Hog killings were also cooperative enterprises. Though
not so many men were needed as at the cuttings, log rollings,
barn raisings and corn shuckings. Butcherings were hilarious

33

occasions. They gave rise to the phrase, "We had the hog killin'est time". The men with whom my father exchanged butchering service usually arrived before daylight and had breakfast with us. I could never eat breakfast on butchering day. I would go into the dining room, however, to appear brave, though I was full of a feeling akin to nausea. My legs would tremble, and I was often on the verge of tears. I smothered my feelings as best I could, for I knew everybody would laugh at my squeamishness. Immediately after breakfast, the killing would begin. The pigs were usually stunned by an ax blow on the head, after which their throats were cut. I would stop my ears to shut out the dull thuds of the ax and the subsequent squealing. I saw a pig rise one day and run across the lot, after its throat had been cut. I ran to the house, hid myself, and wept. It was weeks before I could get that sight out of mind and out of my dreams. As soon as their throats were slit, and often before they were still, the pigs were submerged in the scalding vat. This water had been heated almost to the boiling point by shoveling into it the rocks which had been heated in the burning wood pile. After a pig's bristles had been picked off, and the viscera removed, the carcasses were taken to the smoke house where they were cut into hams, shoulders and middlings. The ribs were removed, and the sausage meat was cut for grinding. Nothing was wasted. The meat from the heads and feet was made into head-cheese and "souse". The fat was cut from the entrails for the making of lard. And even the entrails were carried to the creek, washed, and made ready for soap-grease. It was a cold, nauseating task.

The Franklin County farmers grew little hay. They pulled pulled the blades from the corn stalks instead. These blades were called fodder. The fodder pulling began as soon as the grain in the ears hardened, which was in August and September. This was also tobacco cutting season. The two jobs coming together made a busy period. If labor was scarce and work pressing, the blades were stripped from ground to ears and the stalks with the blades on them were cut just above the ears and bound in shocks. These were called tops. The fodder blades were tied in bundles by a withe made of three or four blades, and suspended for curing in the crotch between the ear and the stalk. Both fodder and tops had to be carried on one's back to the wagon or "slide" at the edge of the field. To have driven into the field would have broken down a few ears of corn. These might have spoiled before gathering time. Easier methods of doing work were always being sacrificed for little things like that.

Daily newspapers were rare, even at the county seat, and almost unheard of in the area of which I write. Lack of fashion plates, style journals, and contact with the outside world guaranteed originality of dress. In no quarter of the world have women ever taken more pride in apparel. Indeed it was almost a fetish. The plainest of girls seemed to implicitly believe that the proper clothes would make them irresistable. Sunday clothes, like the parlours, were regarded with near reverence. Many people, old and young, walked to church. Some because they did not have buggies, and were ashamed to ride in farm wagons. Others because they did not even have a wagon. Many of the girls, in order to save their Sunday shoes, would wear their every day shoes, and carry their Sunday shoes in their hands, or let their escorts carry them, until they were near the church. Then they would change. As a lad, riding to Church in the farm wagon, I have frequently seen the neighborhood belles sitting on logs and stumps by the roadside, putting on their Sunday shoes, and hiding their old ones to be picked up on the return journey.

No greater sociability, hospitality, and general neighborliness existed anywhere than prevailed in Franklin County in the day of my boyhood. Many phases of work required the combined strength of many men. As most farmers were financially unable to employ the necessary labor, they pooled their efforts in the interests of one another. Their very dependence drew them together. These occasions called "workings" were happy social gatherings, as well as business combinations. As a rule, when the men gathered at a farm for a barn-raising, log rolling, corn shucking, grain harvesting, wheat threshing, hog killing or other cooperative "working", the women of the community also came together to quilt and sew, and also to cook for the entire company of workers. At the end of the day, men and women united in dancing, or in some other form of merry-making.

There were a great many kissing games associated with the social functions of the younger folk of the county. Apple peelings, husking bees and all sorts of "bees" closed with such games. Dancing was frowned on, but such marchings and singing games as "Old Phoebe", "Hog Drivers", and "The Cherry Tree", were not considered wrong. There was no logical connection between the ballads which the rude swains and rustic belles shouted so vociferously, and the kissing which invariably followed. The kissing, though treated outwardly as a joke by the boys, and as an unpleasant ordeal by the girls, evidently gave satisfaction to both, or the games would not have been so popular.

There were other games which did not provide for songs and marches, but they did provide for kissing as rewards and forfeits. Such games as "Frog in the Puddle", "William Trimble Toe", "Puss Want a Corner", and "Grind the Bottle", were very popular in Franklin during my boyhood, though these games had been long forgotten in less backward counties. Young people, who in winter flouted the laws of the Churches against dancing, would "repent" during the "protracted meetings" of the next summer. Whereupon the Churches would restore them to "good standing and full fellowship".

Apple peelings were distinctly affairs of, by and for the young people. Courting bees would have been more truly descriptive nomenclature. There are still many married couples in Franklin whose romances began at apple peelings. These "sociables" (for the apple peeling was incidental) were always held at night. On the day preceding them, the apples (chiefly windfalls) were picked up and placed in boxes and barrels on the lawn where the peeling was to be held. Tubs and buckets were provided for the peeled fruit. Barrels and boxes were placed for the parings and cores. As dark came on, lanterns were lighted and suspended from the walls of the house, and from trees on the lawn. Then the belles and beaux of the neighborhood arrived and set to work, though few of them would have employed the term "work". The group usually divided into two groups, peelers and slicers. After the fruit was peeled and sliced it was put into wooden vessels to await spreading for drying on the morrow. The peelings were put in barrels and boxes to be spread and dried also. Mixed with persimmons these dried peelings greatly improved persimmon beer.

The drying slabs were often made of bark. Huge yellow poplars, that would now be worth many dollars as lumber, were felled for no other purpose than to procure bark for fruit drying. They were always cut when the sap was "up". When the tree was down the bark was ringed around with an axe at three foot intervals. Then, with the aid of a "bark-peeler" (something like a crow-bar with one end flattened and curved), a three foot section of the bark was removed in one piece. This section of bark was then spread out and striped of board tacked around the edges to hold it flat. When these sheets of bark had dried, they made receptacles which were light and easily handled. On them both the fruit and parings were spread. Then they were placed on scaffolds in the sun. During the drying process these scaffolds were fearful places for one who was afraid of bees, hornets and yellow jackets. These insects would swarm over the drying fruit to suck the sweet juices. They were as "terrible as an army with banners" to the timid ones who had to take the slabs down hurriedly and carry them to shelter against approaching showers. The insects seemed to be most numerous when the sky darkened and the thunders began to roll.

The apple peelings were usually enlivened, or saddened (according to one's temperament), by the singing of ballads. The

36

older folk present were often relied on for leadership in this phase of the peelings. If some ballads happened to be unknown to any considerable number of the younger set, one of the older folk would "line it out" for the singing. By "lining it out" I mean they would repeat the ballad line by line. After a line, or two lines at most, had been repeated, all would join in the singing of such songs as "The Weeping Willow Tree", "Lord Thomas and Fair Elender", "The Demon Lover", "The Gypsy Laddie", "Lord Batemon", and others of a kindred nature. Some of them were lugubrious in the extreme but the more mournful they were, the more popular they seemed to be. Sometimes there were two or three fiddlers and banjoists present, in which case the group would be regaled with such airs as "Billy in the New Ground", "Callahan", "Fire in the Gum", "Liquor All Gone", "Old Dan Tucker", "Sugar in the Gourd", "Honey in the Gum", and a host of others, any one of which heard today by an expatriated Franklinite would recreate for them an age that has vanished into the limbo of the eternally lost.

I can remember the strange and unexpected death of my maternal grandfather, John Fontaine Motley, which occurred in Roanoke May 1, 1898. Mother's overwhelming grief on receipt of the news is indelibly impressed on my memory. She had just finished transplanting a cutting from a greening apple tree, according to a method recommended by Dr. Green, a traveling dentist. The method consisted in sharpening the end of a twig from the apple tree, and inserting it in a huge Irish potato. The potato was planted and supplied moisture while the sprout rooted. The tree she set out after that fashion still stands before the north kitchen window of the old home. It is a giant tree now, and yields many bushels of apples annually, but they do not taste nor look like the apples of the parent tree. They taste like they inherited too much from the potato which helped the tree to root.

As a lad I never tired of listening to the older men of the community. They had little interest in "book-learning" as they termed it. Their parents had gotten along well without it, so had they, and so could the "younger generation". They were of robust health, and their uproarious laughter was contagious. Many of them were octogenarians but they could ride to Rocky Mount and back home the same day and still be fresh enough to lead the conversation around the fireside after supper. My maternal great-grandfather, George Motley, rode regularly across Turkey Cock Mountain to his Masonic Lodge at Snow Creek until he was past eighty years of age. Under the influence of the stories told by the native African cook in his father's kitchen, he had run away to sea when he was thirteen years old and did not return

37

home until he was past forty.  On returning he found his parents
still living.  He married near his old home, reared a large
family, and died at an extreme old age.

Recreation, as the present day understands it, was
quite unknown to the Franklin of my boyhood.  There were no foot-
ball, baseball, or basketball games; no moving picture shows or
amateur dramatics; no picnics; and no vacations.  There were
apple peelings, singings, school closings, and fishing parties,
with an occasional tournament at some Independence Day celebra-
tion.  I recall several fishing trips down the Snow Creek with
my elders, but memory tells me that I did not enjoy them.  The
fishing that stands out in my memory as the highest peak of pure
delight was the fishing I did with a pin hook in the two small
creeks that flowed through my father's farm.

The creeks were small, and the fish were small, but I
could catch plenty of them, and the catching a "hornyhead" six
or eight inches long gave my boyish heart just as great a thrill
as the catching of the larger fish of Snow Creek gave my elders.
The sheer  joy of dreaming under the willows, whether the "hornyheads" bit or not, was heaven to me, and I am sure my father if
he had known the delight those hours gave me, would have let me
go more often than he did.

The average citizen of Franklin would have considered
himself outraged if the charge of gambling had been laid against
him, yet nothing was more popular among all classes in my boyhood
than the "shooting matches".  All sorts of things were "shot for",
but chiefly cows, hogs, sheep and turkeys.  The owner of a marketable cow would announce the time and place of a shooting match,
and then proceed to sell enough "changes" to amply pay for the
animal.  When the great day came a target was erected, and the
best shot took first choice, second best took second choice, and
so on.  A cow was generally supposed to consist of five parts - - -
two hind quarters, two fore quarters, and the hide and tallow.
It seemed to me that all the men were good marksmen, but in every
neighborhood there was an expert.  One of these would frequently
buy five or six chances and win the whole cow.  Such a marksman
was often bribed by the promise of a choice quarter not to shoot
at all.  I have seen dozens of turkeys "shot for" on election
day at Snow Creek precinct.

# Chapter 6

## TRANSPORTATION AND COMMUNICATION

Franklin County was for over a century one of Virginia's most "backward" counties. Her progress was retarded chiefly by lack of transportation and communication. No other section of the State had such impossible roads. Lack of highways, railways, and navigable streams kept the currents of contemporary life out of Franklin County for over a century. Indeed, communities within the county itself were kept apart by the unspeakable roads as effectively as if mountain ranges had stood between them. As a result, there were still in vogue during my boyhood many customs and contrivances which in most American communities had been discarded so long as to be forgotten.

I have personally known Franklin County adults, and a few of them aged, who had never seen a railroad, steam engine, electric light, gas light, water faucet, kitchen sink, bath tub, fly screen, or telephone. Cooking was frequently done on an open fireplace. The acquisition of a cooking stove was important enough to be neighborhood news. Stove owners of my community were in the minority. Hand cards and flax hackles were common. Spinning wheels were in use in most of the homes of our neighbors, and hand looms in many. Mothers still sang their children to sleep with the ballads of Elizabethan England. I clearly remember when Franklin County children could not reach their schools on account of the roads. But that was not considered a serious matter. Many things of less importance than impassable roads were allowed to interrupt the school life of most pupils so that they never advanced far enough to even enter high school, if there had been a high school.

Franklin County was settled by four distinct groups. Two of these - - - the German and French groups - - - came in together from Pennsylvania over the Wilderness Road. The Scotch-Irish group came in from the north over the same road. The fourth group, largely of English stock, but with a few Hugenots, came over the road which led in from Richmond.

The settlers, after leaving the road by which they entered the Franklin area, seemed to dismiss the matter of roads. They turned, at first, to such impracticable schemes as making the Pigg and Smith Rivers navigable. Among the petitions in the Virginia State Library is one from Franklin dated November 23, 1796, and setting forth that the improving of the navigation of Pigg River from its mouth to the Washington Iron Works would be attended with great convenience to many citizens of Franklin, it having been demonstrated that a boat with eighteen hundred weight of iron would be transported from the said Iron Works in Franklin County to the Staunton River with little difficulty. The petition does not ask for public funds, but proposes to raise the necessary money by subscription. A counter petition was presented under date of December 7, 1797, protesting that such "improvement of navigation" was impracticable, that it would prevent the rebuilding of Colonel Lewis Burwell's Mill, and that it would also prevent the erection of iron works there.

As early as 1796, the Legislature considered a Bill for making the Pigg River more navigable from its mouth to the Washington Iron Works. James Callaway, Benjamin Cook, Samuel Duval, Swinfield Hill and Josiah Wood were named as supervisors of the deepening and clearing of the channel. A proposal for the improvement of navigation of Staunton River, from Booker's Ferry to the mouth of Pigg River, was considered by the General Assembly in 1798. Trustees named to supervise the enterprise were: Charles Callaway, John Law, David Hunt, Bryan W. Nowling, Philip Payne, John Ward, William Ward and William Witcher. Neither of these enterprises proved very successful, but an Act of the Legislature in 1804 resulted in the formation of the Roanoke Navigation Company whereby the Staunton was made navigable from Weldon, North Carolina, to the mouth of Pigg River, and the Dan River was made navigable as far up as Meade, North Carolina.

It was not until 1838, so far as the Legislative Petitions disclose, that any practical effort was made to build a road out of Franklin to intersect at Big Lick (now Roanoke) the Wilderness Road over which the early settlers had come into the county.

The first passenger service to Big Lick was by stage coach. Bob Akers, living in Franklin County as late as 1926, drove the old stage and mail coach between Rocky Mount and Big Lick from 1871 to 1880. He made tri-weekly trips, resting on Sundays. Four horses were required to draw the heavy vehicle over the rough roads. Teams were changed at a Boone Mill livery stable and passengers were given time to get dinner at a tavern there. The old stage coach lines extended southward to points in South Carolina and the Gulf Coast; and northward over the Wilderness Trail to Pennsylvania. There were taverns along the way where teams were changed and passengers rested and refreshed themselves. It is said that Andrew Jackson, Patrick Henry, and other men of distinction were often entertained at one of these wayside hostelries which stood in Franklin, and bore the name Ashpone Tavern. This tavern was noted for its food and drink, and was a favorite gathering place for the fox hunters of a large region.

On December 8, 1832, Franklin County joined five or six other mountain counties in petitioning the General Assembly for a turnpike from Danville to Evansham in Wythe County "to be built after the manner of the Kanawha Pike". The cost of this pike was estimated at $50,000.00, and a map of the proposed course shows that the route through Franklin was almost identical with that of the Franklin Turnpike built a few years later.

Petitions dated in 1837 and 1838 (the latter from a road convention held in Rocky Mount) ask for a charter for the construction of a road from Danville to Rocky Mount and Big Lick to Fincastle. This road was to be a dirt turnpike, and the section between Danville and Rocky Mount was to be built at a cost of $300.00 per mile. This turnpike was surveyed by Crozet, a French engineer, and built about 1840. Known as the Franklin Turnpike, it was a dusty way in summer, and so miry in winter as to be almost impassable. Toll gates were placed ten or fifteen miles apart and the rate of toll for several years was as follows: horses five cents per head; persons five cents each; tobacco five cents per hogshead; four wheel vehicles, twenty-five cents; two-wheel vehicles, ten cents; neat cattle, five cents per head; and hogs, one cent per head.

Over this pike, the drovers, as they were called, passed with their marketable droves, herds and flocks. I have often listened, spell bound, to my grandfather's stories of his adventure on this road. He declared that he had seen "thousands" of turkeys in a single flock being driven along this pike to Danville. The turkey drovers, he said, would start from some point in Patrick, Floyd or Henry Counties with a comparatively small flock and add to it by purchasing small flocks along the way. Some would not need to be bought, for the turkey being the most gregarious of birds, many would add themselves to the flock without the knowledge of their owners. There were no telephones, and the postal system was hardly worthy of the term system. Nevertheless the news of the turkey drover's coming got abroad so that at every intersecting side road there were small flocks with their owners waiting. These flocks had been watched and protected all year from the foxes, minks and weasels, with this peripatetic turkey market in mind.

Then there were cattle drovers who were operating on a plan similar to that of the turkey men. They started from Floyd, Patrick or northwest Franklin, with perhaps a dozen cattle, and added to the herd by purchase as they passed through the countryside. If the herd grew large enough, the drover would hire an extra rider or two, to assist in keeping the animals rounded up and moving.

41

There were also the slow moving droves of hogs and flocks of sheep that had started in a small way on one of the mountain counties, and had grown greater en route. That is to say, they had grown greater in numbers. Lack of food and rest, en route, usually made both sheep and hogs so lean that they were not fit for the abbatoir until they were refattened. Probably hogs were never meant to be driven. At any rate they were so difficult to drive that the patience of the driver was quickly spent. To "cuss like a hog driver" was an expression denoting the acme of profanity. The simile was in common use in my boyhood.

Besides the drovers plying on the Franklin Turnpike, there were the wagons of the hucksters which stopped at the roadside general stores and gathered up the chickens, butter, eggs and pelts which the merchants had received from their customers in exchange for sugar, coffee, cloth, snuff, kerosene and other items which could not be produced on the farm.

A petition dated December 9, 1839, asked for the incorporation "of a joint stock company for the purpose of constructing a dirt turnpike commencing at or near New London and running through the counties of Bedford and Franklin, crossing Staunton River at Hale's Ford, and terminating on the top of the Blue Ridge in Floyd County, at or near the head of Daniel's Run".

The Virginia Legislature received three petitions from Franklin citizens during 1848 asking for an Act to incorporate a company "for the improvement of navigation of Smith's river".

In 1850, a petition was presented to the Virginia Legislature for a "turnpike road", from Dickinson's Store to Asa Holland's place; and in 1851 there were two petitions for a "turnpike road" through the county. A petition dated December 3, 1852, asked the General Assembly for an Act to incorporate a stock company to construct a "turnpike road" beginning at Jacob Naff's and terminating at some suitable point on the Rocky Mount turnpike. The citizens of Franklin joined the citizens of Floyd on December 6, 1853, in asking for an appropriation to build a road from Joshua Underwood's in Floyd across the Blue Ridge at Runnet Bag to the foot of the mountain in Franklin County. In January 1854, a petition was presented for the construction of a plank road "on the Two and Three-fifths Principle" from Martinsville by Helms and Prilliman's Store to Long Branch at the foot of the Blue Ridge in Franklin County. The last turnpike petition which I found was one dated December 7, 1855, asking for an Act to incorporate a stock company to construct a turnpike from some point on the New London and Rocky Mount pike to the Grist Mill in Roanoke.

A reading of these old petitions in the light of subsequent road history in Franklin County, gives rise to the
suspicion that the petitioners, or at least those who framed
and circulated the petitions, were more interested in creating a
corporation in which they could sell stock than in actually building roads. As a matter of fact, some of the turnpikes did pay
the stockholders well through the toll gates and the toll bridges.

These turnpikes cost from $300.00 to $700.00 per mile,
according to the probity of those in charge of construction, and
were nearly always built by chartered corporations with funds
raised by subscription or by lottery. The granting of a charter
did not necessarily mean the building of a pike. Men often bought
stock in pikes that never existed save on paper.

The only reasonably graded roads in Franklin were those
that followed the old buffalo trails. Those which men "surveyed"
were usually steep, crooked and narrow. If they were not rocky,
they were miry from November to April. The road overseers were
more interested in their emoluments than in the roads, and old
records disclose that they were often the subjects of grand jury
investigations. The roads were "worked" by compulsory labor until
the middle of the last century. Then came the enactment of a road
levy. At first this levy was one dollar per capita, or two days
in labor. A man, plow and two horses received one dollar and a
half a day; and a wagon, two horses and driver, one dollar and a
quarter. A surveyor was paid from one dollar to two dollars per
day, and a common laborer fifty cents per day.

It was enacted by the General Assembly on February 19,
1848, "That the Rocky Mount turnpike company be and are hereby
authorized to increase their capital stock by receiving additional
subscriptions to an amount not exceeding thirty thousand dollars,
in shares of twenty-five dollars each; and the said company is
also authorized to extend their improvement from Jacksonville in
the county of Floyd to a point on the Southwestern turnpike at
or near the Seven mile ford in the County of Smyth: Provided:
The said company shall locate their road upon the most direct
practicable route from point to point as specified in this act
and also in their act of incorporation; And provided, That
twenty-five thousand dollars of said increased capital shall be
expended in the construction of said road west of Jacksonville.

"If the said company shall hereafter deem it to their
interest, and promotive of the public convenience, to construct
a branch of their improvement from a point west of Rocky Mount in
Franklin County, to Taylorsville in Patrick County, the said
company is hereby authorized to construct the same in like manner
as they are now authorized to construct their road; for which

43

purpose they may increase their capital stock the sum of ten thousand dollars of which amount the Board of public works shall subscribe on the part of the commonwealth in the same proportions as it is hereinbefore authorized to subscribe to the capital stock of said company, and upon the like terms, conditions and limitations."

It was enacted by the General Assembly on March 22, 1851, "That it shall be lawful to open books for receiving subscriptions to an amount not exceeding five thousand dollars to be divided into shares of twenty-five dollars each to constitute a joint capital stock for the purpose of constructing a turnpike road from Dickinson's store in the county of Franklin to intersect the Lynchburg and Rocky Mount turnpike road at Asa Holland's in said county. The said books shall be opened at Solomon Pasley's, under the direction of Asa Holland, John Booth, Solomon Pasley; at Union Hall under the direction of Benjamin Hancock, Benjamin Williams and Jordan Robertson; and at Dickenson's store, under the direction of Michael Zeigler, Joseph Dickenson and Hopkins Nowlin, or any three of them.

"When sixty shares of the capital stock shall have been subscribed, the subscribers, their executors, administrators and assigns shall be and are hereby incorporated into a company by the name and style of 'The Snow Creek and Hale's Ford Turnpike Company', conformably to the provisions of chapters fifty-seven and sixty-one of the Code Virginia: Provided; That said company shall not be required to pave or cover their road with stone or gravel nor to make a summer or side road; that the said road shall not be constructed less than sixteen feet wide, and that its grade shall nowhere exceed five degrees."

It was enacted by the General Assembly March 29, 1851, "That the Rockymount turnpike company is hereby authorized and empowered to appropriate such portions of the additional capital required by the first section of the act, entitled, 'an Act to provide for extending the Rockymount turnpike', passed February nineteenth, eighteen hundred and forty-eight, as may be necessary to complete the construction of said road east of Jacksonville."

It was enacted by the General Assembly March 22, 1851 "That it shall be lawful to open books for receiving subscriptions to an amount not exceeding fifteen thousand dollars, in shares of twenty-five dollars each, to constitute a joint capital stock for constructing a turnpike road from some suitable point west of Otter bridge, on the Rockymount turnpike in the county of Bedford, to intersect the Pittsylvania, Franklin and Botetourt turnpike at some suitable point east of William H. Dent's in the county of Franklin. Books shall be opened at the Meadows of Goose Creek in

Bedford county under the superintendence of Lewis C. Arthur, Daniel Tompkins, Green Board and Joseph Parker or any two of them; at Union Hall in Franklin County, under the superintendence of Thomas Dudley, James Robinson, Abraham T. Holland, Henry Dudley and Stephen F. Smith, or any two of them; at Glade Hill in the county of Franklin under the superintendence of John S. Brown, Henry Dillard, William Hancock, or any two of them, and at such other places and under the superintendence of such persons as any three of the above named commissioners may designate. The said company may make a further increase of its capital stock of three thousand dollars, in the manner and subject to the conditions and limitations hereinbefore provided, the Board of Public Works to subscribe for three and private persons two-fifths of said increased capital stock for the purpose of constructing a branch of their road from some suitable point on said improvement to or near Dickinson's store on the Pittsylvania, Franklin and Botetourt turnpike".

It was enacted by the General Assembly on March 31, 1851 "That for the purpose of constructing a turnpike road from the town of Liberty in the county of Bedford, to some point on the New London and Rockymount turnpike, it shall be lawful to open books for receiving subscriptions to an amount not exceeding ten thousand dollars, divided into shares of twenty-five dollars each, to constitute a joint capital stock. The said books shall be opened in the towns of Liberty, under the superintendence of Pleasant Preston, Ebin Nelms, Solomon Lindsay, Lodowick McDaniel, Scott, Thomas Robertson, William Wood, William Terry, Nelson A. Patteson and Gustavus A. Wingfield or any two of them, and at such other place or places, under the direction of such agents as a majority of the above named commissioners may appoint. When one hundred shares of the capital stock shall have been subscribed, the subscribers, their executors, administrators and assigns shall be and are hereby incorporated into a company of the name and style of 'The Bedford Southside Turnpike Company', conformably to the provisions of chapters fifty-seven and sixty-one of the Code of Virginia: Provided, That said company shall not be required to make a summer or side road, nor to pave or cover their road with stone or gravel; that the said road shall be cleared not less than thirty-six feet wide and constructed not less than fifteen feet wide, and that its grade shall nowhere exceed three degrees."

It was enacted March 29, 1851 "That the dam heretofore erected by George Hairston across Smith's river at the Blue Falls in the county of Franklin, shall be and the same is hereby legalized".

Since 1891 the Norfolk and Western Railway has contributed to the prosperity and success of industry and agriculture in Franklin County. Crossing the Roanoke River at Roanoke, the line of the Norfolk and Western from Roanoke to Winston-Salem, North Carolina, is dubbed the "Punkin Vine" because of its winding route.

The Franklin and Pittsylvania Railway was built with funds obtained from a county bond issue ordered by the Board of Supervisors on October 7, 1878. A referendum to determine whether or not the bonds should be issued created more political excitement in the county than any other issue ever submitted to the voters. All land owners were qualified voters and the promoters of the bond issue were openly charged with deeding insignificant and worthless plots of ground to equally worthless citizens in an effort to carry the county in favor of the bond issue. The advocates of the issue won; the Board of Supervisors issued the bonds; and the work of building the thirty miles or road officially began in Gentry's field near Rocky Mount on Friday, March 7, 1879. It was a beautiful bright day. The president of the road, Capt. G. W. B. Hale, turned the first spade full of dirt. G. E. Dennis, according to an old newspaper report, "delivered a grandiloquent speech which held the audience spell bound for several hours". Maj. Robert Mason and Major Whitling, of the Corps of Engineers, were there, as were most of the citizens of the county who were proponents of the enterprise. There was a great barbecue and free food for all comers. Whiskey was distributed with equal generosity. There was much rejoicing on the part of the victors, and equally deep disappointment on the part of the vanguished who were at home, cursing the chicanery of the bond advocates.

The laying of the track was completed on Friday, April 16, 1880, and the first train completed the trip over the entire line at twenty minutes of six o'clock that afternoon.

Soon after its completion the road was leased to the Southern Railway Company for thirty-four years, the lessee assuming the mortgage thereupon. The Southern system operated this road until May 1, 1914, when it was turned back to Franklin County. A company was then organized which operated the road until September 1924, when it went to a receiver's sale. The road was then bought by a company whose officers were N. P. Angle, President; C. S. Bennett, Vice-President; and R. E. Ferguson, Superintendent and Auditor. The road was then motorized, and gave one round trip passenger service daily to Pittsville, and two trips daily to Penhook, besides regular freight service.

In 1930, a train struck a farmer at a grade crossing, injuring him seriously. He instituted suit against the road and won. The road and equipment were sold to satisfy his claims. At the time of the sale, trucks were giving a superior service, hence there was no bidder with operation of the road in view.

It was bought as scrap material. The tracks were taken up and the signs of the roads existence are rapidly disappearing. But the citizens of Franklin County are still (1935) paying taxes to liquidate the bond issue of over fifty years ago.

It was enacted by the general assembly on March 6, 1873, "That it shall be lawful for the president, directors and company of the Liberty and Rocky Mount narrow gauge railroad to extend the said road from the town of Rocky Mount, in the county of Franklin, through the counties of Henry and Patrick, or either of them, to such point on the North Carolina line as the said company may determine".

The Franklin County Telephone Company was organized March 7, 1900. At that time there were about twenty-five telephones in Rocky Mount. Within the next four years lines were extended to Boone Mill and Callaway. These lines soon became "loaded", and in order to accomodate others who wanted telephone service, they were split and used as ground lines, thus making four lines instead of two.

In 1904, there was a metallic iron line connection into Roanoke, which was effected through agreement with the Virginia and Tennessee Telephone Company. For several years it extended no further than Roanoke. At that time the Franklin Telephone Company had a total of sixty subscribers. A few years later lines were extended to Taylor's Store by way of Wirtz; to Union Hall by way of Redwood and Glade Hill; and to Patti by way of Sontag.

In 1914, a line was built to Bassett and connected there on the switchboard of the Henry County Telephone Company.

In 1916, the exchange at Bassett was purchased by the Franklin County Telephone Company, together with lines running into Martinsville.

In 1914, service in the Callaway communities had grown so that a board had to be installed at that point, and connection with Rocky Mount and the outside was made by way of Rocky Mount.

In 1912, telephones in Franklin County had greatly increased, service being supplied principally by the Mutual Telephone Companies of Retreat, Boone Mill, Old Glade Hill, Scruggs, Ferrum, and other points. All these companies connected with the exchange at Rocky Mount.

In 1923, there was a demand for common battery service in Rocky Mount. At that time, the company was operating a Kellog magneto board, and nearly all lines were in cable, and practically all the cable was underground.  Until 1923, Rocky Mount had iron circuits for long distance lines, connecting into Roanoke and Martinsville.

## Chapter 7

## THE WAY OF THE WEED

No other phase of farming involves so much labor as tobacco growing. The plant beds require more care than all other beds. One has to select a new and fertile spot, burn enough wood on the ground to kill all weed and grass seeds, and then pulverize it fine as powder. It is then seeded. This work is usually done in January, and sometimes even before Christmas. As soon as spring warmth begins, a shallow wall of logs and dirt is built around the bed, and the whole is covered with a sort of cheese cloth, commonly called plant bed cloth, to keep the tobacco flies from destroying the tiny plants. These beds are usually about twenty yards long and ten yards wide. The plant bed cloth is kept from sagging by sharpening willow switches at both ends, and by sticking both ends in the ground, forming an arch on which the cloth rests. The young plants have to be watered from a sprinkling pot unless showers come frequently, and "hand-weeded" also, for no land is ever burned deep enough to kill all the grass seeds.

When the plants are six or eight inches tall, they are ready to be transplanted in rows three feet apart, and the same distance apart in the row. When the rains known as "the tobacco season" fail to come in time, the plants grow too large and are lost. When the "season" is unusually delayed, tobacco growers haul water to the fields, set out the plants in dry land and then pour a dipper of water at the root of each plant.

After the plants are set out and begin to grow, the cut worms cut off hundreds of them flush with the ground making much transplanting necessary.

No plant is more quickly damaged by weeds and grass than tobacco. Hence much hoe work is essential. Crab grass is the bane of the Franklin County tobacco growers existence. It is especially annoying on old land, that is to say, land which has been cleared for many years. For this reason, every farmer tries to clear some land every year for tobacco. Besides escaping the curse of the crab grass, he does not have to buy so much commercial fertilizer for the newly cleared ground.

The clearing of this "new ground" was, in my boyhood, a cooperative enterprise, and still is to some extent. The farmers of the Snow Creek community, and, I think, of the whole tobacco growing area of Franklin, once pooled their efforts in the interest of one another. The clearing of "new ground" required the combined labor of more men than the average farmer was able to employ. So the farmer had a "cutting". By a "cutting" was meant felling the larger trees on a forest tract and cutting them into ten or twelve foot sections. The smaller trees and the underbrush had previously been cut and burned by the owner. Much of the smaller growth had been hauled to his residence for fuel, or to some nearby spot for the burning of plant-beds. These cuttings cost the farmer nothing but a jug of whiskey, a big dinner, and the obligation to assist at similar cuttings all the men who had assisted him.

After cuttings came log rollings, also cooperative enterprises, which cost the same as cuttings. Log rolling was a misnomer. The original method might have been to roll the logs into heaps for buring but, if so, the method had passed before my day. Log rolling was really log carrying. Sometimes a log was actually rolled to the pile, but it was the exception and not the rule. I am tempted to say that the carrying method was adopted, like many other farm methods, because it was the hardest way to do the job. The cuttings were usually held in the coldest weather. The log rollings were held in the spring. The machinery used was simple. Hand spikes, six or eight feet long and four inches in diameter, were cut from dogwood and allowed to season. Four or five of these were put under a log, and a man took his place at each end of each spike. In this way men often carried logs so large that a man could not see his lifting partner across the log at the other end of the spike. Frequently the hand spikes were so close together that one could not step over ten or twelve inches at a time without treading on the heels of the man in front of him. It was the hardest of labor, and developed great strength in some men, and ruptured others. Sometimes a crew would lift a log so heavy they could not take a step with it. The load would be too great to lower gradually. It then became a matter of every man dropping his handspike and springing away from the log at the same instant. If one man became frightened and released his end out of time, all might be injured. When a crew had all they could carry, no one dared stumble or weaken lest he hurt his team mates with the increased burden. There were great feats of strength exhibited at log rollings, and much brandy, whiskey and food were consumed. If a question arose as to the superiority of strength in any two men they would "pull it out" by placing a handspike under a log that they could not lift. Each would seize an end and lift with all his might and he who let his end go, or had his hands pulled to the ground, was considered "pulled down" and vanquished.

Timber that would now be worth a fortune for building material was destroyed in clearing new ground. The best and most accessible of timber was wasted before the coming of saw mills to Franklin. Prior to the saw mill, the whip saw was used to manufacture boards for the finer houses. A pit was dug and a scaffold was built over it. Then a log which had been squared with a broad ax, and lined according to the thickness of the board desired, was placed on this platform. One man stood on the scaffold and another in the pit, blindfolded, and drew the saw perpendicularly along the line painted on the log. In this fashion two able bodied sawyers could cut two or three hundred feet of boards per day. The day of the whip saw had passed, and steam and water powered sawmills were in vogue, when I was born. Yet many were still building their houses of logs as their fore-fathers had done. My grandfather, Pinckney Green Wingfield, insisted on having a log house when he removed from his "upper place" (which I now own) to his "lower place" (which I sold on January 16, 1937). This log house was under construction when I was a school boy. With my schoolmates, Charles and Alice Lovell, I would stop when going to and from "The Mountain School", to watch the broad ax wielder as he hewed the logs for this building. Every sleeper, still, plate and joist that went into this house was hand hewn. Using a broad ax is an art. I wondered, and still wonder, how one could take such a heavy, unwieldy, ugly looking tool and make a log into such splendid building material. In the process the hewer would "scalp" the logs, line it, score it in, then hew to the line. That's how we got our simile for plain speech and square dealing, "hewing to the line and letting the chips fall where they will". I clearly recall that the hewer who was preparing the logs for my grandfather's house was "lining" his logs with pokeberry juice instead of with a crayon or common paint.

After the rolling and burning of the logs, comes the "coltering" of the new ground. By "coltering" is meant the first plowing of the new ground. A sharp piece of steel, about two inches wide and ten inches long, called a colter, is bolted to a "single shovel" plow, and to this plow two mules are hitched. The older and slower the mules the better. Woe to the colterer whose team becomes fretful and fiery! There are too many un-breakable roots that stop such a team so suddenly as to throw them on their haunches. There are also too many roots that break, fly back, and bark the shins of the colterer. There is no danger from the handles of a coltering plow: they dip when a root is struck. They act quite unlike the handles of the popular turn-ing plow of my boyhood called "the Farmer's Friend". Never was a plow so misnamed. In bottom land it ran so deep that one needed an elephant to draw it. In rocky land it required both a giant and a gymnast to keep it in the ground at all. If the point struck a rock, or a root, the handles, instead of dipping, would fly up and strike the plowman in the chest or under the

chin. I think that if the Devil had given Job a Farmer's Friend
plow, that gentleman, whose name is a synonym for patience, would
hardly be supplying texts for sermons today.  I can, in imagination, still feel those sickening wallops in the solar plexus.
All farm implements were simple in my boyhood.  In addition to the
foregoing,there were the shop made hoes, mattocks, drag harrows
and double shovel plows.

        After the coltering, a drag harrow was pulled over the
"new ground" to collect the turf and separate it from the dirt.
Then great turf piles were collected, and after March winds
seasoned these piles for a few days, they were burned.  The "new
ground" was then "crossed".  That is to say, it was plowed across
the colter furrows.  For this operation, a "bull tongue" was
bolted on a single shovel plow.  A "bull tongue" is very much
like a colter except it is a bit broader.  The land was then
harrowed again, and "laid off" in furrows three feet apart.
Fertilizer was sown in these furrows, and a "list" made on top
of them.  By "list" was meant a small sharp ridge made by running
a plow on each side of the open furrow piling the dirt to the
center.  Up to 1900, not many farmers attempted to "list" new
ground.  Little mounds of soil - - - "hills" they were called
- - - were made with a hoe over a handful of fertilizer.  The
plants were set in these hills.  It was hard labor.  A strong
man could make 1000 hills per day.

        After the tobacco plants grow beyond the cut worm's
power, the hornworms attack the leaves of the growing plants.
The hornworm comes from the egg of a large moth, called a tobacco
fly.  This moth is not to be confused with the tiny tobacco fly
against which plant beds are screened.  These hornworms can eat
as much as a silk worm, and they often grow to be three or four
inches long, and as large as a man's finger.  They have to be
picked off the plants by hand and killed.  This was a "child's
job" in my boyhood, and a shuddery one for a child who was afraid
of the wriggling, spitting things.

        Tobacco must have two or three hoeings, and the same
number of plowings.  The "worming" continues throughout these
several "workings", and on to the harvesting of the crop.  After
tobacco is "laid by", that is to say given its last "working",
each plant has to be "topped", leaving from ten to fifteen leaves
on a stalk,  Of course, as soon as it is topped, suckers begin
to put out at the jointure of the leaves with the stalks, and these
have to be pulled off regularly, lest they sap the strength from
the leaves.

        In my boyhood, after corn and tobacco were "laid by",
and suckering and worming time had come, the children were put

52

in the fields, and the men began to haul wood to the several tobacco barns for burning in the flues in which the plants were cured. And frequently this season was used to "raise" a new barn. Barn raising, like cuttings and log rollings, was a cooperative enterprise. The average two horse Franklin farm had from three to six of these buildings. The logs, about twenty feet in length and from eight to ten inches in diameter were dragged to the site where the stone foundation had been laid. Then the neighbors came together and "raised" (and sometimes roofed) the barn in one day. The finishing touches, such as hanging the door, building rock flues, and chinking and daubing the cracks between the logs, were left to the owner. By "chinking" is meant the placing of pieces of wood between the logs. By "daubing" is meant the throwing of soft mud, made of red clay, against the chinking to make it stick fast between the logs, and so keep out the air. In curing tobacco the heat was to be regulated if the proper color is to be obtained. This means that the barns must be reasonably tight. The interior of an old fashioned tobacco barn was divided into four sections, or "rooms", about four and a half feet wide, and running the length of the building. These rooms were six or eight tiers high, the tier poles being approximately three feet above each other. Tobacco sticks, riven from oak or chestnut trees, and about five feetlong, were laden with six or eight tobacco plants each, and placed in these rooms, each end of the stick resting on a tier pole. These tier poles had to be nearly as large as the logs from which the barn was built, so they would not spring, when men stood on them to hoist the tobacco in its place, nor sway under the great weight of the green tobacco. The barns were usually roofed with riven oak boards three feet in length and about six inches wide.

At the beginning of this century, tobacco was harvested exclusively by splitting the stalk to within six or eight inches of the ground, then cutting the stalk off and forking it over a tobacco stick. The tobacco knife was a curved six inch blade sharp on both edges. As the demand for bright cigarette tobacco increased, cutting down the stalks decreased, and growers would strip the leaves from the plants when they began to ripen at the ground. The leaves are then looped over the tobacco sticks with twine. This method of harvesting enables the growers to make bright tobacco even of the top leaves which formerly did not have time to ripen and so had to be sold as "green tips" at an extremely low price. Nearly all tobacco is harvested now by pulling instead of cutting.

After tobacco is strung on sticks and hoisted into barns, it is allowed to hand a few days, without fire, for the "yellowing" process. When of proper color, fires are kindled in the flues and temperature is kept at between 90 and 100 degrees

53

fahrenheit for a day or two for the "shrinking" process. Then the fires are gradually increased until the leaf is dry. During the last day or two of firing, the temperature ranges from 200 to 240 degrees, thoroughly seasoning the stems, or stalks and stems if the whole plant has been cut. During the curing process one has to stay at the barn day and night to tend the fires and keep the thermometer at the proper point.

In the old days there were a great many professional "tobacco curers" who went from farm to farm taking charge of a barn as soon as it was filled, and staying with it until the fires died. For this service they usually charged a fee of five dollars per barn, which was reasonable enough when one considered that each barn required six or eight days of unremitting watchfulness. These professional "curers" were elderly men, usually without farms or families - - - ne'er-do-wells who drifted from place to place. They had almost disappeared before I came upon the scene.

It was a high occasion in my childhood when I was permitted to spend a night with my father at a tobacco barn. For the curing season, a bed was made by stuffing a cheap cloth "tick" with wheat, straw or corn shucks. This was placed on the ground, in the light of the glowing flues, and on it the "curer" reposed and snatched a few minutes' sleep between feeding wood into the flues, and reading the thermometer. When one man had cured six or eight barns of tobacco in succession, he was so broken from loss of sleep that he deserved a vacation. But there were no such resting spells for the tobacco grower.

I shall never forget the romance of curling up by my father on his straw bed and watching the stars, and listening to the honking of the wild geese flying over to the south. Having no responsibility for the curing, I would soon fall asleep to be awakened far in the night by the ring of the ax as my father, or his helper, chopped more wood for the fires. At daybreak I would return to the house expecting such a reception from my mother as was fitting for one who had been away for such a long time, and on such a marvelous adventure! To say "I stayed at the barn last night", was sufficient to excite the envy of all younger or less adventurous playmates. But tobacco curing was anything but romance for my father. I did not understand then the meaning of his tired eyes, and of his weary appearance. Now I know the price he paid in rearing his children.

When curing season was over, and frequently before it was over, marketing began. We had to wait for a damp or rainy spell, or else cover the dirt floor of the barn with wet, green, boughs, so as to get the tobacco "in order". By "in order", I mean that the leaves had to be soft and pliable, so they might

54

be taken down from the tiers, assorted, and tied in bundles for market, without crumbling or shattering them. Much of this sorting, and bundling into "hands", was done by lamp light after a laborious day had been spent in the fields sowing wheat, or getting wheat land ready for seeding. When five or six hundred pounds of tobacco had been assorted and "bundled", it was hauled to a warehouse in Danville or Martinsville. My father never sold tobacco at Rocky Mount, the county seat.

Tobacco warehouses or "inspections" were erected throughout Virginia at an early day. In many instances, they became the nuclei of towns and villages. Danville and Lynchburg began as tobacco inspections. Inspectors were public officials, and their salaries were regulated and paid by law. In the archives of the State Library at Richmond are numerous petitions to the Legislature from these inspectors and their friends asking that their salaries be increased, and that the tax on the inspectors themselves, as well as the rent on the warehouses, be reduced. There were frequent requests that more money be allowed for nails and coopering. There were protests from proprietors that the upkeep of the warehouses amounted to more than the rent allowed them. The equivalent of all our modern cupidity prevailed. The inspectors were responsible for the loss of all tobacco in their warehouses, yet we frequently find in the Legislative Petitions, appeals asking relief when tobacco had been lost. They declared that if they were forced to pay for the loss of the tobacco, and for the hogsheads, it would ruin them. Legislation by petition had its good points, for when such a petition from an inspector and his friends was read there would invariably follow a counter-petition declaring that the inspection had been without fence, gate, door or lock for months, and therefore the loss was inexcusable.

In my youth there was intense rivalry between operators of warehouses for the sale of leaf tobacco. Each warehouseman claimed that a better price was obtainable at his particular house, though the same buyers operated at all sales. Such "advantages" as better lighting, first sales, better display, closer attention from the proprietor, were played up in much the same manner as modern cigarette and toothpaste advertising. The equivalent of all our modern specious advertisements existed in "the good old days".

There was keen rivalry among inspectors and owners of inspections. Tobacco pickers, as well as inspectors, were appointed by the County Court, and each inspection claimed the best pickers. "Your tobacco will yield greater returns if properly picked or assorted. Bring it to our pickers. They know how." How modern reads this ancient advertisement!

The growers protested at the necessity of hauling, or rolling, their crops great distances. Groups were constantly petitioning the Virginia Legislature for the establishment of more accessible inspections. Then the inspectors, pickers, and warehouse owners of established inspections would become active, representing that the proposed new inspection would increase the duty on tobacco and add to the burden of the already over-taxed citizens. Already, they claimed, the salaries were so low that it was difficult to get capable men for the inspections then in operation. Such a protest was made when George Cabell and his neighbors petitioned, in 1805, for the establishment of an inspection on the Cabell lands on Blackwater. It appears that the inspection was built, but that the citizens of Franklin continued to haul or roll most of their tobacco to Lynchburg.

Many planters did not own wagons suitable for long distance hauling. Tobacco was often prized into large hogsheads of thick, riven, oak staves. A spindle and shafts were then attached, and oxen or mules pulled it to Lynchburg. The hogshead rolled through mud and water, but without damage to the tobacco, so well made were the casks, and so firmly was the tobacco pressed therein. I recall seeing at the Becker and Cook places in Franklin, during my boyhood, many "prizing trees" where these hogsheads were packed. Prizing trees were trees with a mortise about six by ten inches, and eight or ten feet from the bround. Into the mortise the end of a twenty foot pole or "sweep" was placed, and under this lever the hogshead was set to receive the tobacco. Two or three men at the end of such a lever could prize tobacco into a very solid cake.

A petition was presented to the Virginia Legislature in the early 1800's asking that public inspectors "break all hogshead in four different parts in order to detect the many impositions practiced in prizing, and that inspections where such caution is over-looked, or fraudulent prizing connived at, should be closed". Out of this breaking of hogsheads, for inspection, arose the phrase "tobacco breaks" which was later applied to auction tobacco sales and, later still, to those extremely heavy sales which amounted to a glut of the market.

When good wagons became common, tobacco rolling was supplanted by tobacco hauling. I recall many rides in a covered wagon to the Danville tobacco market with my father, or with a hired man. Danville was forty miles away, but the roads were so bad that we could never complete the trip the first day. We would "camp out" at some country store, or by the roadside, where tobacco haulers camps had been erected, and where such food as we had not brought along, might be bought. After an hour or two of conversation with other tobacco haulers, we would climb into the covered wagon, or into the bunks of the camp houses, wrap ourselves in the bed quilts we had brought along, and try to sleep. At four o'clock next morning, or earlier, lanterns would be lit, horses fed, and the journey resumed. Country storekeepers, with an eye to business, often built crude stalls for horses, as well as camps for men, to shelter them from rain and sleet, and to obviate tethering for the night. Such stores were popular, and one often found, on arriving at them, that all the accomodations had been preempted.

On arriving in a tobacco town one found stalls for the horses under the warehouses. As a lad, these places were a terror to me. Unhitching the horses, the driver would lead them away, leaving me to follow him with the horse feed. The stalls were in rows, three or four hundred feet long, with a very narrow aisle between. Sometimes one had to walk to the far end to find space. What an ordeal to walk down that narrow aisle flanked on both sides by the heels of strange mules and horses! As a rule, one end of the main warehouse floor was shut off by a partition, and equipped with stoves and "sleeping racks" fastened to the wall, two or three berths high. After supping in a nearby restaurant, or eating the food brought along, we would arrange the bedding on these shelves, climb up, and try to sleep. It was invariably a vain effort. Usually a group of old friends, or relatives, who had not met since the last marketing season, would get together and sit around the big-bellied stove and talk the night away. Many farmers who were quiet neighbors, and good church members at home, took advantage of these marketing trips to sample such saloon goods as were not procurable at home. As a rule, there were several half-drunken farmers to make the night hideous with their maudlin songs and silly boastings.

When packed on the wagon for market, tobacco was separated according to quality. In unloading, the several lots were weighed separately and placed on the warehouse floor in piles according to grade. At the time of which I write, the professional pickers had disappeared, and each grower graded his own crop before hauling it to market. There were the "lugs" or leaves which grew next to the ground and were full of sand holes; the bright leaves from the middle of the plant, called "wrappers"; and the top leaves of the plant, called "green tips". There were always these three grades and, usually, two more "in between" grades. The "wrappers" were so called because, being the finest leaves, they were used to wrap the plugs which were pressed for chewing. At the beginning of the twentieth century, there was an increase in the use of cigarettes and a decrease in the use of chewing tobacco, with the result that the bright, chaffy "lugs" began to bring more than the leaves of greater strength. Today the very name "wrappers" has almost faded out of the vocabulary of the tobacconists.

Each pile of tobacco had a tag affixed by a sharp wooden peg about the size of a pencil. On this tag, or ticket, was written the weight of the pile, and the name of the grower. As the auctioneer walked down the line of piles "crying the bids", he was followed by clerks who added to the tags the amounts paid for the piles, stating the price per pound as well as the total.

The arrival of the auctioneer was the signal for the sale to begin. The first sale usually began about eight o'clock, and lasted an hour or longer, according to the quantity on the floor. Then the same buyers, and sometimes the same auctioneer, would go to the warehouse that had the second sale. As a rule each warehouse had its own auctioneer. Where there were several warehouses, as in Danville, there was an agreement whereby the order of sale rotated, so that all warehouses might have an equal number of first sales. The warehouse having the first sale had a decided advantage. Unless the farmer was obligated to some particular warehouseman, he would, on arriving in Danville, inquire as to what house would have the first sale next day, and then he would drive to that house and unload. To be at the warehouse having the first sale meant that he could get away from town earlier for the long drive over the muddy roads back to the farm. When there was only one warehouse in town, as was the case for many years in Rocky Mount and Martinsville, the sale would begin about nine o'clock, and the grower could be on his way home by noon or shortly thereafter. Originally, when these auction sales or "breaks" were about to begin, the public was notified by several long blasts from a ram's or cow's horn. The horn had disappeared when I began to go to market, but by then, at every warehouse entrance, there was a common farm bell, atop a fifteen or twenty foot pole, whose peals, announcing the beginning of sales, could be heard all over town.

The town merchants attended these sales, or sent "runners" with handbills to announce their bargains. They seemed to think the farmer an important man. These auction sales also drew patent medicine vendors, fortune tellers, horse traders, politicians, book agents and dealers in all sorts of cheap and shoddy wares. The tobacco growers were considered gullible and "good-picking", so when the marketing season began to bring them to town in large numbers, these tricksters, like vultures, came from afar.

My father was a shrewd man, and the way he would "cuss out" these sharpers always trilled my boyish heart. I have always discouraged swearing but, looking back from these years, I do not find it in my heart to say my father was not justified when he cursed these cheats who preyed upon his more gullible neighbors.

When the sales were over and he turned toward home, he still had his tobacco money. He also had a pity, mixed with contempt, for those who were so foolish as to squander the proceeds of a hard-earned crop - - - a crop which, he often said, required thirteen months of the year to grow and market.

# Chapter 8

## MILLING

Blackwater derived its name from the color of its water when first seen by the settlers who came to Franklin. It is said that its inky appearance was caused by the numerous black walnuts which grew along the banks and fell into the stream.

Furnace Creek derived its name from the old Washington Iron Works.

Crump's Branch derived its name from "Billy" Crump whose grave is in the barn lot of D. A. Bowman, about 500 yards from where the Branch empties into Pigg River. The tomb is built of sandstone and is about one foot high and eight feet square. An old forge and furnace once stood near the grave.

There are branches in every section of the county which bear such names as still-house, tan-yard, and cane-mill. The names were derived from the early association of these brooks with the manufacture of spirits, leather and sorghum.

Franklin County is one of the few places where one may still see the old covered wooden bridges of long ago. They still span a number of Franklin County streams though some of them are no longer used. The author recalls crossing such bridges over the Staunton River at Hale's Ford, over Snow Creek at Snow Creek, over Chestnut Creek between Snow Creek and Rocky Mount, over Pigg River at Rocky Mount, and over Gill's Creek on the Lynchburg Turnpike. The bridge at Rocky Mount was built by Larkin T. and N. C. Cassell in 1857. Its timbers were hand-hewn and fastened together with locust pins. James Moir's carriage broke through the Gill's Creek bridge many years ago but without fatalities. The bridge at Hale's Ford washed away in 1877, just a few minutes after William Booth had crossed it with a four-house team and wagon.

The covered bridge was a meeting place for the boys of the neighborhood. The names of most of them were carved on its timbers. Its walls were often plastered with the gaudy posters of the circus that had been or was coming to Rocky Mount, Martinsville, Roanoke or Danville. The less colorful posters of tobacco warehouses, clothing stores and patent medicines were in evidence the year round. It was a good place to eat water melons on a rainy day and, generally speaking, served as a sort of community hall.

In Franklin, too, may be seen the old grist mills operated by water which rushes along from the mill pond through the "mill race" and into the troughs of the old "overshot" wheel. The author cannot name all of these mills, most of which have ceased to grind, but the following are a few: Altick's Mill on Chestnut; Angell's Mill on Little Creek; Barbour's Mill on Story Creek; Belcher's Mill on Crabtree; Bernard's Mill on Guthrie's Run, a tributary of Snow Creek; Boone's Mill on Maggoty Creek; M. G. Booth's Mill on Gill's Creek; Andrew Brook's Mill on Walker's Creek; Brook's Mill on Crabtree Creek; Callaway's Mill on Blackwater (south fork); Cassell's Mill on Story Creek; William Cassell's Mill on the headwaters of Chestnut Creek; Choice's Mill on Snow Creek; Dillon's Mill on Blackwater; Draper's Mill on Gap Branch; Dry Land Mill on Nicholas Creek; Gentry's Mill on Furnace Creek, one-half mile from Rocky Mount; John Hale's Mill on Blackwater; Hancock's Mill on Pigg River; Zachariah Helm's Mill on South Pigg River; Hickman's Mill on Blackwater; Ira Hill's Mill on north Pigg River; Holt's Mill on Blackwater; Hopkins's Mill on Pigg River; Horsley's Mill on Grassy Fork Creek; Hundley's Mill on Reed Creek; Hurt's Mill on Story Creek; King's Mill on Town Creek; Laprade's Mill on Snow Creek; Lynch's Mill on Powder Mill Creek; Sam Montgomery's Mill on Turner Creek; Morgan's Mill on Bull Run; Nowlin's Mill on Runnett Bag Creek; Armistead Parsell's Mill on Little Chestnut; Bob Pinckard's Mill on Grassy Fork Creek; Pinckard's Mill on Doe Run Creek; Charles Pinkard's Mill on Snow Creek, near Doyle's; William Pinkard's Mill on Grassy Fork Creek near W. J. Wingfield's old place; Saunder's Mill on Blackwater; Esom Sloan's Mill on North Pigg River; Tom Snead's Mill on Long Branch; Spencer's Mill on Nicholas Creek; Tate's Mill on Little Chestnut Creek; Teel's Mill on Teel's Creek; Tyree's Mill on Doe Run Creek; Powell M. Wade's Mill on Big Branch, four miles west of Rocky Mount; T. Webb'e Mill on Gap Branch; Webster's Mill on Blackwater; White's Mill on Snow Creek; Wysong's Mill on Indian Run' Wysong's Mill on Linville Creek; and Zeigler's Mill on Pigg River.

Tradition has it that Charles Pinkard, during a freshet, mounted his horse, rode down to his mill, cut a notch on a sycamore by the creek, and dared the Celestial Powers to let the river reach his mark. Regardless of the tradition, the mill was washed away. Many of the mills, in addition to grinding corn, wheat and rye, carded wool into rolls which were then spun and woven by the thrifty housewives into cloth for the family clothing.

These long-ruined mills once played an important part in the lives of our Franklin forbears. They were their first applications of water power to industry. Here the farmers' ox-carts and wagons brought grist and wool for grinding and carding,

while the farmers themselves held social intercourse in the mill-
yard, exchanging news and ideas as they waited for their goods.

The miller was a man of importance. Statutes were made
for his regulation and for the ordering of his tolls. From his
constant stream of patrons he gathered the neighborhood gossip,
and insured it proper circulation.

Some of these mills were equipped for bolting four, but
the large flour mills of the cities, by the superior quality and
smaller price of their product, long ago put them out of that
business. As makers of cornmeal they persisted until well into
the new era, when the more conveniently located steam and gasoline
powered mill drew away their customers. They persisted for a
time on the local belief in the superiority of waterground meal
to that made by other mills.

Many of the old mill ponds which supplied water for
turning the ponderous overshot wheels have survived the mills
for which they were constructed. These add much to the scenic
beauty of Franklin. They also afford the finest fishing places
in the world.

I have fished in the waters of nearly every country of
our globe but, aside from angling for "hornyheads" in Grassy Fork,
I have never known such sheer fishing enjoyment as was mine when
I caught the shining perch from the old Franklin Belcher and
Billy Pinckard mill ponds. Before I was ten years old my father
would put me on the back of a gentle old plow-horse, with a bag
of corn in front of me, and send me away to the mill. The mill-
sack held about three bushels, and when only a bushel of corn was
put in it there was no difficulty in keeping it on the horse.
The same amount of grain in each end of the sack made a perfect
balance. How proudly I rode away! The years that have passed
have taken me to the far places of the world, but I found a greater
thrill riding away with my bag of corn than I have ever found in
walking up the gangplank to sail for some foreign shore.

I can still feel something of the chagrin that was
mine one day when I had to dismount to open a gate and in trying
to remount pulled the "turn" off the horse and could not put it
back. How humiliating to my pride to have to go back home for
some one to replace the "turn"! It was the worst sort of way of
confessing that I wasn't as big as I thought I was. I have twice
used the word "turn" and, for the benefit of "outlanders", hasten
to explain that in Franklin County the word has always meant a
bag of grist. As a rule there would be several "turns" ahead of
mine, so while waiting for my "turn" to be ground--not waiting
my turn, mine you--I would fish in that awesome body of water--

the largest I had ever seen--the mill pond.  I usually had an hour or two with the perch and carp, for the mill ground slowly. It is said that a newcomer to the neighborhood when he visited one of these mills for the first time snorted contemptuously, "I could eat bread as fast as you grind meal to make it!"  "Yes", said the mild mannered miller, "but how long could you hold out?"

"Until I starved to death", said the newcomer, after which the miller took a fresh chew of tobacco and was silent.

# Chapter 9

## BLOCKADING

The term "blockader" was and is nearly always used in Franklin County for the unlicensed distiller rather than the term "moonshiner". The exciting and dangerous experiences of ancestors in running boats through an enemy's blockade gave rise to the term. The interference of revenue officers and especially the meddling of disgruntled and grudge-bearing neighbors make the blockaders extremely secretive about their operations. The secrecy is not due to any sense of guilt or shame for the blockader feels he has as much right to make a part of his corn into whiskey without license as he has to make the other part into bread. He considers that a tax of a dollar on a quarter's worth of whiskey is an morally wrong as robbery.

But the chief motive for "blockading" in Franklin is no longer to supply one's family and social requirements. The motive now is economic. Life was never especially easy in Franklin, and with the decreased prices on all farm commodities life has become increasingly difficult. Franklin citizens, no longer landlocked, knew what the world outside was enjoying, and they wanted their share. Those who went away "to the public works" (as industrial centers were called) did share in the automobiles, bath tubs and other modern comforts and conveniences. Those who could not get away turned to making and distributing liquor. It meant, besides the spice of adventure, money for doctor's bills, taxes, pianos, automobiles and other things which ordinary tobacco and corn crops could never procure. It was not because blockading offered more ease and comfort than tilling the soil. On the contrary, it was hard nerve-racking, sleep-robbing work.

Since I have not been in Franklin County for more than a fortnight at a time since as a mere lad I went away to college, I dare to speak of the distilling process without fear of having the reader suspect me of being an ex-blockader.

I hasten to confess that I did glean this information after I began to study for the ministry. Nor am I ashamed of the fact that my old neighbors trusted me sufficiently to hide nothing from me though they knew I disapproved of their business. I have seen their corn moistened and warmed for sprouting and spread for drying afterwards. I have been in the mill where this sprouted corn was being ground and I have tasted the sweet mash made from this meal and warm water. I have listened to the sad tales of men who lost their mashes because they chilled down before the "beer" fermented properly. I have been present when

65

a "run" was being made. No, happily not, a run from revenue
officers, for it would have been very embarrassing to a ministerial
student to have been taken with blockaders. The distilling of a
lot of beer which had fermented the same week was always called
a "run". The liquor which came through the "worm" at the first
boiling was called "singlings". When the still was emptied of
the mash and the "singlings" poured in and boiled, that which
came through was called "doublings", or whiskey. The finished
product was then hauled to the surrounding towns and cities and
distributed to the prominent citizens, many of them leading
churchmen and government officials. From the proceeds thus
derived the blockaders and distributors were enabled to buy
automobiles with which to haul their wet goods and frequently
to buy good plantations and even town houses. The traffic was
expecially heavy toward the end of the year for most families in
town and country seemed to feel that they must have some whiskey
to make egg-nog with which to celebrate Christmas and New Year's
Day. And of course there had to be whiskeys for cuttings, log-
rollings, shuckings and other cooperative "workings".

     I have seen some crude distilling outfits in use in
Franklin County. One at least was made by driving an oak cask,
open end down, into a common wash pot. Into an augur hole in
top of the keg one end of a pipe was inserted. The other end,
which was bent into a spiral called a "worm", lay in another keg
of cold running water to condense the vapor discharged from the
boiling pot. I have seen other distilling outfits which were of
copper and quite pretentious - - - indeed I found several of these
on a farm of mine which was unoccupied for a decade. I have often
said jestingly to my friends that I proposed to convert my non-
productive farm lands into revenue producing acreage by renting
distilling sites along the streams.

     There was and is little sentiment in Franklin County
against dram drinking. The man who habitually got drunk was
considered a "no-count" fellow and a man who championed "teeto-
talism" was a fanatic. They were faithful to what they considered
their obligations, but abstinence from drink was not conceived to
be one of their duties.

     Distilleries were numerous until the imposition of a
tax on liquor manufacture. My grandfather's distillery stood
in a little house built for it near the spring. After the tax
there was set up in each community a larger distillery to which
the farmers hauled their surplus apples and peaches to be "made
up on halves". That is to say the distiller kept half of the
brandy as payment for the distilling. Our common distiller was
a man named Peter Finney. I have picked up "windfalls" many a
day to be hauled to his place.

Like most of his neighbors, my father laid in the annual supply of brandy as regularly as the supply of meat and bread. I can well remember the rise of opposition to liquor in Franklin. It was very feeble, indeed never grew strong, and was led by non-resident preachers who came in from some nearby city to fill their regular appointments. The native born preachers frowned on such "meddling" with the personal rights of the people" and often quoted Paul's advice to Timothy to "take a little wine for thy stomach's sake". When the matter became an issue in some of the churches, the conservatives got the reins and forbade joining temperance societies, on pain of expulsion from church membership. I cannot name but two preachers of my boyhood who refused strong drink as a beverage. The two ministers (previously referred to) who made our home theirs during their monthly visits, never declined the invitation to the sideboard where the wicker-covered decanter sat the year around. And my father would have considered it a distinct discourtesy to lead any of his gentlemen guests to the dining room without first inviting them to "have a dram". The sideboard was provided with a pitcher of water, goblets, spoons and sugar. Every man prepared his own drink and stood while he drank it. As a lad I got the impression that our preacher guests, and men generally, never talked quite so well until they had stopped at that old walnut sideboard enroute to the dining room.

I can recall only one instance when any one at our house drank to excess. That was at a cornshucking. My father sent him home without ceremony.

Most reforms move slowly but the attempted liquor reform never moved beyond a snail's pace in Franklin. When prohibition came the few licensed distilleries closed and hundreds of block-aders began operations. There had been blockaders from the first imposition of a tax but not comparable in numbers to the post-prohibition crop. Since it was a most profitable employment and as few peiple if any believed distilling morally wrong, the whole county soon appeared to be engaged in the manufacture and distri-bution of liquor. The county became so notorious as a producer of illicit whiskey that the newspapers of the entire nation carried stories about it. While living in Idaho, I saw an Associated Press item declaring that Franklin County led the country in lawlessness so far as moonshining and bootlegging were concerned. The sons of the citizens who were community leaders in my boyhood days became involved in the traffic. Some of them shot prohibition officers, others were shot by officers, and still others hot one another. In recent years the roofs have been torn from my vacant houses to shelter boxes of mash and keep it from "chilling down", and the houses themselves have often been occupied by these blockaders. In one of these houses an erstwhile neighbor of mine, and the father of one of my boyhood sweethearts, was slain by the son of an old neighbor who owned the farm adjoining my father's land. His act was supposed to have been done in revenge for what city bootleggers term "hijacking". He was sent to the State Penitentiary for a long term. Nowadays when one passes a particularly good house or farm in Franklin he may frequently be reminded that the owner procured it with proceeds of his illegal traffic in liquor. Prohibition may have been good for the nation as a whole--I will not argue that point--but I will argue that it was distinctly unfortunate for Franklin County.

The repeal of the Eighteenth Amendment is but a year behind us as this is written (1934) yet in so brief a period there are distinct signs that Franklin may soon yield its unenviable position as "the illicit whiskey center of Virginia". The County News and Franklin Chronicle, published at Rocky Mount, stated in a front page article on July 26, 1934, that "A severe setback was given the illicit whiskey business by the A.B.C. (Alcohol Beverage Control Board). The sales have decreased seventy-five per cent. The ancient industry which once manufactured three million dollars worth annually will soon be mere history. Selling corn by the gallon must now be through legal channels if Franklinites want to be free and prosper. The people who have made whiskey 'since the memory of man runneth not to the contrary' have been good citizens. They have supported movements for the county's good while violating an unpopular law. They have built beautiful homes for their families, have been good neighbors and have not frowned on anything for the moral good of the community. At the same time their 'stills' have turned out whiskey by the thousands of gallons. It gained a reputation in scores of cities despite the brand made of sugar which was so generally unpopular. But these days are gone forever! In all towns and cities where Franklin whiskeys were formerly in such demand even better whiskeys are now dispensed legally through the A.B.C. and at prices with which Franklin's illicit manufacturers cannot compete. The numerous 'foreign' automobiles once seen on Franklin roads are thinning now. Some of the leaders among the illicit distillers propose continuing in the whiskey business in a legal way. If they succeed the immense revenue from whiskey will continue to flow into Franklin County pockets and in a manner perfectly legal. Thus from developements in Franklin, reputedly the nation's leader in illicit whiskey manufacturing, it is evident that President Franklin D. Roosevelt's theory about delivering the nation from the hands of illicit whiskey makers and dealers was eminently correct. At least Franklin County is passing from the ranks of the law breakers".

## Chapter 10

## SOME NEGROES

Tobacco culture made slavery a popular institution in
Franklin, though the Brethren (Dunkard) population kept it from
the unanimous favour it had in Eastern Virginia. The tobacco
growing section had a large Negro population. There were comparatively few slaves on Blackwater.

The lot of the Negro slave in Franklin was no happier
than elsewhere. The same restrictions were imposed. Slaves were
not permitted to possess poisonous drugs or firearms. It was
illegal at certain periods to teach Negroes to read and write.
The penal code which applied to whites did not apply to Negroes.
The county court could sentence a Negro to be hanged for arson
or theft. Capital punishment could also be assessed against a
Negro for assaulting a white man or for poisoning live stock.

Free Negroes were in disfavour. Slaveholders feared
their influence on the slaves. These "freemen" were often excluded
from the State. Their petitions to the Legislature, to be allowed
to remain in Virginia, are numerous in the Archives of the State
Library. Free Negroes were required to register every five years,
giving all possible marks of identification. That there were
several of these "freemen" in Franklin is attested by the numerous
petitions to have them removed from the county. There is at least
one case of record in which one of these Franklin County "freemen"
was himself a slaveholder.

The county records show that the county court appointed
captains to patrol specified areas of the county. Each captain
had a squad of five or six men under him each of whom received
from thirty to sixty cents per night for patroling. The Negroes
corrupted the word patroller to "patterroller", I have listed
spellbound in my boyhood to stories told by aged Negroes of how,
when caught beyond bounds without a pass, they would outrun or
outwit the "patterroller" and so escape a flogging.

The Negroes of Franklin, as in the South generally,
showed great fidelity to their masters during the fateful years
1860-65. They cultivated the land and protected the families
of the men who were in the army. One of these Franklin Negroes,
Silas Green by name, volunteered for service in the Confederate
Army. His master considered him "Too valuable a piece of property
to be permitted to endanger his life". Not discouraged by his
thwarted plans, he organized a company and drilled it for the
field. He had high hopes of serving with it, but at the last

moment his master refused to let him go, and he dejectedly
watched his company march away, then he turned back to his
master's blacksmith shop which he operated with great skill.
After the war Silas Green removed to Lynchburg where he spent
his last years as a teamster.

My own relationships with the Negroes of Franklin
County have been pleasant. Like many Virginia children, I had
a black nurse - - - in fact three of them --- - but I called
none of them Mammy, according to the conventional formula in
the story books about the South. I have never heard a white
child call a Negro woman Mammy. As children we were taught to
call every Negro woman "Aunt", and every Negro man "Uncle". A
birching awaited the child who neglected this courtesy. An
equally severe birching would have been administered to the child
who used the title Mister or Mistress.

Memory is etched with the faces of the Negro men and
women who blest my childhood. There was "Aunt" Aggy, "Aunt"
Lucy, and "Aunt" Caroline. The last named had a son-in-law,
"Uncle" Robert Trotter, who was a tenant on my father's planta-
tion from my very earliest recollection. Many were the times
he rode post haste for Dr. George P. Dillard, Dr. Robert R. Lee
or Dr. R. J. English when I was ill. "Uncle" Robert is still
living (1934) though twenty-five years and more have passed
since I left the old home. One of the pleasures of my annual
home-going is in seeing him. The last time I visited in Franklin,
he rode his mule over to see me and greeted me with an affection
which is quite impossible to describe.

"Aunt" Aggy Muse, with her husband, "Uncle" Horace,
lived for years on my paternal grandfather's "lower place". He
must have been nearly a hundred years old when I entered my teens,
though he always insisted that he was born in 1818. He had a
great fund of stories of Indians and bears with which he held me
spellbound. He was particularly fond of telling about one of
his young "Marsters" of the Muse family who had a pet bear named
Cudjo. According to "Uncle" Horace Cudjo could do some wonderful
tricks. I suspect now that the facts were considerably overlaid
with fancy in order to enhance a small boy's happiness. If that
was his purpose he succeeded well, for I never tired of hearing
about Cudjo and his amazing stunts. I well remember when "Uncle"
Horace died. It was wintry weather, and we had a house full of
Christmas guests, but father insisted that all of the family
should attend the burial. The roads were quite impassable for
vehicles, as they usually were in winter, so we walked to the
graveyard three miles away. I recollect, too, how we openly
conjectured, as we trudged along with father in the lead, whether

"Aunt" Aggy would shout at the funeral. She was very emotional and would march up and down the Church aisles and shout "Glory to God!" "Hallelujah!" She was one of the few Negroes of the community who attended the services in the Churches of the white people. She was much younger than "Uncle" Horace and their uncongeniality was notorious. Father tried to put an end to our irreverent speculation about the shouting at the burial, but we sensed the half-heartedness of his protest and kept up our silly chatter until we were within sight of the open grave.

"Aunt" Lucy was the wife of "Uncle" Marshall Gravely who had belonged to a Gravely family that lived near my mother's girlhood home in Henry County. She was also the mother of two of "Uncle" Robert Trotter's wives. He ("Uncle" Robert) had many wives, though but one at a time.

When one of my playmates would grow angry with me he would say that the Marshall in my name belonged to a Negro. Then the fight would begin! That was supposed to be a terrible insult. I smile sadly now at the recollection of a pale little white lad fighting just because an angry playmate said he was the namesake of a Negro. I mention this to show how even the children were given to understand that the gulf between the races was quite impassable. Today I can name three Negroes who have so befriended me that I should be proud to name a child of mine (if I had a child) for any one of them.

One of the Negro men I liked best was "Uncle" Anthony Wingfield who had been the slave of my great grandfather. And next in my affection was "Uncle" Horace Muse to whom reference has already been made. Of the Negro women "Aunt" Lucy was my favorite. The others were entirely too stern for me. "Aunt" Lucy was a mild-tempered, child-loving old soul with a vast store of songs and superstitions. I wanted no better entertainment than to sit and shudder at her ghost stories. I would often lie awake all night as a result but the stories were worth it!

Several of "Aunt" Lucy's sons-in-law, besides "Uncle" Robert, worked on my father's farm. One of them, "Uncle" John Woody, loved me dearly. From him I learned "the facts of life". He died very mysteriously - - - it was rumored as the result of a blow from his wife, "Aunt" Margaret. I was disconsolate when he died. His widow soon followed him. Another of "Aunt" Lucy's sons-in-law, "Uncle" Dick DeShazo, died under equally strange circumstances. He was a Primitive Baptist preacher. According to my recollection, he could neither read nor write. His wife's name was Alice. She became the wife of "Uncle" Robert Trotter shortly after "Uncle" Dick's death. When "Aunt" Alice died her

71

youngest sister Berta (too young to call "Aunt") succeeded her
as the wife of "Uncle" Robert.

Still another of "Aunt" Lucy's sons-in-law comes to
mind. His name was Charley Gravely and he worked for my father
for many years. He was a stammerer and prefaced nearly every
word he uttered with something that sounded like "enifer". Behind
his back nearly everybody called him "enifer", but they took care
not to use the nickname in his presence, because he was exceed-
ingly hot-tempered. His stammering seemed to bother him less
when he was swearing than at any time. I have often seen him
beat his wife outrageously, but she seemed to like it. She would
remark afterward that a man was not much of a husband if he did
not beat his wife when she crossed him. I was tremendously afraid
of her. She would say to me occasionally, "Honey, old Emma is a
blue-gummed 'oman, and ef'n I bites you you is dead sho. I'se
mo pizen than a rattlesnake". I took her at her word, and kept
at a safe distance.

"Uncle" Horace and "Uncle" Anthony ministered to my
youthful life by mending my broken toys and fishing tackle. And
they helped me to find the nests of wild birds, and the haunts
of the minks and muskrats.

"Uncle" Charlie was devoted to me and gave indispensable
aid when I ran away from home to attend college. I was only
sixteen at the time. My father was violently opposed to my going
to college, though not on the score of my youthfulness. Twice
he took from me my railroad fare to Knoxville which I had earned
working for George T. Pearson and James J. Okes at fifty cents
a day. President Johnson had promised that if I could manage to
reach his college I would not need anything but the labor of my
hands to pay for the college education coveted. Despite the
double loss of my hard earned railway fare, I was not discouraged.
But I saw that I must use strategy. I pretended that I had dismissed the idea of going to college and father believed it. He
tried then to atone for the wrong he felt he had done in taking
my money. He sent "Uncle" Charlie to Danville with a load of
tobacco and sent me along with him to handle the "business end"
of the sale. I asked for enough money from the proceeds of the
tobacco to buy a suit of clothing. The request was readily
granted. I took out the sum requested which was enough to buy
a good suit, but bought instead a cheap suit for six dollars.
The difference I put in my purse to take the place of that which
my father had wrongfully taken from me. On returning from Danville he asked to see the new suit. When I showed it to him he
swore roundly at me for allowing myself to be so badly cheated.
He said the suit would disgrace any white man who put in on and
that he, personally, "would not wear it to a dog hanging".

A few days later father had another load of tobacco packed for Martinsville, wishing to try both markets so as to determine where to sell the bulk of the crop. The wagon was loaded in the afternoon, so the driver could get away on the morrow early enough to sell as the "first sale". When loaded it was pulled under the wagon shed. My cheap cow-hide trunk had been packed and ready for going to college for some time. That night, when the household had retired, I managed to get the trunk on my back and started down the stairs with it. In the dark I stumbled and almost fell down the steps but caught the hand rail and so saved myself. But I made enough noise to arouse my father, who was a light sleeper, and he called out in his stentorian voice demanding to know who was making that noise. I almost held my breath as I stood there still as a mouse waiting until I thought he was again asleep. It appeared like an eternity to me. The trunk seemed to increase in weight at the rate of a pound a second. Finally I got outside with it and stumbled through the darkness to the wagon shed on the hill. I burrowed a hole in the tobacco, stored the trunk in it, covered it with the tobacco and with the fodder which had been put aboard to feed the horses at noon the next day, and returned quietly to my room, but not to sleep. I was too excited over the great adventure of the morrow,- going away to college.

Early next morning "Uncle" Charlie "hitched up" and started up the "bottom road" for Martinsville. I was sent along, as I knew I would be when I put my trunk aboard, to open the numerous gates and "draw-bars" between home and the public highway. I was not expected to accompany the "load" to Martinsville, but when I had opened the last gate for the driver, I fell in behind the wagon, holding on the the tail gate to make walking easier. I did not disclose my presence until we were several miles from home. "Uncle" Charlie was amazed when he found I had come along. He was even more astonished when, in unloading the tobacco, he came to the hidden trunk. I had told him nothing more en route than that I was going with him to Martinsville. I now told him the whole story and enlisted his help in getting the trunk to the Norfolk and Western station. The story of that journey, and the hardships that followed, as I strove for an education, would make a long chapter.

# Chapter 11

## NEWSPAPERS

The first newspaper published in Franklin County was "The Franklin Whig" established in 1834. The Whig was succeeded by "The Franklin Gazette", owned and edited by Randolph Dickinson. The first issue of The Franklin Gazette appeared in 1872. Mr. Dickinson disposed of this newspaper to W. A. and C. J. Griffith who continued its publication until the spring of 1876, when the name was changed to the "The Virginia Monitor", and the property was acquired by W. R. Murrell and W. A. Belcher. The Monitor was soon consolidated with "The Conservative" of Salem, and W. A. and C. J. Griffith again became editors and publishers.

In August 1876, Gabriel Banks and W. I. Boone revived the old Franklin Gazette but their partnership was brief. Banks disposed of his interest to William Bush. Bush sold to John W. Stump of Bedford County, who kept it only a few months. It was purchased by Abraham Hancock and W. A. Belcher in the summer of 1877. Landon Scott of Amherst County was the next editor and publisher. He acquired the property in 1880, but soon disposed of it to George B. Thompson of Amherst County. Thompson sold the paper to George T. and Henry Lee. In 1883, N. W. Floyd was publisher. A man named Davis had charge in 1885. Frazier Otey Hoffman of Bedford succeeded Mr. Davis, and changed the name of the paper to "The Franklin Times". It was transferred to Barnhardt and Moss in 1893.

On account of dissension on political questions, Hoffman started another paper in opposition to The Franklin Times and named the new paper "The Franklin Democrat". Hoffman subsequently reassumed control of The Franklin Times, and consolidated the papers adopting the name "The Times-Democrat".

"The Franklin Chronicle" succeeded The Times-Democrat, and was first owned and edited by A. W. Robins of Bedford. The Franklin Printing and Publishing Company inaugurated the publication of "The County News", the first issue coming from the press on Sept. 20, 1923. The original organization of The County News consisted of N. P. Angle, president; John O. Martin, vice president; C. J. Davis, treasurer; Frank Watkins, secretary; and J. L. Merrylees, editor.

On Feb. 1, 1924, R. P. Dickinson became editor.

A few years later, The Franklin Chronicle, owned by Col. Peter Saunders, was consolidated with The County News.

According to information received from A. W. Robbins and M. T. Harrison, Frazier Otey Hoffman was the son of Samuel Hoffman, a merchant of the town of Liberty in Bedford County. He was born about 1840, and served in the Confederate Army. In early life, he established "The Bedford Star" which was merged in 1885 with "The Bedford Sentinel". The publication of the Star-Sentinel was discontinued in 1886, and that year Mr. Hoffman removed to Rocky Mount. He had a brilliant mind, and married two brilliant women. His first wife was Blanche Douglass, a talented musician and a woman of the finest culture. His second wife was Julia Wyatt Bullard of Bedford. The citizens of Radford erected a monument to her memory. Hoffman developed a love for strong drink early in life and was cursed by the appetite to the end of his days. Toward the close of his life, he was such a confirmed inebriate that his friends ceased to care for him, and he was committed to the Franklin County Poor House. He wandered off toward Rocky Mount one day, and died alone by the roadside.

## THE "CHRONICLE BUILDING"

In 1935, Rocky Mount's oldest landmark was purchased from Peter Saunders and J. N. Montgomery, Jr., by Robert Perdue and Ruffner Price. This building was erected for a tavern at the very beginning of the 19th century, and was over 125 years old when it was razed to make way for a modern structure. It was generally known as the first brick structure erected in the county. Tradition has it that Andrew Jackson lodged in this tavern. The structure came to be known as the "Chronicle Building" because for years it housed The Franklin Chronicle.

Shortly before the Civil War, the tavern was operated by Creed Adams of Snow Creek. In 1847, it passed into the possession of J. T. Turnbull, who continued to conduct a tavern. From Turnbull, it passed into the hands of Capt. G.W.B. Hale who renamed it "The Early House", in compliment to Gen. Jubal A. Early. During Captain Hale's ownership of the building, the hotel was under the management of Allie Binford of Richmond. When it ceased to be used as a hotel, the building housed the newspaper above mentioned, and also supplied law offices for several members of the Franklin County Bar.

## Chapter 12

## SOME OTHER BUSINESSES

### FRUIT GROWING

In the early days of the county, apple trees received but little care. Modern spraying and pruning were unknown. Even then, much of the fruit was good enough for distant markets, though most of it was converted into apply brandy at home. Today, high-powered spraying machines are in common use, and trees are scientifically pruned. Standard sizing machines are used for grading apples. Only the malformed fruit is discarded. Small fruit, if well formed, is as marketable as any. Only in one year since 1900 has the apple crop in Franklin been seriously damaged, and that was by hail. There has been only one complete crop failure during that period.

An illustration of the possibilities of the apple industry is found in the Algoma apple orchards. At the beginning of the 19th century, Peter Guerrant came from Buckingham County, and purchased a large acreage in this valley from two brothers by the name of Anderson. Being a student of horticulture, Guerrant immediately set out an apple orchard. Some of the pippin trees set out by him are over a hundred years old, and are still bearing. He also planted a vineyard with a view to wine making. The place was called "Ash Grove" during his lifetime.

The estate passed from the possession of the original purchaser to his son, John R. Guerrant; thence to his grandson, Peter Moss Guerrant; and thence to his great grandsons John R. and Samuel S. Guerrant, both of whom became physicians.

Dr. Samuel S. Guerrant practiced medicine in Roanoke for ten years, but the call of the ancestral acres caused him to return to Algoma in 1903, and since that time the orchards have been his chief concern and pride.

Since purchasing his brother's interest in Algoma, Dr. Samuel S. Guerrant has frequently packed 500 barrels daily, and the yield has gone as high as 20,000 barrels per year. In 1933, Dr. Guerrant had 180 persons employed in the orchards. The crop is frequently marketed in England. Barrels for shipping purposes are made on the estate, which has a saw mill, planing mill, grist mill and blacksmith shop.

The trees in the Algoma orchards are of all ages from one year to one hundred. A single pippin tree has produced over twenty barrels of fruit in one season. Algoma apples were awarded

prizes at the International Apple Show at Spokane, and won the
Emerson cup in 1907. In 1926, they took over a score of ribbons.
The St. Louis and Jamestown Expositions awarded gold medals to the
apples from these orchards. Dr. Guerrant has a letter written by
General Robert E. Lee on February 23, 1865, expressing thanks to
the doctor's mother for a barrel of apples from Algoma. He also
has a letter from the late President Woodrow Wilson thanking him
personally for a barrel of apples which, Mr. Wilson said, "were
especially good, because they were flavored with friendship".

Dr. Guerrant's fifteen room brick residence is unique
in that many of the rooms are finished in apple wood.

## FURNITURE MANUFACTURING

The largest manufacturing industry in Franklin County
is the Bald Knob Furniture Company at Rocky Mount, established by
N. P. Angle and B. L. Angle in 1906.

## TALC MINING

The Blue Ridge Talc Company located at Henry, is an
important Franklin County industry.

The original owners and operators were known as the
Henry Mining Company. This company began operating in 1914,
directing its efforts toward producing hot plates for fireless
cookers, soapstone griddles, soapstone footwarmers, and small
electrical insulator units. The business was sold about 1916
to the Franklin Soapstone Products Corporation. This company
continued the operation of the plant until the fall of 1918, when
the plant was closed until June 1920, when it was sold to the
Blue Ridge Talc Company, Inc.

Pulverized soapstone is produced in four grades to meet
the demand of the various trades in which it is used. It is
shipped in crude form, loaded in bulk, and pulverized form, packed
in paper bags, plain jute bags, paper lines jute bags and wood
barrels. Operating at the present capacity, there is sufficient
deposit of this material to last a century.

Ochre has also been discovered near the soapstone quarry,
and laboratory tests show the quality to be of exceptional high
grade. So in addition to producing soapstone, the company has
become the largest producer of mineral colors in Virginia. These
consist of cement and mortar colors and paint pigments. The
cement and mortar colors are produced in the following  shades:
brick red, dark red, brown, chocolate brown, dark chocolates,
buff and black. The paint pigments consist of metallic browns,
Venetian reds, white, yellow and gray ochre, and mineral blacks.

78

## MICA MINING

In 1909, George K. Cooper began to work the mica deposit on his land in Chestnut Mountain on the Snow Creek road about twelve miles from Rocky Mount. He soon interested several men from southwest Virginia, who planned to develop the mine on a large scale. Their plans were not executed, and the property, after lying idle for a considerable period, was sold to a group of Danville citizens.

In 1915, H. C. Fields, representing the Chestnut Mountain Mica Company, bought the property. This company operated the mine for a few years, when it was purchased by the Clinchfield Mica Corporation of New York.

A survey by engineers revealed that the mica veins are so extensive, and the quality so superior, that the mine may be worked profitably for many years.

## PIEDMONT WOOLEN MILLS

One of the most interesting manufacturing establishments in Franklin County was the Piedmont Woolen Mills at Callaway, owned and operated by James A. Martin, his brother-in-law Robert A. Martin, and his cousin Philip C. ("Buck") Martin.

These mills were established in 1880, and remodeled and enlarged in 1884. When James A. Martin went to Philadelphia to buy the machinery from M. A. Furbush and Son, he stopped in Washington and attended the inauguration of President Cleveland.

The machinery consisted of pickers, carders, spinners, looms, nappers and dyers, and was operated by a picturesque old overshot water wheel.

The raw wool was purchased in Franklin, Floyd, Craig, Montgomery, Bedford and Giles Counties. The finished products - - - blankets, carpets, linsey, cashmere, jeans and flannels - - - were sold in the same area, and even in a wider territory. The purchase of raw material and delivery of finished products were made by P. C. Martin. His covered wagon and dun colored mules - - - "Pete" and "Rock" - - - were familiar to a wide area.

As the isolation of Franklin passed away, the mills became less remunerative, and a lumber yard was added. Soon J. A. Martin gave all of his time to operating lumber mills in the mountains, and to building houses throughout the county.

In 1903, Mr. Martin became a stockholder and purchasing agent for Bald Knob Furniture Company of Rocky Mount, and served

79

in that capacity for fifteen years. His reliability was proverbial. When the author visited his daughter Carrie, wife of Dr. L. G. Pedigo of Salem, in 1935, he was 84 years old and had never tasted whiskey or tobacco. He was a public-spirited citizen and built (on land donated by H. M. Turner) and donated to his community its first school house. For many years he and his saintly wife furnished board and room for the school teachers of the community. Their home was open for all civic gatherings. They were members of the Methodist Church. He donated the land for the Highland Methodist Church and parsonage, and erected both buildings. His name and that of his devoted wife will be cherished in their little valley when the names of the rich and mighty are forgotten. He removed to Roanoke in 1918, and his wife died there in 1924.

## TOBACCO MANUFACTURING

Though now a vanished industry, so far as Franklin is concerned, the County once had a score of tobacco factories.

One of the pioneer tobacconists of Franklin was Thomas Keen. His factory was located about two miles from Snow Creek store on a tract of land later known as the Becker place. About 1840, three young men came to Franklin County from Germany, two of whom securing employment from Mr. Keen in his factory. One was Henry Batsche, and the other was Lewis Becker. Batsche married Keen's daughter, Martha, and became a partner in the business. He died a few years later, and Lewis Becker married his widow, and also succeeded to his place in the tobacco business. On the death of Mr. Keen, the firm became Becker and Sons and shortly after the death of the elder Becker, the sons, Thomas and William, discontinued the business.

Capt. Mordecai Cook operated a factory near Snow Creek.

J. R. and F. R. Brown operated a factory on Snow Creek.

The famous "Brown's Log Cabin" tobacco was first manufactured by Wm. A. Brown at Dickinson's Store.

Ferdinand Cook and Company manufactured tobacco between Snow Creek and Shady Grove, about a mile from the author's old home.

Preston Bondurant conducted a manufactory at Shady Grove.

Booker and Sheffield had a factory at Shady Grove.

The earliest manufacturers at Shady Grove were Shelton and Watkins, about 1835.

There was a factory at Taylor's Store, conducted by a man named Ferguson.

A man named Childress also manufactured tobacco at Taylor's Store.

Preston Bennett owned a factory about two miles from Snow Creek Store.

There was a manufactoring establishment at Gogginsville owned by a man named Darnell.

Stephen T. Willis manufactured tobacco near Callaway.

A man named Showalter had a factory at Bonbrook.

John Brown had a factory at Union Hall.

There was a factory at Hatcher's and a factory at Glade Hill.

George Helms had a factory at Rocky Mount, as did Tazewell Helms.

John S. ("Pad") Hale had a large factory at Rocky Mount operated by the labor of his slaves. He was an uncle of G. W. B. Hale.

One of the early tobacco factories was located at Algoma, the present estate of Dr. S. S. Guerrant, which was then known as Ash Grove. The chief brand manufactured was called "Monican". The output was sold largely in the far south.

## WASHINGTON IRON FURNACE
### (Also called Saunders Furnace)

The Washington Iron Furnace located near Rocky Mount is the oldest landmark in the county. It was originally owned by Col. Jeremiah Early (born 1730, died 1779), in partnership with his son-in-law, Colonel James Callaway, of Bedford County. Colonel Early willed it to his sons, Joseph, John and Jubal, who soon afterwards moved to that part of Henry County which is now a part of Franklin. Joseph died leaving his inheritance to his two brothers, John and Jubal. Jubal married about 1790, but died two or three years afterwards, leaving two infant sons, Joab and

Henry. They were placed, by order of court, under the guardian-
ship of Col. Samuel Hairston, whose daughter Ruth Hairston married
Joab Early. Her mother was Judith Saunders of "Flat Creek",
Campbell County. Col. Joab Early was left a widower with ten
children. After rearing this family he settled at Buffalo,
Putnam County, West Virginia.

There were other Saunders alliances with Early's. John
("Pad") Hale of this Saunders connection, married Mary Judith,
daughter of Joab and Ruth Early. At her death he married
Margaret Saunders, his wife's and his own cousin. Thus the
Saunders-Hale families acquired the Washington Iron Works. A
descendant, Miss Annie Saunders, still owns it. The old iron
works were operated from 1755 to 1850. It supplied war materials
during the Revolutionary days as did Oxford (Ross) furnace in
Campbell County, owned by James Callaway and Henry Innes, his
son-in-law. There is a tradition that a venturesome young man
named Stirling Cooper, (whether the Revolutionary soldier I know
not) once rode his horse around on the top of this furnace. The
feat was not impossible as a bridge connected the top with the
hillside so that carts and wagons might dump their ore.

In an article entitled, "Notes on Some of the Magnetites
of Southwestern Virginia and the Contiguous Territory of North
Carolina", by H. B. C. Nitze, Baltimore published in 1892, the
magnetite occurring in the Rocky Mount section of Franklin County
is described as follows:

"Just outside and to the west of Rocky Mount, were
situated the Rocky Mount or Clark mines, on a vein of magnetite
which was worked many years ago by the Pennsylvania Steel Company,
and abandoned on account of the cost of transportation.

"Ore near Rocky Mount was mined at an early date for the
Washington furnace. As late as 1880 these ores were mined by the
Pigg River Mining Company and shipped to Pennsylvania. The ore
is a fine-grained magnetite within walls of dense hornblende
schist dipping 60 degrees southwest.

"The deposit exists in a long, low ridge, parallel to
Grassy Hill. The outcrop is very distinct and has been stripped
to a great extent by the Pennsylvania Steel Company. There are
also a number of old shafts on the vein, which were caved in and
filled with water, so that I was unable to make an inside examination of the mines.

"The last shaft was put down by the Virginia Development
Company, to a depth about seventy-five feet, but this was also
filled with water. I understand that the vein pinched out entire-
at this depth."

On the western bank of the Pigg River, at the foot of a hill on Dr. Taw William's place, were some old pits in which the ore showed up very well.

The Washington furnace is said to have produced from local ores a very superior iron which was wagoned to North Carolina and Alabama.

Pyrrhotite, carrying a small amount of intermingled chalcopyrite, was reported several years ago from the Howell mine, located about a mile from Huff's store, near the Rocky Mount-Floyd Courthouse road.

Gossan was mined in Franklin County near the Floyd line, a few miles northeast of the Toncray Mine, for a nearby local furnace.

A crack in the furnace at Rocky Mount is explained, traditionally and fantastically, by a freshet which is said to have occurred about 1850. A dam above the furnace is said to have been broken by the flood, hurling a wall of water against the huge hot structure and producing the crevice. This story is probably more fanciful than factual. It is a fact, however, that the furnace has not been used since about 1850.

Another landmark of Franklin County was the old furnace on Story Creek. It was operated by Capt. Richard Saunders from 1850 to 1860. A forge stood nearby. When the Norfolk and Western Railroad was built, the furnace was torn down, and the material used for constructing culverts. Of the forge, nothing remains but the name "Forge Place", by which the farm on which it stood is still known.

Just across the Franklin line on Back Creek, south of Starkey Station, stood another old furnace and forge established by the Harvey and Boone families about the middle of the 18th century. Both furnace and forge were washed away by the flood of 1812.

There was still another furnace and forge on Smith River in the late 18th and early 19th centuries. The ore for it was mined in what is now Patrick County.

## RIFLE MANUFACTORY

A very superior grade of rifle was manufactured at one time in Franklin, and there is a tradition that there were two items in qualifying as a member of the military group known as The Franklin Rifles: The applicant had to own a rifle made in the county, and he had to accompany the captain to the woods and kill a squirrel by shooting it through the head.

## FELT HAT MANUFACTORY

The isolation of Franklin caused the manufacture of nearly all necessities within the county. The felt hats made by the Booth family were famous for a long time.

## BANKS

There are four banks in Franklin County.

At the close of business in 1934, the Peoples National Bank of Rocky Mount had resources of $2,027,827.23. The officers of that date were C. J. Davis, cashier; and N. P. Angle, Randolph Perdue, H. N. Prilliman and R. L. Kent, directors.

The Bankers Trust Company of Rocky Mount had, on December 31, 1934, resources of $301,452.50. The officers were R. N. Whitlow, cashier; and C. L. Hunt, C. C. Lee and W. N. Shearer, directors.

The Farmers and Merchants Bank of Boone Mill had assets, on December 31, 1934, of $165,760.92. The officers at that time were G. W. Bowman, Jr., cashier; and C. L. Dillon, J. M. Emswiler and Jack Garst, directors.

The First National Bank of Ferrum had, on December 31, 1934, assets of $325,680.36. The officers at that time were C. L. Ross, cashier; and C. M. Turner, G. M. Thomas and Frank B. Hurt, directors.

# Chapter 13

## EDUCATION AND EDUCATORS

For nearly two hundred years education in Virginia was regarded largely as a matter of personal and private concern. Schools were thought of as luxuries which the State was no more obligated to provide than other luxuries.

The early settlers of Franklin County soon discovered that in such a primitive region, the ax, gun plow and spinning wheel had more to do with successful living than books and schools. Succeeding generations did not even bother about "book larnin'" as much as the first settlers had. And when pioneer conditions had largely passed, it was still difficult to make education seem a matter of importance, so completely had other interests crowded schooling out of the thought of the people. But in this attitude toward schooling Franklinites were not peculiar. Nor were these uneducated Franklinites mentally deficient just because they were illiterate. Illiteracy and ignorance are not synonymous terms. Many who were unable to read and write, operated prosperous mercantile establishments. Some of them actually invented a system of their own whereby they kept their accounts. The most prosperous merchant at Mountain Valley, near my old home, but in Henry County, had such a system. I have often heard the story told that at "settling up time", just before Christmas, he reminded one of his customers that the account included a box of cheese. The customer insisted he had not bought any cheese. Whereupon the merchant re-examined his record and said, "You are correct. That was a grindstone you got. I just failed to put a dot in the middle of the picture". Franklin was not alone among Virginia counties in this indifference to education.

In Franklin, the school houses were usually centrally located with reference to the communities they were to serve. The sites generally chosen were in old fields, which had been turned out to briars and broom sedge. This custom gave rise to the name "old field schools". The buildings were log cabins, about sixteen by twenty feet, with rock chimneys. The fire places would accomodate logs four feet long. These logs were cut from nearby woods by the larger boys, and brought in on their shoulders. During the years I attended Mountain School (the actual name) no wood was ever brought to the building on wagon or sled. The boys thought it fun to be assigned to the task of wood cutting. They were sent out by twos, and kept strict account of their turns, and jealously claimed their "rights" when their turns came.

The mountain School had no windows except such as were provided by sawing part of a log out of the wall. Into this opening immovable panes were placed. In the log beneath the opening holes were bored and into these holes pegs were driven. A wide plank was then nailed to the pegs and thus the writing-desk was made. There was one long bench for this writing board. Like the rest of the benches, it was made of a puncheon. Pieces of sapling were driven into the two auger holes at each end of the puncheon and thus the bench was "legged". The legs of the writing board bench were not long enough to enable the smaller children to use the desk while seated, so they stood for their writing exercises. We had real ink, and steel pens. My father often told me how he used a quill pen and ink made of copperas and green walnut hulls.

The floor of Mountain School, like the benches, was made of puncheons. In winter the wind whistled through the cracks and almost froze one's legs, despite the roaring fire at the end of the room. My old home was over 3 miles from this school, but the walk morning and evening was not considered a hardship. The real hardship was sitting on those backless benches. In imagination, I can still feel the discomfort which came after two or three hours. I do not wonder now that the boys were glad to take the ax and go for wood, or the bucket and go to the distant spring for water!

We had no wall maps and no blackboards. There was, however, uniformity of text books, which was more than my father had when he went to Mountain School, then taught by Dow Brock and Mordecai Cook, McGuffey's Reader and Webster's Blueback Spelling Book were still in use when I started to school. My early teachers were Miss Nannie Mitchell, Miss Elizabeth Brodie, Mrs. Eliza Pearson, and Bluford Cooper, in the order named.

The phase of school I liked best was the spelling hour. That was because I excelled at spelling. Recitation gave me a chance to show off. We were lined up. The teacher stood before the line, book in hand, and gave out page after page of words. If the pupil up the line "missed" his word, the teacher "gave it out" to the pupil next below. If that pupil spelled it correctly he "went up", that is, he exchanged places with the pupil who had "missed". If more than one "missed", the speller took the place of the first one who had "missed". This process of taking another's place was called "turning him down". By it alone could one reach the head of the line. To "turn down" three or four on one word was sufficient justification for foregoing the after-school games and running home to tell about it. Memory points to one of these occasions as the highest point in my school career. I had been sick for a long time. When I returned to school, I was placed at the foot of the line. That very day a word passed all the way down and was misspelled in every conceivable way. When it came to me, I spelled it. No president taking oath of office, no king at his coronation, ever experienced greater pride than I felt as I walked to the head of the line.

All of my early teachers are now (1937) living except Bluford Cooper, and he lived to see me ordained to the ministry and signed my certificate of ordination. He was Clerk of Snow Creek Church (Disciples) at the time, Nov. 10, 1912. His widow lives at Boone Mill.

There were many stories told by the older boys when I first entered school of how they had made the life of Mr. Cooper miserable. There were stories of how they would arrive at the schoolhouse early and bar him out until he made certain concessions. They claimed they often climbed to the roof and obstructed the chimney and "smoked out" the whole school. Mr. Cooper was called a "strict teacher", and it is said did not hesitate to enforce his discipline with the rod. One was not considered a first class teacher in those days unless he applied the rod freely. That was the chief objection to women teachers during my boyhood. They would not or could not whip hard enough! I bear personal testimony here that this objection was not always well founded. The only whipping I ever received at school was administered by a woman. At the time I thought it was ample. The teacher, Mrs. Eliza Pinckard Pearson, had a rule against small boys smoking. My cousin, Beverly Wingfield, and I thought we could evade the rule. We knew nothing about modern cigarettes or cigarette tobacco. We rolled our own cigars from tobacco leaves from our father's barns. I do not think either of us enjoyed the cigars. Smoking them, however, made us feel we were more than mere boys. After the terrible nausea which attended the first attempt, we smoked quite nonchalantly, that is when we were away from our parents and teacher. All pupils brought their lunches in baskets or buckets. The teacher probably noticed now quickly my cousin and I ate our food, and plunged into the woods. At least she followed one day, and came upon us just as our homemade cigars were well-lighted and going good. The sequel almost cured us of smoking. Indeed, it cured us altogether so far as smoking at school was concerned.

There were games at the noon recess, such as hare and hound, hop scotch, corner ball, town ball, antny over, leap frog, prisoner's base, bull pen, and numerous others. The sport I liked best had no name. It consisted of climbing a slender oak sapling until it was too supple to longer bear one's weight, then swinging off to the ground, or near enough to the ground to jump. It was a great ride! Oak saplings were tough and easy to ride down. I tried a sapling of another sort one day. It broke instead of bending, and I fell so hard that I was stunned. After that I was afraid to trust even the oak saplings which had never failed me, and so I abandoned my best loved sport.

The day of days in Mountain School was "school breaking", or the last day of the school year. All the people of the community came early, bringing baskets, boxes, and even trunks of food. A crude stage was erected on the school yard, and on it the rustic lads and lassies, dressed in their best clothes, displayed their elocutionary powers. On such a platform I recited the poem about the boy who stood on the burning deck. A vivid memory tells me I was far more uncomfortable than Casiabanca was! From that crude stage we buried Moses again on Nebo's lonely mountain, raked hay with Maud Muller, crossed the Delaware with Washington and joined Patrick Henry in his demand for liberty or death. There we retold the legend of the organ builder, blew Tennyson's bugle song and made the nations rise and fall. There we brought McGaffey's chickens home to roost, joined Lowell in watching the first snow fall, lost and found Grandpa's spectacles, according to both versions, saw Riley's little white hearse go by, and went riding on a mouse-gray mustang by the side of Lasca.

By that time the audience was so exhausted that food was necessary to revive it. The master or mistress of ceremonies announced an hour's intermission for refreshments. As if by magic, the yard bloomed out with tablecloths, or their equivalent in bed sheets, and soon food enough for an army was in sight and out of sight!

Before the feast ended the lively strains of a string quartet set even the church-members to patting their feet. That was as far as anybody dared go! Dancing would have scandalized the occasion.

The "school-breaking" program was limited to the pupils, with the exception of the string music. But the affair would have been considered a failure without the banjoists and fiddlers. With the eyes of memory I can see them now,-Will Brodie, Charlie Barbour, Syd Belcher and Pierce Kidd- as they sat, knee to knee, on the crude platford and attacked their instruments with all the enthusiasm of men trying to "whip out" a nest of yellow jackets.

After an hour of exciting music, the school play was announced, and the embryo thespians trod the board in their magic hour. Dramatics, however, could not satisfy that mountain audience.

Poetic recitations were wanted and there had to be brave, gay or
tearful. So after the play, came the explanation of why the dog's
nose is always cold, the gray-headed sexton told where wicked folk
were buried, Tommy's prayer was prayed again and Watson's wounded
soldier started home. By that time everybody was ready to follow.
the wounded soldier's example. So we clasped hands, forming a
circle, sang "Auld Lang Syne", and the day of days was ended.

## THE BOATWRIGHT SCHOOL

Professor Charles Boatwright was a pioneer in higher
education in Franklin County. He established a coeducational
school at Chestnut Level, near Dillon's Mill, in 1870. He planned
to build suitable quarters on a beautiful spot which he had
selected that the young people of the community might have educational advantages which had been denied them. His purpose was
never realized because of a lack of financial aid. After conducting the school for several years he moved to Gogginsville,
where he died. His daughter Miss Eudora Boatwright, was also a
teacher in the county for many years, until she removed to Hunt-
ington, West Virginia.

## MISSION SCHOOLS OF THE EPISCOPAL CHURCH

St. Peters-on-the-Mountain, an Episcopal mission school,
is located in the western portion of Franklin County, near the top
of the Blue Ridge Mountains, and about twenty miles from Rocky
Mount. This school was founded in 1906 by Rev. W. T. Roberts and
endowed by A. C. Needles, then president of the Norfolk and Western
Railway. It is known as the Phoebe Needles Memorial School. The
average enrollment is from 100 to 150. The buildings consist of
two large native stone structures, one is the church and the other
the school building. The object of the school is to prepare girls
of the mountains for worthy home life.

St. Johns-on-the-Mountain is another Episcopal mission
school. This school was founded in 1914 by Rev. W. T. Roberts.
It is not endowed. The average enrollment is from 75 to 125.
This school is located twenty-one miles southwest of Rocky Mount.
Its mission is to imbue the girls of the mountains with high
ideals of life and home making.

## ALGOMA MISSION SCHOOL

Algoma Mission School is on "Algoma" estate, owned by
Dr. Sam S. Guerrant. It is maintained principally by the Montgomery Presbytery. The school was established in 1910, composed of
a single room building. It was a hard struggle to keep alive,
but there was no adequate public school in Algoma Valley, and

89

Dr. Guerrant said the opportunity for the education of the many children in the Valley was slipping away. So he constructed the one room building near his home, and interested himself in securing pupils. The school stands as a monument to his generosity and his interest in children.

The present school is an eleven room building, four of which are used for school purposes. It is located on the slope of a hill at the foot of the Blue Ridge Mountains. The average daily attendance is fifty. There are seventy enrolled. Three of the rooms can be thrown together for auditorium purposes, while the upper floor is devoted to home quarters for the teachers and a considerable accomodation for a dormitory. The largest number of children to occupy dormitory quarters so far is five. The building is equipped with hot and cold water, bathroom, sanitary drinking fountains, telephone, wiring for lights, and heat. The water is piped from a spring on the mountain. The school property includes thirty acres of land which embraces an area of woodland that is utilized for fuel, pasture for stock, and garden. The view from the porch on the third floor is one of the most picturesque in the state.

There are three teachers. The days work opens with chapel exercises. The children are taught the catechism and the Bible. The influence of the school is such that a more Christian atmosphere has been built up in the community. The teachers assist in Sunday School work, and home visiting and social service work besides conducting the sales of partly worn clothing which helps the poor of the community.

Dr. P. C. Clark was for many years in charge of the mission schools of the County and gave inspiring influence in the work. On completion of the school at Algoma, the building and land was presented to the Montgomery Presbytery. It is grouped with four other schools of similar nature in the Presbytery, and known as the Harris Mountain Schools in memory of Rev. J. K. Harris, who for many years carried on mission school work in Floyd County.

### FERRUM TRAINING SCHOOL

Ferrum Training School was established in September 1914, by the Virginia Conference of the Methodist Episcopal Church, South, and the Woman's Missionary Society of this Conference.

The school owns a farm of 376 acres. The buildings are situated on about 50 acres of this land, on a knoll that slopes gently in every direction. It would be hard to find a more beautiful piece of ground for the location of an educational institution. Many trees have been set out on this acreage, and are now large enough to afford shade as well as to beautify the grounds.

For many years Ferrum Training School was under the management of Rev. B. M. Beckham, D.D., and to him is largely due the credit for the remarkable success of the institution and its branches. After Dr. Beckham's retirement, the school was directed for a time by Prof. John W. Carter, formerly of the Martinsville High School.

## MANSFIELD'S SCHOOL

Mansfield's School was one of the first of its kind in the Franklin area. Mr. and Mrs. Thomas Mansfield came to Franklin, ca. 1850, and engaged in educational work. They were pioneer members of the Presbyterian Church. Their school prospered and blest hundreds of Franklin boys and girls. It was located about four miles west of Boone Mill and near Fairmont Baptist Church. Mr. Mansfield was ably assisted in his work by his wife, Mrs. Cassie Mansfield, and by his daughter, Miss Mildred Mansfield. Prof. Mansfield died in 1884, and the school was discontinued.

## PUBLIC SCHOOLS

There were in Franklin, in 1915, a total of 177 schools, of which 151 were one teacher schools, 22 two teacher schools, one partially accredited high school at Rocky Mount, and only 4 schools with more than two teachers.

The school population in 1915 was 8,736 with 6,821 enrolled. Of these 6,298 were in one-teacher schools and 523 in consolidated schools. Only 40 pupils in Franklin were doing high school work.

The average daily attendance was 3,875 in 1915.

In 1915, one teacher held a collegiate professional certificate; six held normal certificates; nine held elementary certificates; fifty-four held first grade certificates; thirty-four held second-grade certificates; and eighty-two held local permits.

In 1915, there were 30 school libraries with 2,500 volumes.

The average annual salary paid teachers, in 1915, was $215.28.

91

The per capita cost of education in 1915 was $8.15.

Following are names of men who have served as Superintendents of Franklin County Schools: Dr. James, William Duncan, Richard Brown, W. A. Frith, H. D. Hillard, W. D. Rucker, J. L. Waid, R. A. Prillaman, and Harold W. Ramsey.

In the Snow Creek District of Franklin County is a section known as Briar Mountain. In 1928 there were forty-two Negro children in the Briar Mountain area who were suffering for lack of educational advantages. There was not a school in the area, and there had not been one in that section in twenty-one years. A first class highway had been built through the Briar Mountain community, and the Rev. Morton H. Hopkins, a Negro Baptist minister, thought it a shameful thing for such an illiterate group of people to be exposed to the eyes of the nation. He went to the County authorities and asked for a school in the Briar Mountain community. Though the request was not acted upon favorably, he repeated it annually for three or four years. When he had almost lost hope of favorable action, he met W. D. Gresham of the State Board of Education. He told Mr. Gresham the story, and was advised to make one more effort, and report results. When Pastor Hopkins reported that this effort was also unavailing, the State Board of Education came into the matter and instructed the county School Board to either build a school house in the area or provide bus transportation for the children of the area to enable them to attend school. In the year 1929, Pastor Hopkins saw his long efforts crowned with success when Franklin County's first school bus for Negro children was put in operation.

## Chapter 14

## CHURCHES, CHURCHMEN AND CHURCHWOMEN

Church services have always been social events in Franklin County. Monthly meetings, as well as revival meetings, are still used to further various non-religious enterprises. Men used to go not only to hear a sermon, but to invite "hands" to cuttings, log rollings, road workings or corn shuckings. They still go to swap or sell horses and mules, "electioneer" for office, rent land, buy seed potatoes or other farm seeds, and to get the neighborhood news. There was a time when a farmer-preacher frequently announced from the pulpit that he was in the market for certain field seeds or for a few pigs "old enough for 'killers' next winter".

The old time revival meetings in Franklin were religious sprees. The attendance at regular monthly services was always large, but the revival crowd was "too large for man to number". People came from miles around in wagons, buggies, and on foot. Around all country churches were crude tables on posts which stood through the years. On these great quantities of food were spread two or three times during the protracted meetings. The food from the various baskets, boxes and trunks was put together as though it had been brought by one person. Each ate what pleased his fancy, and in this way all enjoyed an amazing variety.

When "laying by" time came the revivals began. In a addition to the "revivals" the Baptists held their association, the Dunkards their love feasts, the Methodists their conferences, and the Disciples their cooperations. The Presbyterian and Episcopal churches of the county had few antidotes for the dull drab life of winter, and the summer monotony of plowing endless corn and tobacco rows. Perhaps that is the reason these denominations did not grow like Baptists and Methodists.

Revivals frequently took the form of camp meetings. They were usually held where there was no church building, in a grove and near a spring. A brush arbor was built to keep out the sun, also the brunt of a possible thunder shower. Many of the attendants came from afar and stayed throughout the meeting. Some slept in or under the covered wagon and cooked over a camp-fire. Others improvised tents. The singing at the camp meetings made up in volume what it lacked in quality. The community singing master was usually there and drilled the campers between services after the fashion used in teaching his scattered singing classes which ran throughout the year. What he lacked in musical knowledge, he made up in posing and boasting. As I remember the genus, he usually believed he was the reincarnation of Apollo.

93

The camp meeting preaching was usually done by the "Arminians", as believers in freedom of the will were called. They spent most of their time declaring that salvation is free, and all men free to accept it. The Calvinists spent most of their time "explaining", and emphasizing the doctrine of predestination and election. Their explanation usually put the matter beyond the ratiocination of man and left the hearers no alternative but to "take it by faith". It was a very comforting doctrine as it put man's salvation beyond his own efforts, and so left him little to worry about.

The Presbyterians and Protestant Episcopalians laid so much emphasis on classical education as a pre-requisite for the ministry that native Franklin County men were practically excluded. Lack of preparatory schools kept most of the local boys out of college. The "imported" ministers did not like the rough life, which seemed so good to those born and bred to it. Consequently those denominations which overlooked classical requirements, and ordained the most suitable of local men, flourished and grew strong. The rank and file of the people being uneducated themselves were not as hospitable to college trained ministers as to the self-made men.

The people of Franklin County enjoyed religious debate more than any other people I have every known. As a rule, that sermon was accounted a failure which did not show up the fallacies of other religious bodies. The chief topic of debate was predestination and free will.

Near my old home was a Primitive Baptist Church. My father gave all the pews for it. Services were held there on the first Saturday and Sunday of each month. Elder William S. Minter preached on Saturday morning, and Elder Taylor Turner (my father's cousin) on Sunday morning. There were no services at night. These two preachers made our home their headquarters, and the family usually attended their services. Memory brings back the sing-song monotone in which their sermons were delivered, but recollection evokes no discourse that did not "ring the changed" on predestination and election, and the final perserverance of the saints. In debate on the issue, a Disciple (called Campbellite where whiskers and celluloid collars are still worn) preacher used the illustration of salvation as a rope cast to a drowning man. In catching and holding on to the rope, one exercised free will. Elder Moore, the Calvinist champion, insisted that the unsaved man is "dead in trepasses and sins", and that a dead man can't catch or hold a rope. Divine grace must tie the rope around him!

The sermons of these elders were usually from two to three hours long. When two or three of them preached in one

service, which frequently happened, one got home in the middle
of the afternoon. It usually required about half an hour for
one of them "to get warmed up".

A wooden pail of water from the nearby spring usually
sat on the edge of the platform. It was customary for the thirsty,
especially mothers with little children, to go forward and drink.
Those who craved a stronger drink, or who wished to trade horses,
retired to nearby trees. To leave the building during the sermon
was not considered disrespectful. There was a sense of fair
play - - - a mutual respect on the part of preacher and hearer of
each others rights. When the preacher had said all he wanted to,
he would stop. When the hearer had enough, he would go out and
talk, swap horses, or take a drink. It was his privilege. He
could go back for more preaching after he rested.

The elders served without pay and sought their liveli-
hood in the same fashion as the members of their congregation,
not even excluding horse trading and distilling. Their religion,
like their sermon themes, was quite remote from every day life.
The sermons contained much of such themes as death, the judgment,
the priesthood of Melshizedek and the work of the Holy Ghost.
The cataclysmic, mysterious, magnificient and speculative prevailed. Religion had more to do with the future than the present.
It was intensely personal rather than social.

Despite the seeming harshness of the foregoing criticisms,
I had, and have, a profound respect for the faith of these people.
It gave them strength in the hour of trouble. They were certain
that they could not have borne some of their burdens if they had
not trusted in the Lord. They were sure God would give strength
to bear whatever came. They loved one another. Even as a lad,
I sensed the depth of their love at their "feet washings" and
love feasts. The latter was exclusively a Brethren ceremony,
and included a full meal. It was held on the evening of a full
moon in late summer or early autumn. Primitive Baptists had
feet washings as well as Brethren. I have seen the members go
forward to the front benches where the elder waited with towel
and basin. He began the rite by washing the feet of some of the
men. They in turn washed the feet of others. The women did the
same for one another. Instead of youthful amusement, I was awed
by their silence and their tears. Even now, when memory brings
back the scene, I think of an upper room in Jerusalem nearly two
thousand years ago.

Church going gave the belles of Franklin their greatest
opportunity for displaying their finery. The dresses of thirty
years ago were "fearfully and wonderfully made". My powers of
description are unable to do justice to Franklin's ambitious

leaders of fashion, but from memory, and from old photographs, I can assure the reader that they had the merit of originality.

Funerals and burials were two different things in Franklin County. The burial was simply the interment of the body accompanied perhaps by a hymn and a prayer. The singing did not begin till the neighbors began to fill the grave. For one to have gone away before the mound was smoothed and the flowers placed, would have been extremely disrespectful.

The funerals were held months after the burials. It is generally supposed that bad roads gave rise to this custom. When one died in winter, or early spring, the roads were usually impassable and the numerous relatives and friends were thus hindered from attending the burial. And it was highly important that they hear what the preacher had to say about the deceased. In many instances, the funeral preacher had been chosen long beforehand, and had been entrusted with life secrets unknown to any other. Funeral sermons might give historical information and clear up old mysteries. Besides, the deceased often had remembered his kinsmen and friends, and even his enemies, with certain messages and these usually formed a part of the funeral sermon. It would never do therefore to miss the funeral. So, if roads were bad, a Sunday in the forthcoming summer, or fall, was named as the funeral day. It soon came to pass that the funeral was announced for a distant date, regardless of the state of the roads at the time of the death. Funeral services finally became merely memorial services and were then discontinued. I recall that my maternal grandmother's funeral was held over two years after her death. It was simply a memorial service.

These postponed funerals were usually capitalized by the preachers to glorify their own denominations. The loyalty of the deceased to his denomination was always stressed. Those of similar persuasion felt that they were on the safe road, consequently the funerals greatly strengthened them in their denominational loyalty. Christians of communions other than that of the deceased were given to understand that while their faith might possibly give entrance to heaven by a tight squeeze, the faith of the deceased was so undoubtedly right that "an abundant entrance" was certain. Funeral sermons often kindled in the minds of people of differing denominations serious doubts as to the validity of their particular brand of religion!

Persons who were non-church members were told rather plainly that they were without God and without salvation. The preacher was never equivocal as to the final destiny of the deceased. He told just where the departed had gone and why he had gone there. And the fact that the departed had talked so confidently with the preacher gave the sermon great weight.

As a lad, I was often puzzled as to why all the dead were located in the realms of the blest. Of what use was hell anyway? Even those who died outside of the church were assigned to heaven when funeral time came, though in the funeral sermon, live non-church members were assured of hell, unless they joined the church. The result was that I became a thoroughgoing universalist before I ever joined any church.

During the period between the burial and the funeral, widows and widowers were not supposed to do any courting. Any evidence of new matrimonial arrangements were frowned upon. It was supposed to be a period of mourning. Yet I have known many who, during this period, seemed to be far more interested in contemplation of the future than in any sort of retrospection. The story is told of a Snow Creek widow whose husband had died one November. The funeral was announced for the following August. In the meantime the widow remarried, and at the August funeral she sat by her new husband and wept copiously on his shoulder.

Sentiment must not lead me to overlook the fact that the native Franklin preachers were quite illiterate. But what they l lacked in education, they made up in "direct revelations" from God. They claimed (and many believed them) that they were in such direct communication that whatever theme they discussed was given of God. To make preparation on a given subject, or even to select a text for it before going into the pulpit, was considered presumptuous. God would direct the preacher to the right text, illuminate it, and fill his mouth with the proper words. As a result, passages from the Bible without any connection whatsoever were brought together and given an application so far fetched that one really had to admire the imagination of the preacher even while pitying his ignorance.

Many preachers could scarcely read, and comparatively simple words were grotesquely mispronounced or given definitions that were ludicrous. They rarely failed to misquote and some have even been known to base sermons on sayings from Poor Richard's Almanac supposing them to be verses from the Bible. I personally heard a sermon on the text, "Every tub shall stand on its own bottom".

One preacher commented at length on the "town clock" at Ephesus and was not even made aware of his error when his host at length asked him after dinner if the phrase in the seventeenth chapter of the Book of Acts was not "town clerk".

Another took the phrase "Damnable heresies" from the second Epistle of Peter, and preached a rousing sermon on "Damnable heresay".

97

Most of the hearers swallowed everything, believing the preacher had been called of God who had also chosen his texts, arranged his sermons and guided their delivery. No wonder the people also believed the preacher spoke infallibly when he declared the destiny of the dead in his funeral sermon.

Further proof that the preacher was God's man lay in the fact that he had never been contaminated with "book-learnin", and that he accepted no pay for his preaching, but worked with his hands just like his hearers. There was no gap between preacher and congregation. He was as poor as any of them, and frequently had walked a long distance to reach his appointment. His clothes were no better than theirs, and he was not so proud that he chewed plug tobacco like the imported preachers. The natural leaf was good enough for him. His sermon was not to be measured so much by what he said as by the way he said it. If his gesticulations were as vigorous as those of a man fighting hornets; if he raced from one side of the platform to the other; if he stamped his feet like he was killing snakes; if he bellowed like the bulls of Bashan; if he frothed at the mouth and perspired; if he drank frequently from the gourd in the cedar bucket on the platform - - - if he did these things, then he was an earnest man and a great preacher. His atrocious grammar did not matter for there were few present who knew anything about grammar any way.

It is said that when the Disciples decided to raise the academic standards of their ministry, their first problem was silencing an old minister who "butchered the King's English". He was known for his saintliness as well as for his picturesque speech and his brethren were reluctant to proceed against him. However, they were sure that his uncouth language put his whole communion in a bad light. He was present at the meeting and his brethren were embarrassed about beginning. Knowing their purpose the old minister asked for a statement of the case against him. One by one they pointed out his outlandish speech. Finally the last speaker arose and said, "Why Brother, you even say "gwine" and "agin". The accused then asked what further charges were against him. On being told there was nothing but his speech, he said, "Wal, brethren, if that's all you got agin me, I's a gwine on".

## BAPTISTS

The best account of early Baptist history in Franklin County is found in the writings of the notes of Jeremiah B. Jeter. He informs us that when he and Witt first went into Franklin County they had an appointment to preach at the house of Aquilla Divers. It was a sparsely settled neighborhood, but the news had spread that two boys from Bedford would preach. People came from all the surrounding region. Witt preached. He laid off his coat and rolled up his sleeves, not in vanity nor affectation, but for comfort and convenience. It meant earnestness and labor. When the discourse was ended, there was suppressed weeping. It was the commencement of a revival which brought hundreds into the Baptist Church.

Soon after Jeter and Witt labored in Franklin, the strife in the Baptist denomination concerning missions commenced. The ministers generally took the anti-mission side. They were good men, but of narrow views and scanty information. They were afraid missionary efforts would take the work of salvation out of God's hands and transfer the glory to men. Most of the churches in Franklin withdrew from the Strawberry Association, and organized the Pigg River Association.

Jeter gives an interesting sidelight on Elder Moses Greer, one of the best known preachers in Franklin County. Dr. Jeter writes: "He was of a highly respectable family, and fully sustained its respectability. He was rather above the ordinary stature, quite lean, and very plain in his dress, as were all the preachers of his region. His manners were simple and unaffected. He was past the meredian of life when Witt and myself were entering on our ministry. He was of very tender feelings,,rarely failing to mingle a profusion of tears with his prayers and exhortations. He was free from ambition. In a small circuit in his county he passed his life in unostentatious efforts to do good. In his latter years he was led off from the main body of the Baptist denomination by the anti-mission faction. His means of information were very limited, and the missionary work, as it was presented to him by the leaders of the faction seemed to be a very evil thing. I record, with gratitude and pleasure, this testimonial of his hospitality and kindness to me when I visited his neighborhood."

Elder Greer was remarkable for two things. The first was intoning. He carried this art to the highest perfection. He sung his hymns, prayers, sermons and exhortations all in the same tune, and a most mournful tune it was. No one not greatly given to levity could hear it without solemnity. All in sympathy with the intoner had their hearts stirred within them. If a stranger, unacquainted with his language, had heard his intonations he would have concluded that the old man was in fearful distress. If Brother Greer were living, with his voice unimpaired and his sympathies unblunted, the clergymen who are reviving the art of intoning would find themselves much profited under his instruction, and by imitating his unaffected example.

The second thing for which he was notable was spiritualizing the Scriptures. "I believe", he said, "That every tex' (a common pronounciation in that day) in the Bible, and every word, and every letter, and every crook and dot of every letter, has a spiritual meaning".

Of one of his sermons, I have a distinct recollection. He preached from I Peter, 1:13: "Wherefore gird up the loins of your mind, be sober, and hope to the end". His discourse was based principally on the work "loins" which he pronounced as if it had been spelled lines. He considered the different uses of lines, lines for the guidance of workmen, lines for the division of lands, lines for governing plow horses, and lines for the driving of coaches. From these various kinds of lines, he ingeniously drew spiritual instruction. The reader must not judge of the merit of the sermon by its fanciful outline. He contrived to mingle much sound religious instructions with his wild fancies.

## BAPTISTS (MISSIONARY)

Beulah Baptist Church, near Sontag, was organized Dec. 9, 1888, by J. V.Dickinson in a small log school house. The charter members came from Rocky Mount, Stony Creek and Providence Churches.

The first house of worship, a small frame structure erected largely through the efforts of William D. Stone and wife and C. T. McBride and wife, was later enlarged, then replaced by a commodious brick building in 1924.

Joseph Parker located in Franklin County in 1845 on a large farm near the mouth of Blackwater River. His spacious dwelling erected about the time of the Civil War was of brick, made mostly by his own slaves. It still stands. There he reared a large family, three of whom followed the Confederate flag in the War Between the States. The eldest son, Lieutenant William A. Parker, was killed on his 24th birthday, March 1, 1864.

Mr. Parker was a minister of the Baptist Church before the division of that body. He used his influence to prevent the rupture. When the split came, he went with the missionary branch.

William Parker Stone, grandson of Joseph Parker, was graduated from Baltimore Medical College of Physicians and Surgeons at the age of 21. He located at his childhood home near Sydnorsville. Here he gave his life in service to his friends and neighbors, dying in 1898, at the age of 28.

## BOONE MILL BAPTIST CHURCH

The Boone Mill Baptist Church was organized in Nov. 1877, as the result of meetings held by J. Lee Taylor and his father, Nathaniel Taylor, assisted by Davis Lancaster, a young minister from Floyd County. These meetings were held in an old log school house on top of the hill about one half mile from the present building which is on the Carolina-Big Lick Turnpike in the northern part of the town.

Pleasant Brown, who lived between Bon Brook and Hale's Ford, preached for the community several years before this church was organized.

J. Lee Taylor was the first pastor of the Boone Mill Baptist Church. Among the charter members were: Jabez L. Abshire, Asa Wright, O. D. Wray, T. J. Phelps, O. J. Phelps and his wife and daughters, and Mrs. Isaac Boone.

The first deacons were: O. D. Wray, Jabez L. Abshire and T. J. Phelps. The last named was the first clerk and the last surviving charter member. He died in Bluefield, W. Va. in 1935.

The ministers who have served this church are: J. Lee Taylor, Gabriel Wheeler, J. E. Poteet, J. W. Wade, H. H. Martens, W. P. Brooks, S. B. Moses and G. W. Ferrell.

The present officers are: G. W. Ferrell, pastor; J. M. Emswiler, clerk; C. O. Murray, treasurer; J. W. Carbaugh, Dr. C. L. Dillon, C. O. Murray and F. D. Wray, deacons; G. W. Wade, C. L. Dillon and G. W. Mills, trustees; and G.F. Murray and T. A. Flora, Sunday School Superintendent and Assistant Superintendent, respectively. The membership is approximately 200.

## EBENEZER BAPTIST CHURCH

Ebenezer Baptist Church, seven miles west of Rocky Mount, was organized in 1909. The first house of worship was erected in 1912, and dedicated in 1913. T. P. Mason (Maban?) was the first pastor, and served until his death. Booker Mullins, George W. Meadow, Robert Milliron, Charles Mullins, S. S. Stanley and John Mullins were among the first officers of the congregation.

## FAIRMONT BAPTIST CHURCH

Fairmont Baptist Church was organized April 29, 1855, at Charity Chapel, near Gogginsville, by Elders John L. Pritchard, Pleasant Brown, George W. Leftwich and Thomas C. Goggin, with the following charter members: Elijah B. Wade, Octavia Wade, Mary J. Wade, John A. Smith, Tenah Smith, Sarah A. Smith, Elizabeth Claiborne, Elizabeth Turnbull, Ursula Levasey, John Nunley, John Hartman, Lockey Hartman, Catherine Hensley and George W. Leftwich, Acting Clerk.

On Dec. 6, 1856, the church appointed as building committee and trustees, David S. Webster, John A. Smith, Elijah B. Wade, Creed T. Webb, Daniel S. Simpson, Ferdinand Price and Cyrus Price. Elijah B. Wade was elected treasurer. The building committee met Dec. 11, 1856, at Three Forks, and decided on a site and also to begin work at once. The building was completed in the year 1857. The first meeting was held in the building Dec. 5, 1857. The revival meetings of the church were held at Charity Chapel till Nov. 10, 1856, then at the Blackwater Meeting House until the Fairmont Church was completed.

Blackwater Meeting House was a large log building, used principally by the Primitive Baptists. It was also used as a school house. It was located on Mirey Branch between the two small branches on the south side of the public road to Fairmont, midway between Dillon's Mill and the James R. Mitchell place.

The following was taken from the record books of the church, which have been carefully preserved by Owen B. Jamison, Boone Mill: On June 23, 1855, Creed T. Webb and John A. Smith were elected first deacons of Fairmont Baptist Church. On July 7, 1855, they were elected delegates to the Strawberry Association. On May 10, 1856, Creed T. Webb was elected a delegate to the General Association, and Thomas C. Goggin his alternate. On June 7, 1856, Creed T. Webb and John A. Smith were ordained first deacons by Thomas C. Goggin and Pleasant Brown. Elijah B. Wade and John Hartman were elected delegates to the Strawberry Association on the same date. On July 4, 1857, Creed T. Webb and John A. Smith and Elijah B. Wade were elected delegates to the Strawberry Association.

The first Sunday School was organized in April 1859.

Three former members of Fairmont Baptist Church became ministers: John W. Mitchell, Wilson Mills and Samuel L. Naff.

Gogginsville Baptist Church and Boone Mill Baptist Church are both branches of Fairmont Baptist Church.

The following were pastors of Fairmont Baptist Church from 1855 to 1922: Thomas C. Goggin, June 23, 1855, to May 10, 1866; C. W. Wood, May 10, 1866, to Feb. 23, 1867; J. W. Stine, Feb. 23, 1867, to Nov. 9, 1867; T. N. Sanders, Dec. 28, 1867, to

Feb. 27, 1869; T. E. Reynolds, Feb. 27, 1869, to Oct. 13, 1869;
Thomas C. Goggin, Nov. 12, 1870, to Oct. 21, 1876; J. L. Taylor,
Nov. 18, 1876, to Oct. 17, 1880; Gabriel Wheeler, Dec. 19, 1880,
to Feb. 14, 1891; R. D. Haymore, Mar. 15, 1891, to Oct. 18, 1892;
J. W. Wade, May 20, 1893, to Dec. 20, 1902; M. W. Royal, June 20,
1903, to Aug. 15, 1908; W. L. Naff, Aug. 15, 1908, to April 17,
1909; F. P. Robertson, April 17, 1909, to Dec. 20, 1913; J. W.
Wade, Dec. 20, 1913, to Nov. 18, 1917; H. H. Martens, Dec. 15,
1917, to June 18, 1922; P. W. Brooke, 1922-

The following are the clerks and treasurers since organi-
zation; Elijah B. Wade, from June 23, 1855, to June 2, 1858; Creed
T. Webb, from June 2, 1858, to April 7, 1860; Henry Jamison from
April 7, 1860, to April 14, 1888; George W. Price from May 19,
1888, to Jan. 1, 1905; C. L. Dillon, from March 18, 1905, to
July 15, 1906; C. L. Naff, from July 15, 1906, to Feb. 20, 1915;
Parker C. Jamison from Feb. 20, 1915.

## MILL CREEK BAPTIST CHURCH

Mill Creek Baptist Church was organized in 1885 and the
house of worship erected in 1886. Among the charter members were:
W. P. Williams, W. G. Goode, Robert Stone, and Andrew Stone.
Pastors of Mill Creek include J. Lee Taylor, J. W. Wade, T. P.
Pearson, J. E. Poteet and S. C. Fulton.

## PROVIDENCE BAPTIST CHURCH

In the years 1828-32, when the Baptists of Virginia
were dividing over missions, most of the Baptists in Franklin
County remained anti-mission. Town Creek Church was the only
church that had enough missionary sentiment to cause a division.
The Pigg River Association, of which Town Creek was a member,
passed a resolution in 1832 declaring non-fellowship with all
organized missionary effort. This resolution led to the organization, in 1833, of Providence Missionary Baptist Church by seven
former members of Town Creek.

The land on which Providence was built was given by
David G. Goode, Sr., and deeded to Joel W. Meadows. Thomas
Williams, John Thornton and David G. Goode, and their successors,
as trustees.

The following item from the first records has happily
survived: "In accordance with an appointment of the Strawberry
Baptist Association at their last session Elders John S. Lee and
Ebner Anthony attended at Chestnut Meeting House, in the County of
Franklin, and State of Virginia, on the 18th of Nov. 1833, and
after due examination of the circumstances and character of the

103

brethren who petitioned for the constitution of a church, proceeded to constitute themselves into a church upon the principles of the United Baptists of this country. Whereupon the church assumed the name Providence and proceeded to the choice of deacons and it appearing that the following persons, viz: Brethren John Mason, John Thornton were unanimously chosen, the presbytery immediately proceeded to choose a clerk. Whereupon Bro. Samuel G. Mason was unanimously elected to that office. Thereafter divine service commenced in church order and the following persons were received as candidates for baptism: Edward Hiatt, Starling M. Thornton and Anna Compton". Samuel G. Mason was clerk.

For seven years Providence was the only Missionary Baptist Church in the area now composing the Blue Ridge Baptist Association. The church grew rapidly and when it entertained the Strawberry Association in 1855, only two churches of the Association (Mount Zion in Bedford and Lynchburg Church) excelled it in white membership. Two other churches, located in strong slave territory, excelled it in membership when the colored members were counted.

The Blue Baptist Association was organized in 1858, and Providence Church led all churches in the Association in membership for 48 years. Today the church ranks eighth in membership among the 41 churches of the Association.

This church has given to the Baptist ministry Samuel G. Mason, Skelton Coleman, R. G. McGhee, Gilbert Mason, J. R. Harrison, John W. Wade, Andrew J. Ramsey, T. P. Mason and T. P. Pearson. Tom P. Mason was pastor of Ebenezer Church. He married Maude Mills. T. P. Pearson, born 1830 and died 1909, married a Miss Hoy. He served as pastor of Providence, Mill Creek, Ebenezer and Trinity Churches. Skelton Coleman and R. G. McGhee lived near Providence Church at which they received their call to the ministry.

William Hankins was the first clerk of the Association. He was known as the "Walking Preacher", and is buried near Providence Church. His grave is enclosed with an iron fence and marble slabs erected by the Blue Ridge Baptist Association.

A partial list of pastors of Providence Church include Pleasant Brown, T. Webb, S. G. Mason, H. C. Ruffin, M. B. Major, J. Lee Taylor, F. P. Robertson and John W. Wade, An incomplete list of clerks of the church include Samuel G. Mason, John Thornton, W. D. Williams, S. Coleman, R. G. McGhee, W. J. T. Hankins, John W. Wade, L. V. Ramsey, Milton L. Goode, S. A. Mason and M. M. Young.

## ROCKY MOUNT BAPTIST CHURCH

Rocky Mount Baptist Church was organized in 1879. Among the charter members were:  D. D. Divers and C. F. Hudson. Pastors of this church include J. Lee Taylor, Thomas Morris, E. Y. Poole, T. P. Robertson, C. K. Hobbs, E. E. Dudley, T. H. Francisko and R. M. Pleasants. The present house of worship was erected in 1923.

## STORY CREEK BAPTIST CHURCH

Story Creek Baptist Church was organized in 1855. The present building, erected in 1910, stands on land purchased from Ira Hurt. Among the charter members were Mr. and Mrs. Ira Hurt, Mr. and Mrs. E. B. Wade, Mr. and Mrs. Edmund Wade, and Charles R. Mason. Pastors include Joel Meadors, R. D. Haymore, S. G. Mason, J. W. Wade, F. P. Robertson, E. Y. Poole, W. L. Naff and M. B. Major.

## OTHER BAPTIST CHURCHES

Antioch (Negro), near Waidsboro; Boone Mill (Negro); Belleview (Negro); Chestnut Grove (Negro) near Sontag; Cole's Creek (Negro), about 5 miles west of Rocky Mount; Glade Hill; Hale's Ford, near Hale's Ford; Henry Chapel; Mt. Ivy, near Scruggs; Mt. Carmel, four miles north-east of Snow Creek Store; Morning Side (Negro), on U. S. Highway 311, three miles south of Rocky Mount; Rocky Mount (Negro); Rock Ridge (Negro), near Waidsboro Postoffice; Snow Creek (Negro), near Becker's old tobacco factory; Sandy Ridge, near Wirtz Station; Truevine (Negro), near Dickinson's Store; Trinity, 1874, in upper Snow Creek Valley, near Henry County line; and Union Hall (Negro).

## BAPTISTS (PRIMITIVE)

The only information gained from many letters to Primitive Baptist churches is that some of the early members of the Snow Creek Church (organized in 1858 and now extinct) were: Greenville P. Cooper, Lawson Williams, Gideon B. Cooper, Carter B. Terry, James White, Anna Finney, Sarah Hix, Polly Wingfield, Elizabeth Law, Sallie Cooper, Frances Finney, Celia Belcher, William T. Cooper, Sallie Bousman, G. F. Tench, Mollie F. Cooper and Maude A. Bousman.

## OTHER BAPTIST (PRIMITIVE) CHURCHES

Bethel, three miles northeast of Glade Hill, J. P. Dudley, Clerk; Black Rock, G. W. Wood, clerk; Blue Hill (Negro), two miles west of Snow Creek Store; Canton Creek, on Canton Creek,

Reed McGhee, clerk; Carolina Springs (Negro), about five miles west of Rocky Mount; Chestnut, near Chestnut Creek, W. C. Hodges, clerk; Cross Roads, in northeastern part of the county; Endicott, on Runnet Bag Creek; Ephesus; Fork Mountain (Negro); Gill's Creek, J. A. Perdue, clerk; Knob, six miles west of Henry Station; Little Creek, five miles west of Rocky Mount, L. T. Webster, clerk; Long Branch, near Endicott, and eight miles west of Ferrum; Lynville, near Staunton River, J. P. McGuire, clerk; Old Chapel, J. J. Oakes, clerk; Pigg River, on headwaters of Pigg River, S. M. Prillaman, clerk; Republican, three miles west of Ferrum, W. P. Stanley, clerk; Rocky Mount, T. G. Spencer, clerk; Rocky Mount (Negro); Town Creek, two miles east of Henry Station, A. M. McGuffin, clerk; and Union Hall (Negro).

## BRETHREN

The Brethren Church (known variously as Dunkard, Dunker, Tunker and German Baptist) is the fruit of a pietistic movement which spread over Germany in the seventeenth and eighteenth centuries. When they first came from Pennsylvania and New Jersey to Maryland, the Brethren settled in two sections. One was the area now in Shenandoah, Rockingham and Augusta counties. The other was the area now in Franklin, Botetourt, Floyd and Roanoke counties. The first of them came in 1775 and 1776. Elder Jacob Miller, who came to Virginia in 1783 began his ministry in Franklin County in 1786. Miller came with the Garber, Myers, Flora, Naff, Bowman and Glick families whose property had been confiscated because of their pacifist views. William Smith was a co-worker with Jacob Miller in Franklin and Botetourt counties. Miller would speak in German, and Smith in English. Other co-workers were Christian and John Bowman, Abram and Isaac Naff, Daniel Barnhart, Austin Hylton, Samuel Crumpacker, David Rife and Henry Snider.

The Franklin County Brethren went out on missionary expeditions as far as North Carolina and made many converts. They prospered despite the fact that most of them repudiated the slave owning which was practiced by their neighbors. The church as a whole disapproved of slavery a half century before the Civil War. With the coming of the Civil War, the Brethren suffered persecution much as their ancestors had in the days of the Revolution. The indignities heaped upon them makes a pathetic page in Virginia history. But most of them stood true to their pacifist convictions. Elder John Kline encouraged the Brethren in Franklin County to stand firm against military service. This greatly enraged the militarists, and he was shot from ambush and killed June 15, 1864. He was buried at Linville Creek Church.

Elder Daniel Peters married Mary Brubaker of Franklin County, Jan. 17, 1850, and was made a minister in 1872. He

106

preached much in Franklin, and was among the first Brethren
ministers to preach in Patrick, Floyd, Henry and Pittsylvania.
He continued to preach after he became blind.

Isaac Naff also preached much in Franklin.  He spoke
both English and German fluently.  The Franklin County Brethren
so increased in numbers that their communions could no longer
be held in their dwelling houses, so the Germantown meeting house,
40 by 100 feet, was built in 1848.  Abram Naff and Abram Barnhart
were in charge at the time.

It was decided in 1870 to divide the Franklin County
Brethren into three congregations.  Accordingly, the Antioch and
Bethlehem congregations were formed.  Their houses of worship
were built in 1873.  The Snow Creek church was organized in 1906,
with twenty-five members, and a house of worship was erected in
1910.  The Brethren in Franklin County now have (1935) eight
church buildings and a score of preaching points.  Through the
efforts of the Franklin County Brethren, churches have been
established in Campbell county.  The elders of the Franklin County
congregations in 1908 were:  Germantown-Abram Barnhart, Henry
Ikenberry and R. L. Peters; Bethlehem-Daniel Peters, David Bowman,
D. A. Naff and Geroge Bowman; Antioch-Riley Flora, Isaac Bowman,
Samuel Ikenberry and L. E. Brubaker.

Boone Mill Church of the Brethren functioned for a long
time as a part of the Bethlehem congregation.  Though the present
building was dedicated in July 1925, it was more than a year
before the congregation ceased to be a part of the Bethlehem
congregation.

On Dec. 19, 1926, the first independent meeting was
held.  L. A. Bowman, who had been in charge of the mother congregation was elected elder of Boone Mill Church, G. W. Bowman
was elected treasurer, and agent for the publishing house, and
Miss Gladys Flora correspondent.  Other ministers, in addition
to the elders were: E. E. Bowman, F. M. White, J. H. Murray,
C. B. Boone and J. T. Cummings.  There are now three other houses
of worship within this congregation, and a new house has been
completed at Red Hill just beyond Back Creek.

Since its organization, the following men have been
inducted into the ministry:  J. E. Bowman, C. W. Bowman, Jr.,
W. D. Abshire and I. D. Hoy.  The present ministry is composed
of E. E. Bowman, elder in charge, J. H. Murray, G. W. Bowman, Jr.,
W. D. Abshire, I. D. Hoy and L. A. Bowman.  These men make their
living independently of the church.  R. B. Barnhart is clerk and
Mrs. Gladys Greene is correspondent.

The names Boone, Bowman, Barnhart, Brubaker, Cummings, Flora, Ikenberry, Mitchell, Montgomery, Naff and Peters have been prominent in the Brethren Church in Franklin County. The Franklin County Churches have kept a missionary in China for several years.

Other Brethren churches and missions are: Bethany, between Dillon's Mill and Callaway; Bethel, two miles west of Ferrum; Bethlehem, at the foot of Cahay's Knob; Boone's Chapel, three miles east of Snow Creek Store; Brick, two miles west of Wirtz Station; Fairview, on Highway 40, four miles southwest of Rocky Mount; Oak Ridge, near Red Valley; Piedmont, four miles northeast of Wirtz Station; and Pigg River, five miles west of Rocky Mount.

## DISCIPLES
### (also called Christian Church)

G. W. Abell, in the Annual Report of 1859, says in part: "My fourth trip, comprising a part of the months of July and August, was to the counties of Franklin, Henry and Pittsylvania. Here is a vast and needy field. Brother Dillard is our only Evangelist in this section, though there is need for a full score".

## SNOW CREEK CHRISTIAN CHURCH

Snow Creek Christian Church was organized or re-organized on this trip. Plans were made for erecting a house of worship, but before they could be executed the War Between the States broke out, and the house of worship was not erected until the late sixties. The Masonic Order assisted in the building of the house and for 65 years has used the upper floor for its meetings. The Methodists also assisted in erecting the building and have held monthly services in it ever since. Up to the erection of the present building, the congregation had no definite place of worship and met in whatever places were available. Among these places was a house belonging to William Brodie, originally the Tatum house, and vacant most of the time. This building was also used as a school house, and Richard ("Dick") Moorman and his sister, Mrs. Dickinson, taught there at one time.

Among the early members were Mr. and Mrs. Lewis Becker, Mr. and Mrs. Samuel S. Cook, Elizabeth Wingfield, Mr. and Mrs. Morgan Cooper, Mr. and Mrs. George Cooper, Mr. and Mrs. Green Graveley, Mr. and Mrs. William ("Billy") Williamson, Mr. and Mrs. Silas Bernard, Mr. and Mrs. Mordecai Cook, Mr. and Mrs. John O. Bernard, Emeline Pinckard and Mr. and Mrs. Jason B. Hundley. The two men last named were elders and assisted the pastor, Rev. W. C. Clark, at the ordination of the author of this volume in Snow Creek Church on Nov. 10, 1912. J. T. Stone served this church from about the time the building was erected until his death in 1903. W. C. Clark became pastor in 1904, and has served continuously to this day. He has baptized over 300 persons during these years and buried approximately the same number. A cemetery was opened on the church grounds about 1925. Thomas Otis Wingfield is the present clerk of this church.

The Disciple Church in Franklin once called their county and district meetings "Cooperations". The average citizen en route to one of them would have told you that he was on his way to the cooperation. It was not a corporate body, nor a delegate convention. It assembled every year, but it had no authority and assumed no perrogatives over congregations or individuals. It did not attempt to deal with matters of doctrine or discipline. It was simply a mass meeting of ministers and laymen and no one claimed to represent anybody but himself. Through such meetings the Disciple Churches tried to cooperate with one another in promoting evangelism. The spiritual food of these cooperations, like the food spread on long tables under the trees at noon, was varied. From it each man selected such things as were congenial to his taste.

There were few "business sessions", no questions of parliamentary usage, no ponderous committee reports, and no political maneuvering. The chief features were preaching, praying, singing and eating. The singing was without benefit of a professional leader, but everybody knew the old songs and seemed to joy in singing them.

The attendants were plain people in plain apparel. The only men who seemed to be dressed for the occasion were the presidents of the Church colleges who used these meetings to "drum up" students - - - Bethany, Milligan and Virginia Christian College, later renamed Lynchburg College.

The man who appealed to my boyish imagination above all others was T. J. Stone. He was born in Carroll County in 1830, and died in Franklin in 1903. During his forty years in the ministry, he baptized over 2000 converts. Next to Stone in my hero worshipping heart was W. C. Clark. He was born in Henry County, educated in Johnson Bible College and the University of Virginia, and began his ministry in Franklin County nearly 40 years ago, and still continues in his first and only pastorate. When I decided to preach, Mr. Clark, with the assistance of Elders Jason B. Hundley and John O. Bernard, ordained me to the ministry. Believing that all regular ordinations had to be attended with fasting and prayer, I went a few days in advance to the home of Mr. and Mrs. B. F. Williams near the church so as to observe the occasion with due solemnity. My home was only two miles away but my father was not wholly sympathetic with my course. The members of my family for the most part were not church members. I feared levity would attend the process of fasting and prayer if I attempted to carry it out among them.

The ceremony was held in the old Snow Creek Church, Nov. 10, 1912. I had taught a Sunday School class there while yet in my early teens. I still have the little red-back class roll book with these names: Annie Brodie, Mamie Brodie, Carroll Brodie, George Brodie, Will C. Brodie, Peral Barbour, Myrtle Belcher, Ben Belcher, Mont Belcher, Mary Bondurant, Gladys Cooper, Lee Doyle, Walter Haynes, Charles Haynes, Robert Hundley, Ben Hurd, Homer T. Lawrence, Sallie Lawrence, Arthur Martin, Louise Pearson, Kathleen Pearson, John Pearson, Estelle Stultz, Thomas A. Trent, Belcher Whitehead, Ben Whitehead, Bob Whitehead, George T. Washburne, and my sisters, Nannie, Lucy, and Elsie Wingfield.

Writing from Glade Hill, Oct. 3, 1861, G. W. Abell says: "For a few days I have been skirmishing here among the hills of Franklin, but I can't get the people within reach of heaven's artillery. They won't stand the divine fire. Their orthodox ears are too hard to be perforated with the bullets of heresy. Yet a few free spirits are found among them. We have just baptized one such who had courage to stand when a general spirit of fearfulness is prevading the masses".

"I have been in this country (Franklin) six weeks. About 100 have declared themselves on the side of the Lord". It was during these two weeks that Mr. Abell baptized the author's maternal grandmother, Nannie S. Martin, who shortly afterwards was married to John Fontaine Motley.

## COOL SPRINGS CHURCH

Cool Springs Church was formed during Mr. Abell's visit of 1862. Of the ministers of Cool Springs before Rev. J. T. Stone, I know nothing. R. Page Laprade is clerk of this church.

## MOUNT IVY CHURCH

Mount Ivy Church was formed during Mr. Abell's visit referred to in the preceding paragraph. The present building was erected in 1894 through the cooperation of Methodists and Baptists.

## DOE RUN CHURCH

Doe Run Church was organized as a result of the visits of Mr. Abell to Rocky Mount in 1872. The present house of worship was erected in 1897. The trustees at that time were J. L. English, C. R. Bennett, J. H. Divers, S. T. Byrd and Nathan B. Hutcherson. The first pastor of this church was T. J. Stone.

## ROCKY MOUNT CHRISTIAN CHURCH

The Rocky Mount Christian Church, an attractive brick structure, was erected in 1917 and 1918. The first trustees were W. R. Davis, A. M. English, R. E. Ferguson, N. B. Hutcherson and J. S. Hudson. The first pastor was Riley B. Montgomery.

## FOREST HILL CHURCH

Forest Hill Church was organized by W. C. Clark in 1910. He has been pastor since its organization. He has baptized over 100 people into the church and has buried half that number. The charter members of this congregation were: J. W. Pearson, Mr. and Mrs. H. G. Law, Annie Jeter, Ada Fralin, Mr. and Mrs. J. A. Belcher, Mr. and Mrs. S. I. Belcher, Mr. and Mrs. Cooper Law, Martha Pearson, Mrs. I. K. Tench, Mr. and Mrs. Campbell, Mrs. Dink Adams, Mrs. Sam Cooper, Mr. and Mrs. J. L. Lovell, Mrs. Jeff Fralin, Herbert Mills and Mrs. J. J. Oakes.

## BOONE MILL CHRISTIAN CHURCH

The Boone Mill Christian Church grew out of the interest of a few members of the Snow Creek Church who had located in and near Boone Mill. The lot on which the church stands was purchased in 1918. The building was erected the following year and dedicated on June 27, 1919 by F. H. Scott of Roanoke. Mr. Scott served Boone Mill Church in connection with his Roanoke pastorate until the end of 1922. Pastors since 1922 include R. B. Montgomery, O. F. Sherwood, M. E. Turner, J. T. Watson, R. M. Redford, L. B. Riley, Joseph Smith and R. A. White. The charter members were Mrs. G. W. Angell, Mr. and Mrs. S. W. Bernard, Ewell Bernard, Mrs. Mary Beard, Belle Beard, Mr. and Mrs. L. M. Bussey, Mary Bowman, Garnett Bowman, Vivian Boone, Mary Boone, Eulalia Bowman, W. R. Boitnott, R. S. Childress, Jack Garst, Winifred Garst, Virginia Grubbs, Mr. and Mrs. H. F. Hill, Mr. and Mrs. G. P. Penney, Pearl Penney, Mr. and Mrs. J. M. Kendrick, Mr. and Mrs. C. J. Kinsey, Gladys Kendrick, Irene Kendrick, Aubrie Kendrick, Carl Kendrick, Mr. and Mrs. J. W. Kinsey, Blanch Kinsey, Julia Kinsey, Mr. and Mrs. James Mills. Mrs. C. W. Mills, Walter Mills, Mrs. Steve More, Mr. and Mrs. E. L. Montgomery, D. T. Naff, Harry Neighbors, Clara Naff, Frances Peters, A. H. Spielman, Lizzie Sloane, Mr. and Mrs. M. D. Starkey, Harry Sandredge, Maye Terry, Mr. and Mrs. J. H. Webb, Janette Webb, Geneva Webb, Mrs. Fannie Whorlie, Fannie Wray, Reba Wray, Agness Whorley and Sallie Whorley.

From this charter membership the Church was organized
with Elders- J. M. Kendrick and J. H. Mills; Deacons- Jack Garst,
George P. Jenny, S. W. Bernard, C. J. Kinsey and L. M. Bussey;
Treasurer- W. F. Mills; Clerk- L. M. Bussey; and Trustees- S. W.
Bernard, T. F. Montgomery and A. H. Spielman.

## PLEASANT VIEW CHURCH
### (originally Mountain View)

Pleasant View Church was the first church of the
Disciples of Christ north of the county seat. It was organized
in August of 1884 in a log house, near the home of Joel Montgomery,
and called Mountain View after the school of that community. The
organizer, William Huffman of Craig County, had the new church
enrolled as a constituent of his Alleghany District.

When the first house of worship was built in 1889, T. J.
Stone became pastor, the name was changed to Pleasant View, and
for cooperative purposes, the Church was numbered with those of
South Piedmont District where it geographically belonged.

C. W. Montgomery became pastor in 1900, and led the
congregation in building a new house in 1903.

With the centralization of the community in the village
of Boone Mill, a church was built there in 1920, and many of the
Pleasant View members transferred membership to the new congregation. The whole church was merged with Boone Mill Church in
1928.

The charter members of Mountain View were: Mr. and Mrs.
Joel Montgomery, Mr. and Mrs. Cephas S. Montgomery, Mr. and Mrs.
George W. Jamison, Hazel Langston, Charlotte Webster, Mary
Webster, Sarah Patterson, Jane Blankenship and Martha Heckman.
This Church sent out the two well known ministers, J. D. and R. B.
Montgomery.

## EPISCOPALIANS

The Protestant Episcopal Church in Rocky Mount was the
first congregation of that communion in Franklin County. The
organization was effected in the home of the late Judge Hugh
Nelson shortly after the War Between the States. The organizer
was the Rev. John R. Lee, a Pennsylvanian. He was Rector of the
Episcopal Church in Leaksville, North Carolina, and a brother-in-
law of Judge Nelson. He conducted services regularly from 1875
to 1880.

The first house of worship, a modest wooden structure, was erected in 1875. This building was later placed in a more central position on the church grounds, and the present stone building (now ivy clad) was erected around it.

The names of the rectors, in the order of their succession, are as follows: John R. Lee, E. L. Goodwin, J. K, Norwood, Alexander Barr, S. O. Southall, W. T. Roberts, D. I. Hobbs and Allen Person.

## METHODISTS

### BETHANY METHODIST CHURCH

Bethany Methodist Church grew out of a Sunday School held in Cross Roads School House. The organization was effected in 1912 by pastor O. L. Haga, assisted by presiding Elder B. M. Beckham. The lot was bought from R. O. Hale and Aaron Price. The building committee consisted of J. R. L. Wood, C. C. Nash and Mill Ellen Wright. The building was dedicated in 1915 during the ministry of Kenneth Faust.

Stewards of this church are J. H. Brogan and J. W. D. Nash. Mrs. J. H. Brogan is treasurer. Sunday School officers and teachers are Carrie Nash, Louise Brogan, Burbee Lowe, Lola Maxey and Mamie Montgomery.

### BOONE MILL METHODIST CHURCH

A revival held by Rev. J. W. Carroll in May 1887 resulted in the organization of this church. Charter or early members of this church were: Thomas Abshire, Henry Abshire, Samuel Abshire, Lewis Abshire, John W. Angell, Jane Angell, Belle Angell, Minnie Angell, James H. Turner, Mrs. J. H. Turner, Crickett Pate, Empress Turner, Thomas N. Wright, Mrs. Judy A. Boone, E. H. Burchfield, Mrs. Judy R. Burchfield, Tazewell Abshire, Mrs. J. W. Abshire, Annie Wilkes, John Nelson Abshire, Middie Abshire, Miss Johnnie Abshire, Mrs. Lucy Wray, Cora L. Pearson, Ozella A. Pearson, Clifton W. Pearson and Georgia A. Pearson.

At a quarterly conference April 6, 1895, a building committee was appointed consisting of C. T. Abshire, E. H. Burchfield, and J. W. Angell. The cornerstone of the present building was laid July 13, 1895. This building was erected jointly by the church and Isaacs Lodge No. 29 A. F. & A. M., and is jointly owned by the two organizations.

On May 23, 1897, the building was dedicated. The lower floor is used by the church, and the upper floor by the Masonic Order.

The following pastors have served Boone Mill: J. W.
Carroll, J. O. Moss, E. V. Carson, Thomas G. Pullen, E. E. Harell,
J. C. Harry, George W. Watkins, W. A. Tompkins, B. C. Beahm, C. A.
Hamilton, J. W. Parrish, G. B. King, George T. Kesler, S. R.
Drewry, E. G. Kilgore, J. W. Wimbish, Richard H. Shapland, Banton
T. Leonard and Paul R. Best.

Thomas N. Wright and Kinsey W. Sink are Stewards, and
Thomas N. Wright and D. N. Greene, Trustees. The charge known as
Franklin Circuit consists of Boone Mill, Trinity, Red Valley,
Flint Hill and Redwood Churches, and owns a parsonage in Rocky
Mount. For several years Boone Mill was a part of the Circuit
embracing the church at Rocky Mount.

## FLINT HILL METHODIST CHURCH

Flint Hill Methodist Church was organized in 1870 by
David F. Hodges, a native Franklin County preacher. Among the
charter members were Mr. and Mrs. William A. Hurt, Mr. and Mrs.
William Thurman, Mrs. Lucy Chitwood, Mr. and Mrs. J. O. Fisher,
and Mr. and Mrs. John Angle. Ministers who have served this
Church include: D. F. Hodges, J. W. Tucker, J. E. DeShazo, J. P.
Woodward, W. P. Jordan, J. W. Carroll, John O. Moss, E. V. Carson,
R. G. Pullen, L. E. Harrell, J. C. Harry, G. W. Watkins, W. A.
Tompkins, B. C. Beahm, G. T. Kesler, G. B. King, G. W. Wimbish,
R. H. Shapland, B. T. Leonard and Paul R. Best, J. W. Carroll led
in the erection of the house of worship in 1889.

## GOGGINSVILLE METHODIST CHURCH

Gogginsville Methodist Church was organized in 1855, and
the house of worship erected that year by Thomas Hawkins and Ned
Withers on an acre of land donated to the congregation by Meshak
Griffith. The Church was named for Thomas Goggins, a native of
Franklin County and said to have been an early pastor, though his
name does not appear in the list of deceased ministers in the
Virginia Conference Annuals. Ministers who have served Goggins-
ville are: William (Billy) Beach; Andrew Boone, a native of
Franklin; Bedford Shelton; W. M. StClair (grandfather of Walter
StClair of Rocky Mount); J.W. Carroll; J. H. Moss; Harry Green;
R. G. Pullen; J. R. Bradshaw; H. W. Lundrum; H. B. Owen; T. R.
Jarrett; W. L. Jones; M. O. Harvell; N. C. Turner; G. W. Amos;
E. R. Collie; C. T. Boyd; J. M. Trower; and W. B. Estes.

Trustees of Gogginsville are: Robert Akers, Walter
St.Clair and D. E. Wigington. The last named is treasurer of
the Church. The stewards are Walter Overfelt, Mrs. G. H. Plunkett,
D. E. Wigington and Hobart Wright. Sunday School officers and
teachers are: Mrs. H. D. Jones, Mrs. Walter Overfelt, G. H.

114

Plunkett, Mrs. Frank Wright, Mrs. Hobart Wright, Dunnington
Plunkett and Virginia Wigington.

## HIGHLAND METHODIST CHURCH

Highland Methodist Church was organized in 1896 as a
result of a series of meetings held on the ground floor of James
A. Martin's Mill. Mr. Martin gave the lot and constructed the
house of worship. In all his church activity, he had the constant
encouragement of his wife, who was characterized by C. E. Blankenship (pastor during the erection of Highland) as "one of the
saintliest women I ever knew".

The trustees of Highland are: W. E. Angel, J. A. Mills
and C. M. Prillaman. Stewards are: B. G. Fisher, J. A. Mills,
C.M. Prillaman, George Stanley and Mrs. J. M. Robertson. The last
named is treasurer. Sunday School officers and teachers are:
Virginia Akers, J. A. Mills, C. M. Prillaman, Edith, Inez and
Lula Prillaman, E. M. Simpson and Anna Wray.

## NEW HOPE METHODIST CHURCH

New Hope Methodist Church was organized before the Civil
War. The house of worship was built on land donated by James A.
Walker. It is said the first building was burned by Federal
soldiers. Present day leaders in this Church are Mr. and Mrs.
P. C. Walker, Vera Walker, Sybil Shepherd, J. M. Walker and G. F.
Stanley.

## PLEASANT HILL METHODIST CHURCH

Pleasant Hill Methodist dates back to Aug. 5, 1857, when
William Menefee deeded land to a board of trustees composed of
Shelton Lavinder, James T. Waid, Powell M. Waid, Creed W. Waid,
William G. Wagner, James Doughton, Nicholas Cassell and Larkin T.
Cassell.

The charter members of the church are: Larkin Cassell;
Nicholas Cassell, Sr.; John Cassell; Powell Waid; Creed Waid;
James Waid; Mrs. Jerry Barbour; Mrs. Jane Wagoner; Mrs. Sarah
Arthur; Mrs. Susan Ann Taylor; Nathaniel Angle, Sr.; Mrs. James
Doughton, Sr.; Mrs. Ann Jane Doughton; Samuel Lavinder; Mrs. Lucy
Cassell; Mrs. Ann Price; Mrs. Mary Jane Cassell, Sr.; Miss Susan
A. Woody; Miss Cynthia Woody; Mrs. Caroline Frith; Mrs. Jane
Menefee; Shadrach Richards, Sr.; Mrs. Shadrach Richards, Sr.; and
Shelton Lavinder.

Nathaniel Thomas, the first pastor, assisted the workmen
in erecting the first house of worship. John Cassell, Sr., was
the contractor in charge of construction.

115

Pleasant Hill for many years had annual camp meetings. Several camp buildings were on the grounds, one of which was used as a school house for years.

The old building was replaced by a new sanctuary in 1912, the same being constructed by James L. Cassell, a relative of the builder of the first house. The building erected in 1912 was struck by lightning and burned in 1935.

## ROCKY MOUNT METHODIST CHURCH

The first Methodist church built in Rocky Mount was erected in 1845, through the efforts of Capt. R. A. Scott and Col. Samuel Woods. It was a frame structure, and served for about 40 years. It was used as a "union" church for a long time. The Methodists, Baptists, Presbyterian and Episcopalians each had services in it one Sunday per month.

Captain and Mrs. R. A. Scott were probably the first Methodists to settle in Rocky Mount. Mrs. Scott's maiden name was Charlotte Grimes.

Prior to the construction of the frame building, services were held in the home of Capt. Scott. He was superintendent of the Sunday School, steward of the church, and sexton. He rarely missed a quarterly, district or annual conference. The visiting ministers made his house their headquarters. In the absence of the pastor, Capt. Scott conducted the Church services.

Pastors of the Rocky Mount Methodist Church who served in the first building were: John W. Tucker, James O. Moss, W. P. Gordon, John P. Woodward, David F. Hodges (born and reared in Franklin County), and Joseph Potts, three of whose sons became ministers.

Largely through the efforts of Rev. John W. Carroll, a new church was built about 1885. Among the pastors who served in this building were: James O. Moss, T. G. Pullen, John L. Bray, A. L. Franklin and C. A. Tucker.

The present Methodist Church building, one of the finest in Virginia, was completed in 1926. W. G. Bates, Jr., Starke Jett, A. McK. Reynolds and C. O. Tuttle have served in the present building.

## ST. JAMES METHODIST CHURCH

St. James Methodist Church at Ferrum was built in 1896 on a lot donated by James Angle, a brother of N. P. Angle of Rocky

Mount. The bricks were made near the site of the building by a Mr. Haynes, and laid by a Mr. Menefee of Rocky Mount.

C. E. Blankenship, who was pastor at the time the building was erected, bestowed the name of St. James, in honor of his home church in Richmond. The house of worship was dedicated in the spring of 1897 by Presiding Elder W. P. Wright.

The present (1936) stewards are: B. P. Corn, Frank Hurt, C. L. Ross, R. B. Skinnell, and P. T. Slone, The last named is treasurer. The trustees are: D. A. Nicholson, J. P. Pinckard, and P. T. Slone. Sunday School officers and teachers are: Mrs. F. P. Brammer, Ruth Brammer, Coy Brammer, Vera Cannaday, Mrs. J. K. Hurt, Mrs. Ruby King, Mrs. Guy Nolen, T. R. Richardson, Archie Ross, C. L. Ross, P. T. Slone, Mrs. Mary Whitehead.

## TRINITY METHODIST CHURCH

Trinity Methodist Church was organized in 1912. The Church grew out of a Sunday School held in Harmony school house. The house of worship was erected in 1913. Among the charter members were: Dr. and Mrs. W. P. Reese, Mr. and Mrs. J. H. Ferguson, Mr. and Mrs. Carlton Price, Mr. and Mrs. A. L. Hannabass and Mr. and Mrs. T. P. Newbill. The first pastor was G. T. Kesler. The second was S. R. Drewry, a native of Franklin, who died in the first year of his pastorate.

Other Methodist Churches and preaching places are as follows: Bethany, five miles northwest of Ferrum; Bethlehem, at Sydnorsville Boone Mill (Negro); Crafts, five miles north of Glade Hill; Epworth, near Hale's Ford; Fork Mountain, on Fork Mountain; Northfield, between Union Hall and Penhood; Nowlin's Mill Mission, near Endicott; Oyler's Chapel; Red Valley (oldest Methodist Church in Franklin); Redwood; Rehoboth, near Wirtz Station; Shady Grove, in upper Snow Creek Valley, near the Henry County line; and the Union Mission, at Snow Creek.

## PRESBYTERIAN CHURCH IN FRANKLIN COUNTY

There is reliable evidence that there was a Presbyterian Church called Old Chestnut in the southern part of the county, near Sydnorsville, prior to 1850, although the writer has been unable to find any of the records of this church. There is a small cemetery in that community, which is still known as the Presbyterian Cemetery. Services were held by Presbyterian pastors in that community until 30 or 40 years ago. The Fishburnes were among the Presbyterian families of this section, who have moved away.

117

When the Piedmont Church was organized at Callaway, Mrs. Elizabeth M. Burwell was received by letter from Old Chestnut Church, and some time later, Mrs. Cassandra Mansfield was received on statement that she was a member of Old Chestnut, it being difficult to secure a letter.

On Sept. 15, 1850, according to previous notice, publicly given, an association preparatory to a Presbyterian Church was organized by Rev. Robert Gray at Pigg River Church, with the following persons forming the Association: Henry T. Callaway; Elizabeth W. Hairston; Jane S. Woods; Agnes E. J. Hairston; Ruth L. Hairston; Eliza J. Burwell; and Isbel (servant of Col. Robert Hairston). Mr. Gray was requested to come to Callaway, and lead the people in building a Presbyterian Church. During the plans for the building, he made a horseback trip to Norfolk to attend the meeting of Hanover Presbytery, and, on his return, brought $400 for the new building, $200 having been given by his father in Richmond.

On Sept. 21, 1851, during a protracted meeting conducted by Rev. Robert Gray and Rev. W. H. Matthews, the new brick building was dedicated as Piedmont Church.

On April 3, 1852, the above named members of the association, together with Mrs. Elizabeth M. Burwell, Dr. William Hairston, James S. Callaway, Maria Jane Webb and Mary T. Talliferro, were organized into a regular and constitutional Presbyterian Church; and James S. Callaway and Dr. William Hairston were chosen ruling elders.

The Rev. Robert Gray's pastorate of Piedmont Church extended from 1859 to 1866.

He was succeeded by Rev. Horace P. Smith who served as pastor for about the same length of time, and also taught school in the community. The next pastorate of much length was that of Rev. W. M. McPheeters, who came in 1880, and remained about six years. He lived at Rocky Mount, and during his pastorate the Rocky Mount Manse was erected.

The church at Rocky Mount had been organized in 1877, when twenty-two members had been dismissed from Piedmont Church, August 15, to form the new organization; and the church building was erected at about the same time. Rev. P. C. Clark became Pastor of the Rocky Mount and Piedmont Churches in 1887, and served for about four years. During this pastorate he taught a school in Rocky Mount. He has been superintendent of Home Missions in Montgomery Presbytery for over twenty years, and has had a longer association with this work than any other minister. For the past four years he has been preaching once a month as supply pastor at Rocky Mount and Bonbrook. After his pastorate, each of the following ministers served for a few years: Revs. J. M. Holladay, W. A. Hall, F. L. Higdon, W. H. Workman, J. L. Sherrard and A. S. Rachal. During this period the churches were served part of the time by Seminary Students while not having a regular pastor. The church at Rocky Mount seems to have been in a right flourishing condition for some twenty-five or thirty years after its organization, under the leadership of Elder George Dennis and others, but for some years past the local membership has been very small.

Regular services were begun in the Bonbrook community during the pastorate of Mr. McPheeters, and in 1897, largely under the leadership of Elder James Skeen, a church of about thirty members was organized and a church building erected. About 1918, the membership had decreased, and the church organization was dissolved and regular services discontinued. However, in 1928, the building was reparied with a new roof, and regular preaching services were resumed, being continued till the present time.

During the pastorate of Rev. C. W. Reed, in 1912, a new Manse was built at Callaway near the Piedmont Church, and since that time the pastor of the Franklin County group of churches has lived in this new manse. The next pastor was Rev. Thos. B. Ruff, who served for about four years, and then the following who served for shorter terms: Revs. N. W. Kuykendall, Lang, and Y. P. Scruggs.

During the pastorate of Mr. Scruggs, in 1924, the Blackwater Church was organized with thirty-five members, most of them by letter from Piedmont, in the new church that had been erected about a mile below the site of the old Blackwater Chapek, which had been a preaching point for a number of years.

For the past 25 or thirty years the missions of the Piedmont Church have played a large part in the growth and developement of the church. In 1907, Dr. S. S. Guerrant, an elder of the Piedmont Church and Superintendent of the Sunday School, organized a mission Sunday School in his home four miles north of the church. The Sunday School was later moved to the mill, and then to the little school house that had been erected nearby. In 1920, through the generosity of Dr. Guerrant, the Algoma Mission School Building was erected with four school rooms on the main floor and living rooms for teachers and a few pupils upstairs, at a cost of several thousand dollars, and was given to Montgomery Presbytery. Since that time, this building has been used for school, most of the time in connection with the public school system; and quite a

few pupils have been housed in the dormitory; but with the developement of the public schools nearby, the church is now conducting only a one-room primary school at this point.  In 1928,
also through the generosity of Dr. Guerrant, a smaller building
was erected at Pippin Hills four miles above his home, where a
one-room mission school is now being conducted.  At the opening
of this new mission, Dr. Guerrant asked to be relieved of the
superintendency of the Piedmont Sunday School in which place he
had served for 24 years, in order that he might take charge of the
new Sunday School at Pippin Hills.  This gives him a record of
30 years as Superintendent and Teacher of the Men's Class, most
of that time in two schools; and for several years past his wife
has been organist and teacher of the Women's Class in the two
schools.

In 1912 a Sunday School was organized at Coopers school
house, and in 1914, one at Oak Grove school house; and in 1918,
these were combined when the mission chapel was built at Midway,
three miles southwest of Callaway.  This building has been used
for the public school most of the time, since there is no public
school building in the community; and the Sunday School has been
conducted by various men from Piedmont.  All three of these
missions: Algoma, Pippin Hills and Midway have preaching services twice a month, the same as the mother church Piedmont.

During this period of Sunday School extension there has
been a steady increase in the church membership of the Piedmont
Church.  In 1883, over 30 years after the church was organized,
there were forty-four members and thirty Sunday School pupils
(although a number had been dismissed to Rocky Mount), and during
the past five years, although there has been a slight decrease
in Sunday School attendance, the church membership had increased
to 304.

The church has suffered much during its history from
long intervals between short pastorates, also from the constant
drain by removals to the cities.

Rev. Roy Smith became pastor of this field May 1, 1927,
and has had the longest pastorate in this work since the Civil
War, the exact length of the first two pastorates not being clear
from the records.  For three years, Mr. Smith was pastor at Rocky
Mount, in addition to Piedmont, and preached for two of those
years also at Bonbrook.  But for the past four years, he has
given his entire time to the two churches, and the three missions
in the Piedmont Group.

## Chapter 15

## ORDERS AND ORGANIZATIONS

### BOONE MILL MASONIC LODGE

Isaacs Lodge No. 29 was organized in 1884, and worked under dispensation until December 12, 1884, when a Charter was granted by the Grand Lodge of Virginia. It is the only Lodge in the State that preserves the name of William Bryan Isaacs, who was Grand Secretary from 1876 until his death in 1895.

The Masons who organized this Lodge came largely from Lone Star Lodge at Rocky Mount, which had recently surrendered its charter.

The Lodge was first housed in a room over the school building known as "Mountain View", located near Helms Store.

The first list of officers and members reported to the Grand Lodge was in 1885, and, supposedly, the charter officers and members were as follows:

Officers:

| | |
|---|---|
| N. C. Carper, Worshipful Master | T. K. Tench, Senior Deacon |
| O. M. Tench, Senior Warden | E. A. Ross, Junior Deacon |
| J. O. Abshire, Junior Warden | John Lee Taylor, Chaplain |
| C. T. Jamison, Treasurer | E. C. Akers, Tyler |
| O. H. Price, Secretary | |

Members:

| | | |
|---|---|---|
| William B. Akers | George D. Bennett | J. H. Lemon |
| C. E. Akers | W. S. Boon | A. J. Phelps |
| D. T. Abshire | N. C. Cassell | T. J. Phelps |
| J. W. Abshire | George M. Helms | J. H. Turner |
| Jabez Abshire | W. R. Crowder | F. I. Wray |
| John W. Angell | John S. Hale | P. F. Walker |
| John Boon | D. T. Krantz | O. D. Wray |

The Lodge moved to the town of Boone Mill in 1893, and held its meetings in a room over J. W. Abshire's store until 1895, when the store building and all its contents were destroyed by fire, except the charter and the secretary's cash book which had been placed in a fireproof vault in the storeroom.

The Lodge joined with the Methodist Episcopal Church, South, in 1895, in erecting a building in the town of Boone Mill, and both have occupied the building since.

The following members, in addition to the above list, have belonged to Isaacs Lodge since its organization:

Denton Abshire
H. T. Abshire
J. T. Abshire
D. B. Aker
G. E. Akers
R. D. Aker
H. T. Aldhizer
W. R. Arthur

W. J. Baldwin
J. O. Basham
T. O. Basham
Y. L. Bernard
E. H. Birchfield
C. R. Boitnott
J. R. Boitnott
W. H. Boitnott
C. W. Boone
E. P. Boon
G. C. Boon
M. D. L. Boon
J. W. Bradley
L. F. Brickey
J. L. Byrd

T. C. Callaway
D. P. Carner
H. G. Cheatham
B. L. Clements
Josephus Custer

P. H. Dillard
C. I. Dillon
C. L. Dillon, Sr.
C. L. Dillon, Jr.
C. H. Donahue
J. F. Drish

W. P. Emschwiller
J. M. Emswiler

J. H. Ferguson
W. C. Ferguson
J. E. Flora
T. A. Flora
F. T. Forbes
M. G. Forbes

J. G. Gerry
B. S. Gregory
John R. Guerrant
S. P. Guerrant, Sr.
S. P. Guerrant, Jr.
Samuel S. Guerrant
S. S. Guerrant, Jr.

N. S. Hampton
H. H. Hannabass
J. W. Hannabass
A. L. Hartman
L. C. Haynes
F. J. Heckman
W. I. Helie
G. W. Helms
Tazewell Helms
C. B. Hopkins
T. D. Hunt
H. H. Hurt

C. D. Jamison
C. H. Jamison
E. C. Jamison
L. C. Jamison
W. C. Jamison
D. F. Johnson

J. M. Kendrick
C. W. Kennett
S. G. R. Kennett
L. G. Kesler
O. C. Kesler
J. J. Kingery

I. G. Lloyd
J. P. Lovelace, Sr.
J. P. Lovelace, Jr.
R. A. Lovelace

H. H. Martens
M. D. Martin
D. W. Mattox
E. D. Mattox
E. L. Mattox
G. D. Mattox
G. T. Meador
J. F. Meador
W. C. Meador
G. W. Mills
N. H. Mills
D. M. Minnix
P. A. Minnix
Ewd. Moffett
F. L. Moore
S. B. Moses
C. O. Murray
G. F. Murray

C. G. Noell
D. M. Noell
H. L. Noell
S. A. Noell

O. E. Palmer
W. H. Perdue
U. S. Peters
W. S. Phelps
B. E. Price
H. C. Price
J. W. Price
Roy H. Price
Taylor Price
T. L. Price

122

| | | |
|---|---|---|
| Chas. Renick | Frank Sink | George W. Wade |
| C. M. Renick | T. O. Sink | Bedford Wagner |
| A. M. Renick | W. H. Slone | C. F. Walters |
| F. T. Renick | J. E. Smith | J. F. Webb |
| J. R. Renick | J. W. Stanley | J. L. Webster |
| P. R. Renick | R. G. Swanson | George C. Wertz |
| T. W. Repass | J. L. Stover | T. C. Wertz |
| T. J. Richards | | T. A. Wiles |
| T. P. Richardson | James Tanner | R. M. Williams |
| | | F. A. Wray |
| H. L. Sandridge | Walter Via | L. E. Wray |
| O. T. Saul | | C. H. Wright |

The following members have served as Masters of Isaacs Lodge, since its organization, and in order as their names appear:

| | | |
|---|---|---|
| N. C. Carper | J. M. Emswiler | B. L. Clements |
| R. A. Lovelace | L. E. Wray | S. S. Guerrant, Jr. |
| E. H. Birchfield | L. C. Jamison | C. D. Jamison |
| T. K. Tench | O. C. Kesler | C. W. Kennett |
| E. P. Boone | J. L. Webster | T. A. Flora |
| E. C. Akers | C. W. Mills | |

Note: Secretary J. M. Emswiler, in a letter dated Feb. 25, 1935, compiled the above records, adding that in 1895, many of the records were destroyed by fire.

## ROCKY MOUNT MASONIC LODGE

Rocky Mount Lodge No. 75 A. F. and A. M. was chartered January 20, 1852, with James Dinwiddie, Master; J. E. McCrery, Senior Warden; and Samuel Hale, Junior Warden.

The report of 1853 showed additional names as follows: Moses G. Carper, Joseph Dickerson, Lewellin H. Powell, B. H. Tatum and Leroy Downs.

The names of Fleming Saunders and John L. Goodwin appear in 1854.

In 1855, these new names appear: Randolph Dickerson, John H. Choice, Seth R. Richerson, B. T. Tatum, William Dawes and William Martin.

The lodge was marked "suspended" in 1858, and never reported to the Grand Lodge again.

A new charter was granted the Masons of Rocky Mount on December 11, 1867. The new lodge was known as Lone Star No. 75.

David Arrington, M. F. Robertson and Thomas H. Franklin were officers.

In 1868, the members were Thomas B. Greer, W. W. Franklin, J. W. B. Hale, A. M. Hall, George Loring, Jacob W. Webb, William H. Ray, James E. Carper, Hughes Dillard, H. C. Holly, L. C. Bell, P. M. Guerrant and T. L. Reynolds.

Additions in 1869 included J. J. Carper, Nathaniel Ray, H. W. Holly, Thomas C. Callaway, John C. Ferguson, S. B. Willis, John W. Price, H. C. Woods, N. C. Carper, Samuel S. Holly, James O. Abshire, James S. Edwards and John R. Powell. The 1869 report lists George W. Finney as expelled.

New named added in 1870 include M. F. Robinson, J. H. Binford, J. C. Cabell, O. H. Price, William A. Griffith and R. C. Henderson.

Additions in 1871 were A. S. Hughes, W. J. Jones, B. H. Hatcher and D. A. Meadows.

New members in 1872 were P. H. Dillard, J. L. English, W. Y. Jones, J. H. Green and J. S. Edwards.

L. C. Menifee, J. O. Abshire and Benjamin Garrett were added in 1873.

In 1874 three new members were added: John W. Hartwell, J. W. Bolling and B. B. Webb.

Additions in 1875 were: J. S. Hale, Jesse Prunty, William E. Andrews, J. W. Tucker, G. M. Bright, D. W. Dowdy, C. T. Jamison, John B. Saunders, H. M. Turner, W. D. Vaughn, J. W. Webb and T. J. Webb.

In 1876, the new members were H. C. Chapman, W. P. Holland, W. P. Jeter, C. R. Woody, James E. Hartwell, George W. Hartwell and M. F. Brown.

E. G. Beheler and J. W. Bowling were added in 1877, and T. K. Tench in 1878.

In 1879, P. H. Dillard, C. L. Menefee, J. W. Webb, and J. W. Tucker withdrew. George W. Hartwell was expelled. G. D. Bennett and John W. Hartwell were added the same year and J. W. Bowling died. T. P. Guerrant and M. J. Carper were also added in this year.

Lone Star Lodge No. 75 seems to have suffered a decline during the years 1877-1881, probably due to the expulsion of old members, and the "blackballing" of candidates. The 1881 report shows the death of M. F. Brown and J. W. Bowling. There was no report to the Grand Lodge after 1881, and the lodge became extinct.

The present Rocky Mount Lodge No. 201 was chartered on December 10, 1890. M. G. Carper was Worshipful Master; W. L. Garrett was Senior Warden; and P. F. Walker was Junior Warden.

In 1891, the members were William H. Hale, I. M. Menefee, J. H. Austin, Leonard W. Pinkard, J. V. Dickinson, H. H. Powell, N. C. Cassell, S. S. Guerrant, C. L. Menefee, W. S. Tyree, John S. Walker, P. F. Walker and William L. Garrett.

In 1892, new members were George B. Hale, A. L. Noel, W. D. Saunders and J. W. Wade. W. N. Powell withdrew in this year.

In 1893, new members were W. J. Allen, P. H. Dillard and B. R. Powell.

In 1894, William H. Hale and J. B. Beach were added. J. H. Austin died.

In 1895, W. T. Bernard and W. O. Frith were added.

In 1896, C. H. Barnes and J. M. Barbour were added. N. C. Carper died.

In 1897, J. J. Scott, J. C. Shearer, J. F. Henry, G. T. Kesler, C. L. Menefee, G. A. Menefee and J. W. Pendleton were added. B. Z. Wade died.

In 1898, B. S. Preston, E. E. Harrell, J. P. Mathews, J. N. Carper, H. D. Menefee, H. C. Dillard and J. K. Hurt were added.

In 1899, Odell Fizer, B. S. Robertson, A. J. Sims and R. E. White were added.

In 1900, G. E. Goode, D. A. Nicholson, J. R. Hutchison and B. W. Angle were added. A. D. Wood affiliated; J. N. Carper was restored; and J. J. Carper died.

In 1901, J. E. Keen was added. H. F. B. Martin was affiliated.

In 1902, M. O. Lemon was added, and J. A. Booth and Taylor Price were affiliated.

In 1903, George W. Gilbert, S. Preston and Z. T. Richards were added. J. E. Keene and I. M. Menefee both died in this year.

W. L. Garrett and J. H. Binford died in 1904.

In 1905, J. S. Cahill, T. G. Ingrum, W. T. Chitwood and R. H. Marks were added. A. B. Garrett, W. T. Roberts and G. T. Williams were affiliated.

In 1906, W. E. Bennett, C. J. Davis, G. O. McAlexander and D. A. Nicholson were added. Bernard Ingrum died in 1906.

In 1907, M. L. Dudley was added.

In 1908, J. W. Anglin, R. V. Owen and C. E. Turner were added. J. H. Coverstone was affiliated. T. G. Ingram and J. W. Anglin died in 1908.

In 1909, T. J. Beckett, I. V. Canaday, and H. T. Martin were added. F. W. Clare was affiliated.

In 1910, D. W. Divers, W. S. Garrett, C. C. Price, W. M. White and B. E. Walker were added. W. L. Coleman, H. E. Mattox, A. L. McGhee and A. W. Robbins were affiliated. W. E. Andrews died.

In 1911, R. Davis, J. C. Philpot, T. W. Carper and J. P. Dillard were added. J. L. Byrd and J. C. Shearer were affiliated.

In 1912, J. W. Altice, J. A. Frith, J. M. Farron, A. H. Powell and T. G. Perdue were added. S. M. Layne and C. W. Read were affiliated.

In 1913, G. W. Hooker, G. W. Sutherland, J. W. Melton, Walter St. Clair, J. O. Martin and R. L. McNeill were added. J. P. Hill, B. M. Harbould, W. D. Rucker and O. P. Williams were affiliated.

In 1914, G. W. Arrington, Z. Bernard, J. D. Chapman, S. E. Corn, R. S. Carroll, G. C. Dudley, J. W. Hodges, C. H. Hodges, A. H. Hopkins, R. Y. Melton, J. N. Montgomery, Jr., H. F. Powell, A. T. Pinckard and W. E. Woody were added.

In 1915, Edgar Beckett, W. H. Cannaday, N. Morris and C. R. Powell were added. A. S. Adams affiated, and J. L. Byrd died.

In 1916, T. F. Carroll, W. L. Hopkins, H. E. Painter, R. N. Whitlow, B. L. Watkins and Noel Walker were added. G. A. Menefee died.

In 1917, N. P. Angle, C. A. Johnson, H. L. Poff, T. A. Ross and W. J. Sutherland were added. J. W. Hannabass affiliated, and F. W. Clare died.

In 1918, S. H. Holcomb, C. L. Pickett, Daniel Edward Powell and C. M. Young were added. A. J. Ramsey and Elbert Y. Poole were affiliated.

In 1919, Okie S. Skinnell and W. E. Blackwell were added. Taylor Price died.

In 1920, B. B. Angle, L. W. Angle, B. A. Bennett, B. R. Cribb, B. A. Davis Jr., D. H. Davis, C. W. Dudley, H. L. Dudley, N. R. Draper, W. P. Hash, L. A. Hodges, W. D. Peak, R. H. Robinson, S. D. Simpson, H. L. Vaughan, F. H. Watkins and E. C. Whitlow were added. H. G. Cheatham, E. G. Kilgore, A. J. Simms, A. W. Steller and T. G. Wade were affiliated.

In 1921, Ira D. Culler, R. N. Elliott, J. M. Frith, J. L. Goggin, B. G. Garrett, C. R. Hunter, H. L. Laprade, John P. Lee, H. A. Prillaman, R. A. Prillaman, J. T. Sutherland, C. J. Shoaf Jr., and J. A. Wallace were added. H. P. Davidson, R. E. Ferguson, O. P. Williams, C. B. Willis and T. H. Francisco were affiliated.

In 1922, Toner Antisell, W. A. Bennett, W. H. Chestham, R. P. Dickinson, G. C. Greer, T. E. Sloan and W. N. Shearer were added. J. O. Smithers was affiliated, and H. L. Poff died.

In 1923, J. L. Davis, O. D. Deer, H. D. Dillard, J. R. Foster, Aaron Gravely, C. H. Lemon, J. A. Luke, L. M. Menefee, B. V. Reid, John I. Saunders, C. G. Shelburne and W. C. Williams, were added. Ryland Goode, B. H. Perdue and Arthur Wake were affiliated.

In 1924, J. B. Allman, R. N. Anderson, E. L. Barnes, L. H. Bennett, L. P. Bernard, T. O. Bradley, C. Oscar Cooper, C. R. Crook, J. S. Eames, H. F. Fralin, A. M. Goode, S. A. Gravely, W. M. Greer, J. J. Greer, Roy S. Hodges, N. B. Hutchison, Starke Jett, R. L. Kent, R. W. King, E. S. King, W. E. Laprade, C. D. Lee, H. L. McNeill, J. E. Montgomery, E. G. Nash, T. C. Nicholson, C. B. Nolen, G. W. Nolen, Roy T. Pinckard, Paul C. Prillaman, I. W. Ramsey, S. H. Richards, W. G. Richards, H. L. Robertson, J. R. Robinson, Peter Saunders, G. D. Sutherland, Fred A. Turner, E. L. Turner, T. F. Webb and J. W. Wimbish Jr. were added. W. G. Bernard F. P.

Brammer, W. T. Chitwood, K. P. Housman, J. S. Joplin, R. W. Menefee, W. F. Owen, H. E. Stanley, B. W. Taylor and J. B. Zeigler were affiliated. J. M. Barbour died.

In 1925, C. H. Barnes, A. K. Bennett, R. L. Davis, D. H. Goode, C. H. Perdue, James P. Preston, Karl Richards, L. W. Skinnell, M. E. Skinnell, C. B. Wade, B. H. Wray and J. D. Young were added. A. O. Moran was affiliated. A. B. Garrett and C. D. Ponton died.

In 1926, G. C. Pendleton, T. E. Prillaman, Gordon Stanley and G. W. T. Ware were added. D. I. Hobbs was affiliated. C. B. Willis died.

In 1927, A. C. Angle, H. H. Booth, J. H. Ferguson, N. T. Green, E. W. King, J. W. Perdue, H. W. Prillaman, B. T. Turner and F. L. Wright were added. C. L. Pickett and J. S. Walker died.

In 1928, H. L. Maxie and J. W. Wimbish Sr. were affiliated. B. W. Angle, W. T. Bernard and J. A. Luke died.

In 1929, I. Davidman, H. H. Frith, H. W. Ramsey and J. G. Wright, were added. W. H. Cobbs, A. M. Davis and D. E. Stone were affiliated. John P. Lee and F. A. Turner died.

In 1930, S. A. Gravely, J. C. Martin and R. W. Menefee died.

In 1931, Ryland Goode, L. W. Pinckard, Carl Richards, C. R. Powell and J. C. Shearer died.

In 1932, W. A. Alexander was affiliated. L. H. Bennet and J. R. Robinson died.

In 1933, V. G. Bennett was added. R. E. Ferguson and J. K. Hurt, died.

In 1934, J. B. Sink and G. C. Holland were added. H. P. Davidson died.

In 1935, R. E. Weaver was affiliated. G. W. Sutherland, J. L. Davis and R. W. King, died.

Members as of December 31, 1934:

| | | |
|---|---|---|
| A. S. Adams | A. C. Angle | E. L. Barnes |
| W. A. Alexander | B. B. Angle | Edgar Beckett |
| J. B. Allman | N. P. Angle | T. J. Beckett |
| R. N. Anderson | Toner Antisell | A. K. Bennett |
| | | B. A. Bennett |

128

V. G. Bennett
W. E. Bennett
L. P. Bernard
W. G. Bernard
Z. Bernard
W. E. Blackwell
H. H. Booth
T. O. Bradley
F. P. Brammer

T. W. Carper
J. H. Coverstone
Ira D. Culler

I. Davidman
C. J. Davis
A. M. Davis
O. D. Derr
J. P. Dillard
C. W. Dudley
Grover C. Dudley
H. L. Dudley

J. S. Eames

J. M. Farrow
J. R. Foster
H. F. Fralin
J. M. Frith

J. L. Goggin
A. M. Goode
A. A. Gravely
G. C. Greer
J. J. Greer
N. T. Greer
W. M. Greer

W. P. Hash
L. A. Hodges
Roy S. Hodges
S. H. Holcomb
G. C. Holland
A. H. Hopkins
K. P. Housman

Stark Jett
C. A. Johnson
J. S. Joplin

R. L. Kent
George S. Kesler
E. W. King

H. L. Laprade
W. E. Laprade
C. D. Lee
C. H. Lemon

A. L. McGhee
H. L. McNeill

H. L. Maxie
L. M. Menefee
J. E. Montgomery
J. N. Montgomery, Jr.
A. O. Moran
N. Morris

E. G. Nash
D. A. Nicholson
C. B. Nolen
G. W. Nolen

W. F. Owen

W. D. Peake
G. C. Pendleton
J. W. Pendleton
J. W. Perdue
T. G. Perdue
J. C. Philpot
A. H. Powell
D. E. Powell
H. F. Powell
H. A. Prillaman
Paul E. Prillaman
R. A. Prillaman
T. E. Prillaman
W. H. Prillaman

A. J. Ramsey
H. W. Ramsey
I. W. Ramsey
B. V. Reid
W. G. Richards
W. T. Roberts
B. S. Robertson
R. H. Robinson

T. A. Ross

Walter St. Clair
John I. Saunders
Peter Saunders
W. N. Shearer
C. G. Shelburne
C. J. Shoaf, Jr.
S. D. Simpson
I. B. Sink
L. W. Skinnell
M. E. Skinnell
O. C. Skinnell
J. O. Smithers
Gordon Stanley
H. E. Stanley
D. E. Stone
G. D. Sutherland
J. T. Sutherland
W. J. Sutherland

B. W. Taylor
B. T. Turner
E. L. Turner

C. B. Wade
G. W. T. Ware
B. E. Walker
F. H. Watkins
R. E. Weaver
T. F. Webb
W. M. White
E. C. Whitlow
R. N. Whitlow
G. D. Williams
O. P. Williams
W. C. Williams
J. W. Wimbish, Sr.
J. W. Wimbish, Jr.
W. E. Woody
J. G. Wright
F. L. Wright

C. M. Young
J. D. Young

J. B. Zeigler, Sr.

# SNOW CREEK MASONIC LODGE

Snow Creek Lodge No. 90, A. F. and A. M., was chartered December 14, 1869, with Banjamin H. Tatum, master; D. F. Hodges, senior warden, and John R. Brown, junior warden.

The members reported in 1871 were W. P. F. Lee, W. H. McGhee, C. C. Lee, B. F. Bernard, C. S. Cook, Thomas D. Hunt, John W. McGhee, John O. Bernard, F. R. Brown, P. T. Barrow, William A. Brown, Lewis Becker, Mordecai Cook, William H. Dickerson, Jesse H. Turner, C. S. Boothe, William A. Lester, John V. Brown, Creed H. Adams, Henry F. White, Henry T. Brown, George W. Cooper, O. M. Tench, B. T. Semones, S. W. Brown, John P. Turner, Joseph M. Gravely, James M. Montrief and Richard J. Moorman.

In 1872, new members were William Pinkhard, Henry Rau, Samuel Sutherland, G. W. Davis and W. R. Nunn. Henry Fulhite died.

New members for 1873 were Jacob P. Bondurant, John L. Dillard, William A. Pinkard, Benjamine J. Gravely, David H. Hodges, William A. Semones, William G. McGhee, John F. Montrief, Henry C. Pace and Marston Williams.

New members of 1874 were George W. Motley, Christopher C. Law. Ferdinand Phillips, John W. Tench, Otis M. Tench, Bruce A. James, R. Dent Mattox, John A. Street, William G. Davis, M. G. Carper and Samuel Morgan.

New members in 1875 were Henry J. Brown, William Dickinson, Lewis W. Morgan, William P. Burgess, William D. Cook, John M. C. Burgess, William G. Davis and Peyton W. Stultz. Deaths: John L. Dillard and Thomas L. Booker.

In 1876, new members received were Charles F. Belcher, Marshall E. Burgess, Joseph A. Koger, James L. Stultz, Obediah M. Allen, B. F. Campbell, Robert A. Reed, James W. Brown, David H. Hodges and Alexander C. Robinson.

New members in 1877: Samuel G. Mason, George W. Brown, James S. Bondurant and George W. Hundley. Deaths: Alexander C. Robinson and David F. Hodges.

New members in 1878; John W. Burch, Jacob E. Sutherland, Michael E. Draper and Horatio S. Slaydon. Suspended: William A. Lester, John F. Montrief and William G. McGhee.

Charles L. Putzel was the only new member in 1879. Pete Tom Barrow withdrew. Charles C. Lee and Benjamin H. Tatum died.

Peter L. Dent and William O. Minter were the only new members in 1880. Suspended that year were: B. F. Bernard, Samuel W. Brown, John W. McGhee, L. W. Morgan and J. P. Turner.

N. C. Carper was the only addition in 1881. W. R. Nunn, R. A. Reed and J. L. Stultz withdrew.

Ferdinand Cook was the only new member in 1882. (The author of this volume visited him when he was an inmate of the Confederate Soldiers Home in Richmond.)

New members in 1883 were A. H. Bousman, J. B. Fuller and John W. Pearson. C. L. Putzel and W. D. Cook withdrew. J. M. C. Burgess, M. E. Burgess, J. V. Brown, J. W. Turner and P. W. Stultz were suspended.

Accessions in 1884 were T. B. Fuller and L. McGhee. Withdrawals were H. S. Slaydon, J. O. Bernard, George W. Cooper, J. A. Rogers and W. O. Minter.

Additions in 1885 were W. H. Fuller, John W. Pinkard, Thomas W. Pinkard, B. Z. Wade and F. N. Parcell. Reinstated: S. W. Brown, B. F. Campbell and W. T. Cook. Withdrawn: B. F. Campbell. Died: S. W. Brown.

New names in 1886 were C. W. Law, John R. Lawrence and W. S. Tyree. Suspended: W. A. Lester. Withdrawn: M. E. Draper. Died: J. M. Montrief, William A. Brown and J. M. Gravely.

B. F. Williams, J. H. Greer and George W. Cooper were enrolled as members in 1887. Withdrawals were B. J. Gravely, H. F. Brown, John R. Brown and Joseph A. Koger. Died: Lewis Becker.

In 1888. Suspended: F. R. Brown, J. P. Bondurant, J. W. Burch, W. P. Burgess, George W. Davis, W. H. Dickinson, A. H. Bousman, R. J. Moorman, George R. Hundley, B. A. James, W. A. Lester, W. A. Semones and Samuel Morgan. Withdrawn: B. T. Semones, N. C. Carper and H. C. Pace. Died: Creed H. Adams.

New members in 1889 were: G. D. Williams, Mastin Williams, W. O. Frith and Stephen Kesler. Suspended: C. F. Belcher. Reinstated: Samuel Morgan. Withdrawn: O. M. Tench.

New members in 1890: R. W. Menefee. Suspended: Mordecai Cook. Withdrawn: F. R. Brown.

In 1891: Reinstated. W. H. Dickinson, J. M. C. Burgess and L. W. Morgan. Withdrawn: W. H. Fuller, J. M. Bondurant, W. H. Dickinson and W. O. Frith.

New members in 1892: Marshall L. Brock, J. T. Haynes and J. W. Amos. Suspended: A. L. McGhee, J. H. Greer, F. M. Parcell and George W. Cooper. Died: M. G. Carper.

New members in 1893: S. B. Chesler. Suspended: George W. Brown. Withdrawn: Thomas D. Hunt and B. Z. Wade. Died: George W. Motley.

New member in 1894: Samuel Sutherland. Died: Peter L. Dent.

In 1895. Withdrew to join at Martinsville: O. M. Allen. Suspended: S. S. Cook and J. B. Fuller. Died: Mastin Williams.

In 1897, a new member was Virgil White. Whitdrawn: Thomas B. Fuller. Suspended: Ferdinand Cook, E. D. Mattox and W. S. Tyree.

In 1898. Withdrawn: C. F. Pinkard.

In 1899, new members were William T. Legwin and W. S. Bernard. Died: Otis M. Tench. Dimitted: S. R. Kesler.

In 1900, Archie S. Adams was the new member. Restored: J. M. C. Burgess. Died: John R. Lawrence.

In 1901, C. F. Pinkard was reinstated.

In 1902, C. L. Dodd was added to the membership. Restored: John F. Montrief. Dimitted: J. M. C. Burgess.

In 1903, the new members were S. A. Reynolds and W. C. Swanson. Affiliated: H. S. Law. Withdrawn: John T. Haynes. Suspended: J. E. Fuller and J. B. Fuller.

In 1905, two new members were added: Walter H. Cobbs and Walter A. Lawrence. Withdrawn: G.D. Williams. Died: C. W. Law.

In 1906, two new members were S. M. Ziegler and J. B. Ziegler. Restored: J. H. Greer.

In 1907, W. C. Cobbs was added. Restored: S. S. Cook. Withdrawn: T. W. Pinkard.

In 1908, the new members were S. P. Brown, W. C. Clark and Jesse E. Richardson. Affiliated: G. W. Belcher (raided in Vincent Witcher Lodge No. 77). Withdrawn: C. F. Pinkard and W. R. Pinkard. Died. R. S. Brown.

In 1909, new members were W. H. Davis and S. H. Gaulden. Reinstated: M. E. Burgess and W. S. Tyree.

In 1910, the new members were R. G. Bousman, T. G. Adams and James V. Reynolds. Withdrawn: W. C. Swanson.

In 1911, the new members were C. B. Pearson, J. H. Philpott and F. T. Turner. Affiliated: W. R. Davis. Restored: J. B. Fuller.

In 1912, the new members were T. S. Law, J. W. Montrief and I. F. Tench. Died: W. P. F. Lee.

In 1913, the new members were A. C. Martin and G. D. Davis. Withdrawn: J. B. Fuller.

In 1915, J. J. Davis was affiliated.

In 1916. Withdrawn: W. A. Lawrence. Suspended: W. T. Legwin. Died: John O. Bernard and Lewis W. Morgan.

In 1917. New member: Harry C. Yeatts. Withdrawn: W. S. Tyree. Died: W. B. Brown.

In 1918. Died: B. F. Williams.

In 1919. New member: T. B. Rogers.

In 1920, new members were Paul C. Bernard, A. M. Davis and W. B. Turner. Affiliated: C. R. Cooper. Withdrawn: C. L. Dodd and S. M. Zeigler. Died: D. B. Yeatts.

In 1921, new members were C. G. Bernard, J. W. Hundley, George Lawrence, G. C. Martin, R. P. Saunders, Thomas Trent and E. H. Thompson. Restored: J. E. Fuller. Withdrawn: J. W. Pinkard.

In 1922, new members were Buell Martin, Calvin Washburn and Thomas Otis Wingfield. Died: John Pearson.

In 1923. Died: J. J. Davis.

In 1924, new members were J. D. Bousman, Buford Gregory and G. E. McDowell. Withdrawn: H. S. Law and J. V. Reynolds.

In 1925. Withdrawn: R. W. Menefee, J. B. Zeigler and L. P. Turner. Suspended: M. E. Burgess and T. S. Law.

133

In 1926. Affiliated: W. H. Dickinson. Restored: W. T. Legwin. Died: S. S. Cook.

In 1927, new members were L. S. Finney and J. B. Shorter. Died: W. H. Dickinson.

In 1928, new members were J. F. Fralin, B. G. Hurd, J. R. Montrief and L. D. Thompson. Withdrawn: W. T. Legwin, W. H. Cobbs, A. M. Davis and R. P. Saunders. Suspended: G. L. Yeatts.

In 1929. Died: E. D. Mattox.

In 1930, new member was G. W. Gregory. Restored: G. L. Yeatts.

In 1931, new members were W. G. Bernard, W. R. Davis and T. K. Tench. Suspended: C. B. Pearson.

In 1932. Died: Samuel Sutherland.

In 1933. Restored: W. R. Pinkard.

In 1934, new member was B. W. Cooper. Died: J. D. Bousman.

## UNITED DAUGHTERS OF THE CONFEDERACY

The Jubal Early Chapter, United Daughters of the Confederacy, was organized by Mrs. W. N. C. Merchant of Chatham in the home of Judge Hugh Nelson on February 13, 1902, and named for Franklin County's greatest Confederate soldier. His great niece, Mary Early Hale, was elected the first president of the organization. The charter members were:

Mrs. E. W. Saunders
Mrs. John P. Lee
Mrs. Herbert N. Dillard
Mrs. Emily Suttle
Mrs. Crocket S. Greer
Miss Lucy Nelson

Miss Ethel Hale
Miss Mary Nelson Strayer
Miss Josephine Menefee
Miss Eva Saunders
Miss Mary Early Hale

Many companies of the Confederate Army were drilled on the front lawn of the Nelson home, and it was particularly fitting that the first U. D. C. chapter in the county should have been organized in Judge Nelson's home. The intrepid Jubal A. Early found refuge in this home after the war, when Federal soldiers were pursuing him on the charge that he had burned Chambersburg. When finally pressed too closely, General Early sent a boy of this family to Capt. Marshall Waid, who lived a few miles south of Rocky Mount, requesting Captain Waid to furnish him with a horse to ride to Atlanta. Captain Waid not only did so but rode with him. From Atlanta General Early went to Cuba, and thence to Canada to elude his pursuers.

One of the most lasting works of the Jubal Early Chapter was the erection (with the assistance of R. H. Fishburne) of the Confederate monument in the Court House square at Rocky Mount. The chapter added much to the comfort of Confederate veterans of the county at their reunions, held on June 3rd of every year as long as they were able to assemble. Among the noted guests entertained by the chapter was Miss Mary Lee, daughter of Robert E. Lee. She gave the chapter an autographed photograph of her illustrious father.

Other members of the chapter since organization are:

| | |
|---|---|
| Miss Nora Ashworth | Mrs. Robert McNeil |
| Mrs. J. W. Beheler | Mrs. Morton Menefee |
| Mrs. W. T. Chitwood | Miss Mabel Montgomery |
| Mrs. W. H. Cobbs | Mrs. Nat Morris |
| Mrs. C. J. Davis | Mrs. Fanny Webb Neil |
| Mrs. W. R. Davis | Mrs. H. W. Peake |
| Mrs. Robert P. Dickinson | Mrs. T. G. Perdue |
| Mrs. H. D. Dillard | Mrs. J. C. Philpott |
| Mrs. W. W. Dillard | Miss Estelle Price |
| Mrs. Andrew Edmundson | Miss Mildred Price |
| Mrs. B. E. Ferrell | Mrs. O. H. Price |
| Mrs. A. B. Garrett | Mrs. O. L. Reynolds |
| Mrs. G. W. Gilbert | Mrs. A. W. Robbins |
| Mrs. Ryland Goode | Mrs. W. T. Roberts |
| Mrs. George Greer | Mrs. Louise Robinson |
| Mrs. N. T. Greer | Miss Mary Robinson |
| Mrs. D. C. Grubbs | Mrs. Walter St. Clair |
| Mrs. John R. Guerrant | Mrs. C. J. Shoaf |
| Mrs. C. L. Hunt | Mrs. Sula Simpson |
| Miss Belle Hurt | Mrs. W. E. Skinnell |
| Mrs. N. B. Hutcherson | Mrs. G. W. Sutherland |
| Mrs. Annie Price Ker | Mrs. Thomas F. Webb |
| Mrs. O. T. Kittinger | Mrs. S. K. Williams |
| Mrs. Kate St. Clair McDonald | Mrs. Hugh Womack |

## SONS OF THE CONFEDERATE VETERANS

The Franklin County Camp No. 526, Sons of Confederate Veterans, was organized in Franklin County, July 23, 1923. Col. Walter L. Hopkins, of Richmond, formerly of the County, and at

that time, National Adjutant-in-Chief of the Organization, installed the Camp with the following officers and members.

Officers

| | |
|---|---|
| Bedford S. Robertson | Commander |
| Walter St. Clair | 1st Lt. Commander |
| John Edd Montgomery | 2nd Lt. Commander |
| Samuel D. Simpson | Adjutant & Treasurer |
| Sidney H. Richards | Quartermaster |
| B. G. Garrett | Judge Advocate |
| W. T. Chitwood | Surgeon |
| Rufus A. Prillaman | Historian |
| Clyde H. Perdue | Color Sergeant |
| Robert L. McNeil | Chaplain |

Other Charter Members:

| | |
|---|---|
| James N. Montgomery, Jr. | Henry L. Dudley |
| Robert P. Dickinson | Robert Prillaman |
| Carl Richards | Robert Nelson Dickinson |

## AMERICAN LEGION

Franklin Post bear the number "6" yet it was the first
post of the American Legion organized in Virginia, and probably
the second one organized in the United States.

In March of 1919, Walter L. Hopkins, a charter member
of the General John J. Pershing Post No. 1, of Washington, D. C.
(now George Washington Post No. 1), called the ex-service men of
Franklin County to meet at Rocky Mount for the purpose of forming
a World War veterans association. In accordance with the call,
seventeen men met at Rocky Mount, on April 7, 1919, and formed
such an association, adopting a constitution and by-laws. The
following officers were elected:

> Walter Lee Hopkins, commander
> James N. Montgomery, Jr., vice-commander
> A. Newton Carroll, vice-commander
> Allen O. Woody, quartermaster
> Walter M. Greer, adjutant
> Clark Dickinson Hopkins, sergeant-at-arms
> Charlie N. Parcell, chaplin

A committee of this association called a meeting to
decide the national organization of ex-service men with which it
would affiliate. The members met at Rocky Mount, on June 2, 1919,
and voted to affiliate with the American Legion. Application for

136

charter was made, and Franklin Post was chartered July 1, 1919, and assigned No. "6", with the following charter members:

Lewis W. Angle, Buford B. Angle, E. G. Adams, Louis W. Bowles, A. New Carroll, Beverly A. Davis, Jr., E. T. Frith, Gordon G. Fralin, Walter M. Greer, Charles C. Greer, Edwin Greer, Clack Dickinson Hopkins, Walter Lee Hopkins, William Benjamin Hopkins, Leonard A. Hodges, Oscar T. Kittinger, J. N. Montgomery, Jr., Rufus E. McGhee, Bryant M. Morris, D. H. Mills, L. M. Menefee, Richard Y. Melton, Charlie N. Parcell, Word Day Peake, Edward W. Saunders, Jr., A. O. Woody, Dalton D. Webb, Posey Lee Webb and P. A. Young.

The Commanders of Franklin Post No. 6 since its organization are as follows:

Walter Lee Hopkins , '19.  
J. N. Montgomery, Jr., '20, '24.  
R. A. Prillaman, '21.  
Edwin Greer, '22.  
Greenwood Garrett, '23.  

C. N. Parcell, '25, '32.  
B. Andrew Davis, '26, '27, '30,'31.  
B. B. Angle, '28.  
J. B. Allman, '29.  
Sam Eames, '33, '34.  

The work of this Post could not have been accomplished without the assistance of the Woman's Auxiliary of the American Legion organized by Mrs. Walter L. Hopkins during the month of July, 1920. The officers for the first year of the American Legion Auxiliary were: Mrs. Walter L. Hopkins, president; Miss Ann Joplin, 1st vice-president; Mrs. H. W. Paek, 2nd vice-president; Mrs. A. B. Garrett, secretary; and Miss Mabel Montgomery, treasurer.

The charter members of the Auxiliary, Franklin Post No. 6, were:

Mrs. B. L. Angle, Mrs. Minnie S. Bennett, Mrs. Thomas Dudley, Mrs. Raymond Davis, Mrs. J. A. Dinwiddie, Miss Mary Dinwiddie, Mrs. A. B. Garrett, Mrs. C. S. Greer, Miss Flora Greer, Mrs. Walter L. Hopkins, Miss Ann Joplin, Miss Josie Menefee, Miss Mabel Montgomery, Mrs. H. W. Peak, Mrs. W. T. Roberts, Mrs. W. D. Rucker, Mrs. B. S. Robertson, Mrs. E. W. Saunders, Miss Sarah Saunders, Mrs. C. J. Shoaf and Miss Loline Shoaf.

## AMERICAN RED CROSS

The Franklin County Chapter of American Red Cross was organized in October 1917, with the Hon. E. W. Saunders as County Chairman; the Rev. B. T. Candler, Vice Chairman; and Mrs. W. C. Menefee, Secretary. This organization was continued intact until after the World War I came to an end. The Chapter raised $9,139.23. There were sent to training camps and to the front

137

for the use of service men the following:  sewed garments 1,112;
knit garments 1,517; and other articles 1,060.  An active canteen
corps was maintained for serving refreshments to service men while
they were being mobilized in the county.

The present organization of the Franklin County Chapter
is as follows:

C. J. Davis, County Chairman; C. C. Lee, Vice Chairman;
W. C. Brown, Treasurer; Jack Price, Secretary; Mrs. J. C. Shearer,
Chairman Production Committee; and Mrs. E. G. Foster, Roll Call
Chairman.  Executive Committee:  N. P. Angle, Chairman, C. C. Lee,
W. C. Brown, Jack Price, Rev. J. W. Dixon and C. J. Davis.

## LION'S CLUB

The Rocky Mount Lion's Club was organized in 1923 with
twenty members, and the following officers:  Ryland Goode, president; John P. Lee, vice president; and W. D. Peake, N. B. Hutcherson, Edwin Greer, A. N. Carroll and W. N. Shearer.

# Chapter 16

## THE COURTS OF FRANKLIN

County Courts were set up by the appointing of eight or more citizens of the county as commissioners.

The County Court had, in addition to its judicial functions, the authority to erect and repair the county court house; to contract for the construction of roads and bridges; or, in the absence of such contract, to procure labor for the construction of the same by drafting all able bodied, tithable males to perform a certain amount of work under the direction of a surveyor. These courts also had the authority to clear the rivers of obstructions; to procession or "beat the bounds" of parishes; to license taversns; to recommend inspectors of tobacco; to designate the places for tobacco inspections or warehouses; to designate landings along the rivers; to appoint constables; and to nominate for sheriff three of its own members, one of whom the Governor invariably appointed. This County Court was actually a self-perpetuating body. When a vacancy on the bench occurred, the remaining members would, at the next session of court, name a man to fill the place, and the Governor invariably confirmed him. This court system existed until 1851, when the Constitutional Convention made the justices elective officers, and provided certain compensation for their services.

The Constitution of 1869 abolished plurality of commissioners and provided for a County Court with a single judge. Hugh Nelson was appointed first judge in Franklin County. He served until February 1872, when Thomas H. Bernard was appointed. Judge Bernard held office until 1879. In March 1879, Thomas B. Claiborne was appointed, and he served until 1883. He was succeeded by George D. Peters who was appointed February 1884, and held the office until 1898. In 1899, John P. Lee was appointed and he continued in office until 1904 when the Constitution of Virginia was changed and the circuit and county courts were consolidated.

A roster of Franklin County judges includes the following: Thomas Arthur, Thomas H. Bernard, J. L. Campbell, Thomas B. Claiborne, Peter H. Dillard, H. L. Ford, George H. Gilmore, Berryman Green, Moses Greer, Robert Hairston, E. J. Harvey, Swinfield Hill, Abram H. Hopkins, Hugh Innes, John P. Lee, Hugh Nelson, George D. Peters, Jonathan Ricjeson, Fleming Saunders, Peter Saunders, E. W. Saunders, John Smith, Norman M. Taliferro, Henry Tazewell, William Tredway, Robert White, S. G. Whittle, Gustavus A. Wingfield and Edmund Winston.

The first court held in Franklin County convened at the home of Col. James Callaway on March 6, 1786. Present: Peter Saunders, Theo. Arthur, Moses Greer, John Gipson, John Rentfro, John Smith and Swinfield Hill. The last term of this court of General Justices was held in January 1870, with Robert Pasley, W. C. Mitchell and Thomas J. Forbes on the bench. Hugh Nelson was the first Judge under the new system.

The first tavern rates were set by the County Court in March 1787, as follows:

For good West India Rum, per gallon, ten shillings.
For Peach Brandy, per gallon, eight shillings.
For Whiskey, per gallon, six shillings.
For Wine, per gallon, twelve shillings.
For Hot Breakfast, one shilling, three pence.
For Cold Meal, one shilling.
For Stable and Fodder for Night, nine pence.
For lodging, six pence.

# Chapter 17

## DISTRICT BOUNDARIES

Commissioners were appointed to divide the county into Townships under an Act of the General Assembly passed the 2nd. April 1870.

District No. 1- the Township of Rocky Mount, was bounded as follows: commencing at the head of North Chestnut and down it to Jeffrey Woody's ford, thence with his road to the turnpike, and down to the fork of the Snow Creek road, thence northward to the south fork of Doe Run and down it to Pigg River, up it to the Old Forge, thence by Harveys Old Road to the Glade Hill Road, and across to the river at an Ivy Cliff, up it to the Island Ford, thence by a road to the Law's Island Road, with it to Harvey's Road, with it to the Daniel Run Road, west of Germantown, up it to the Carolina Road, with it to the Cam Road on the Grassy Hill, thence along the ridge that divides the waters of Pigg River and Blackwater to Hales Old Road, and with it by Saunders Forge to the Carolina Road and with it to the beginning. All the public roads made boundaries of this Township shall be included within and made a part of the same. The place for holding elections in this Township shall be at the Courthouse in Rocky Mount.

Change made by the order of the Circuit Court held for the County of Franklin, Saturday, March 8, 1919 (Order Book 20, page 413):

Beginning at a point on Pigg River, it being the beginning point on the lands of C. R. Bennett of the present extablished line (old Line), thence up Pigg River as it meanders a distance of five miles to a point on the said river on the old Siras Bennett place where the old line between Union Hall and Rocky Mount Districts intersect with said river.

Change made by the State Board of Education June 10, 1921, so as to subdivide the Magisterial District of Rocky Mount No. 1, into two school districts, as follows: Rocky Mount School District, No. 1, beginning at the bridge across Pigg River, just below the dam of the Rocky Mount Light and Power Co., thence up the river to the Ford just above the farm of R. F. Rakes on what is known as the Soapstone Road, thence in a Northerly direction with the said road to where it intersects with the old Cassell Store Road, thence with the old Cassell Store Road to the location of the said old Cassell Store, at a point where the old Corn Road intersects with the Floyd Turnpike, thence with the old Corn Road to the crest of Grassy Hill, thence along the ridges of Grassy

Hill to the old Hill Hale Place (now owned by N. P. Angle), thence a straight line to the culvert on the Norfolk and Western Railway, just North of the Blue Cut, thence a straight line to the John O. Wray residence on the last side thereof, leaving the residence in the Town District, thence a straight line to the Ad Wade house (now Ben Young's), on the east side thereof, thence a straight line due south to the branch on the north side of Bald Knob in the old J. W. Morris place (now C. F. Hudson), thence down the said branch to where it empties into Pigg River, thence up the river to the place of beginning. The remaining portion of the old Rocky Mount School District was made a separate district, known as the Pigg River School District No. 2.

District No. 2- the Township of Snow Creek, was bounded as follows: commencing at North Chestnut on the road leading by Ramsey's with it to the County line along said line Eastward to Dunn's Gap on Turkey Cock Mountain, thence with the new road to the cross roads near Francis Belcher's thence up the road by Charles Lee's and Antioch Meeting House to Snow Creek, at Silas Bernard's thence up Guthrey's Run and its north branch and Isham's Gap of Chestnut Mountain to a point north of the former dwelling house of Andrew Patterson, decd., thence by his old road to the turnpike, and with it to the southeast corner of the Township of Rocky Mount, with it to the lines of the same to the beginning. All the public roads made the boundaries of this Township and not embraced within the Township of Rocky Mount shall be included within and made a part of this Township. The place for holding elections in this Township shall be at Snow Creek Store.

District No. 3- the Township of Union Hall, was bounded as follows: beginning at the corner of the Township of Rocky Mount and Snow Creek on the Turnpike thence with the line of the Township of Snow Creek to Dunn's Gap, thence with the County line to Reddy's Gap, thence by the road to Anthony's Ford Road, with it to the Robert Powell's Road, with it to Bernard's Ford on Blackwater, up it to Holland's Ford Road, with it to Louis Island Road in the line of the Township of Rocky Mount, and with it to the the beginning. All the public roads made boundaries of this Township and not embraced within the Townships of Rocky Mount and Snow Creek, shall be included within and made a part of this Township. The place for holding elections in this Township shall be at Union Hall.

Change made by order of Circuit Court of Franklin, May 30, 1921: Beginning on top of Chestnut Mountain on line between Union Hall and Snow Creek Districts, thence in a southerly direction along the top of Chestnut Mountain to E. T. McGhee and Charles Hickman's corner, thence following the line between the lands of the said McGhee and Hickman to the corner of Sam Tench and Joseph Webb, thence following the line between said Tench and Webb to Shade Richards' corner, thence following the line between Shade Richards' home tract and the land bought by him from Sam Tench to the Hanging Rock Road (leading from George W. Cooper's house to Hanging Rock), thence with said road north easterly to Hanging Rock on Chestnut Creek, thence up Chestnut Creek to the mouth of Johnnie Cake Branch, thence following said branch westerly to Robert Young's spring head of the branch, thence a straight line westerly to Beulah Church, thence following the line (north) between Mary A. Hodges and W. S. Tyree, Mary Woody and J. H. Parcell and Taylor Woody to Little Doe Run, at a point where the line of Mary A. Hodges intersects said Run, thence down little Doe Run to the Union Hall line.

District No. 4- the Township of Gill's Creek, was bounded as follows: beginning at the corner of the Townships of Rocky Mount and Union Hall at the intersection of Holland's and Louis Islands Roads, thence with the line of the Township of Union Hall to Reddy's Gap thence with the County line to Staunton River and up it to Hopkins Mill, thence with the road by Nineveh Meeting House to Moore's on Gill's Creek, thence by an old road to Elliot's Creek and down it and Maggodee Creek to Blackwater, up it to Davis' Ford in the line of the Township of Rocky Mount and with said line southward to the beginning. The public roads made boundaries of this Township and not made a part of the Township of Rocky Mount or Union Hall shall be included and made a part of this Township. The place for holding elections in this Township shall be at Hatcher's Store.

District No. 5- the Township of Bonbrook, was bounded as follows: beginning at the line of the Township of Rocky Mount at Davis' Ford on Blackwater, thence with the line of the Township of Gill's Creek northward to Hopkins' Mill, thence with the County line to a point on the Blue Ridge opposite the source of a branch that runs into Maggodee at Isaac Boon's, thence with said branch to the Turnpike, with it to the cross roads, at the line of the Township of Rocky Mount with it to the beginning. All the public roads made boundaries of this Township and not made parts of the Township of Rocky Mount or of the Township of Gill's Creek, shall be included within and constitute a part of this Township. The place for holding elections in this Township shall be at Bonbrook Mills.

District No. 6- the Township of Maggodee, was bounded as follows: beginning at the southwest corner of the Township of Bonbrook on the Turnpike and with the line of said Township to the County line on the Blue Ridge, with it to Wimmer's Old Road with it to Blackwater, and by the road leading by C. B. Reynold's and Randolph Abshire's to the Lynchburg Road and down it to the

143

beginning. All the public roads made boundaries of this Township and not made parts of the Township of Rocky Mount or of the Township of Bonbrook shall be included within and constitute a part of this Township. The place for holding elections in this Township shall be at the house of John H. Kinsey.

District No. 7- the Township of Blackwater, was bounded as follows:  beginning at Saunders Forge on Pigg River up it and the Oil Mill Creek to  Ruble's Branch, thence along the summit of Waldron's Ridge to the base of the Mountains, thence by a line due west to the County line, with it northward to the corner of the Township of Maggodee, thence with the boundary of that Township to the corner of the Township of Rocky Mount and with the boundary of the last mentioned Township to the beginning. The place for holding elections in this Township shall be at James S. Callaway's Storehouse.

District No. 8- the Township of Long Branch, was bounded as follows:  beginning on Waldron's Ridge at the Oil Mill Road thence with the line of the Township of Blackwater westward to the County line with it to a point opposite to the mouth of Nickolas Creek, thence across Smith's River and up said Creek to the Old Mill Road and with it to the beginning. So much of the Oil Mill Road as forms a part of the boundary of this Township shall be included within and constitute a part of this Township. The place for holding elections in this Township shall be Long Branch Meeting House.

District No. 9- the Township of Brown Hill, was bounded as follows:  beginning at the northeast corner of the Township of Long Branch on Waldron's Ridge, thence southward with the boundary of the Township of Long Branch to the County line, with it eastward to the southwest corner of the Township of Snow Creek, with the boundary of the said last mentioned Township to the boundary of the Township of Rocky Mount, with said last mentioned boundary to Pigg River at Saunders Forge in the boundary of the Township of Blackwater and with said last mentioned boundary to the beginning. The place for holding elections in this Township shall be at Thomas H. Prillaman's Storehouse.

> Peter Saunders, Jr.
> Silas G. Bernard        Commissioners.
> John A. Bernard
> Paschal Meador

Deed Book 29, p. 164.

District No. 10- Little Creek District. A new Magisterial District was made from the Districts of Maggodee and Bonbrook, by order of the March Term of Franklin County Court, 1879, and bounded as follows: commencing at Retreat in said County, thence with road leading to Fairmont Church as the outside boundary, thence to James Mitchell's (leaving him in Maggodee District), thence with the road leading by his house to the forks of the road at Henry Wood's, thence by Henry Wood's up the branch between Henry Wood's and Edmund Tench's, thence up a hollow to the top of the House Rock Mountain, thence with the top of said mountain to the Roanoke line, thence with the Roanoke line to the top of Flat Rock Mountain, thence in a direct line to the fork of the road at Sade Pater thence with the road by Eller's Mill with the road by John Flora's, with a road around Little Mountain to Abram Barnhart's, thence with road to Brick Church with a road to Peter Angle's gate on the Gogginsville Road, thence with the road to Gogginsville, thence with the road from Gogginsville to Retreat, the beginning, said proposed district containing thirty square miles.

Order Book No. 5, page 469.

It was enacted by the General Assembly, February 1, 1840, "That the separate poll now authorized to be holden at Dickenson's and Keene's old store, in the county of Franklin, for the election of any person or persons in whose election all the lawful voters of the county are required to vote, shall hereafter be holden at the store-house now occupied by Stockton and Choice, about two miles distant from the old store."

It was enacted by the General Assembly, January 12, 1848, "That whenever hereafter an election shall be holden in the county of Franklin, in which all the lawful voters of the county are required to vote, there shall be at the same time a separate poll opened and held for such election at the house now the residence of Joseph Hickman, situate about twenty miles northwest from the courthouse of and in said county."

KEY:  Pvt-Private; Sgt-Sergeant; Lt-Lieutenant; Capt-Captain;
VM-Virginia Militia; MM-Maryland Militia; VCL-Virginia Continental
Line; VST-Virginia State Troops; PCL-Pennsylvania Continental Line;
NCL-North Carolina Continental Line; SCL-South Carolina Continental
Line;POPR when placed on Pension Roll; AWP age when pensioned;
DD date of death.

Abshire, Abraham, Pvt;  VM;  POPR 1/17/33;  AWP 70
Adams, Elisha, Pvt;  VM;  POPR 10/16/33;  AWP 71
Adcock, William, Pvt;  VCL; POPR 11/20/1818;  AWP 91
Akers, James, Pvt.
Akers, John, Pvt;  VM;  POPR 6/15/33; AWP 76
Akers, Simon Peter, Pvt.
Akers, William, Pvt.
Akins, Thomas, Capt.
Asbury, George, Pvt;  VCL;  POPR 6/14/1824;  AWP 78

Barton, Elisha, Pvt;  AWP 80
Bernard, Walter, Pvt;  WCL;  POPR 12/13/32;  AWP 76
Beverly, Sylvester, Pvt.
Boone, Jacob, Pvt.
Boone, John
Booth, Thomas, Pvt;  POPR 10/28/1786
Bowman, John, Pvt.
Brizendine, William, Sr., Pvt;  VM;  POPR 1/17/33;  AWP. 91
Byrns, James, Capt.

Campbell, John, Pvt.
Campbell, William, Pvt;  VCL;  POPR 12/8/32;  AWP 85
Childress, Robert, Pvt.
Claiborne, Nathaniel H.
Cooper, Eiles, Pvt;  VM;  POPR 12/8/32;  AWP 86
Cooper, Sterling, Pvt;  VM;  POPR 12/7/32;  AWP 74
Craig, Thomas, Pvt;  VCL;  POPR 12/8/32;  AWP 81
Cuff, William, Pvt;  AWP 92

Dale, Richard, Pvt;  VM;  POPR 9/16/33;  AWP 74
Davis, Lewis, Pvt;  VM;  POPR 12/8/32;  AWP 78
DeHaven, Isaac, Pvt;  VCL;  POPR 12/8/32;  AWP 84;  DD 5/11/33
DeWalt, Michael, Pvt;  PCL;  POPR 12/23/19;  AWP 77
Dixon, Nathaniel, Pvt;  VM;  POPR 3/15/33;  AWP 91
Drake, William, Pvt;  VCL;  POPR 4/3/27;  AWP 78

Farmer, Mathew, Sgt;  VCL;  POPR 12/7/32;  AWP 73
Ferguson, George, Pvt.

Gibson, John, Sgt;  VM;  POPR 9/16/33;  AWP 85
Gibson, James
Graves, David, Pvt;  VM;  POPR 12/24/32;  AWP 75;  DD 8/20/33
Green, Joseph, Pvt;  VCL;  POPR 6/14/24;  AWP 78;  DD 11/24/32
Greer, Moses, Capt;  VM;  POPR 12/8/32;  AWP 90

Griffith, Chisholm, Pvt; MM; POPR 2/5/34; AWP 75
Griffith, Christopher, Pvt.
Guthrie, John, Capt.

Hale, Thomas, Pvt; SCL; POPR 2/1/19; AWP 77
Hancock, Edward
Hambrick, Joseph, Pvt.
Hancock, Samuel
Hodges, Abednege, Pvt; VCL; POPR 3/31/28; AWP 76
Huff, John, Pvt; VM; POPR 7/16/33; AWP 71
Hundley, Joseph, Pvt; VCL; POPR 12/8/32; AWP 87
Hutts, Leonard, Pvt. VCL; POPR 9/25/23; AWP 73

Jeffries, John, Pvt; POPR 3/4/01
Jamison, Joseph, Pvt.
Jamison, John, Pvt.
Jamison, Reuben, Pvt.
Jamison, Samuel, Pvt.
Jamison, Thomas, Pvt.
Jamison, William, Pvt.

King, Stephen, Pvt; VM; POPR 2/15/33; AWP 82
Kemplin, William, Pvt; PCL; POPR 11/20/18; AWP 81

Law, David, Pvt.
Law, Henry, Pvt.
Law, John, Pvt; VM; POPR 12/24/32; AWP 73
Law, Nathaniel, Pvt.
Law, William, Pvt.
Lesueur, Martel, Pvt; VST; POPR 3/15/33; AWP 73
Lumsden, Charles, Pvt; VM; POPR 1/17/33; AWP 73

Meader, Jeremiah, Pvt.
Mitchell, Henry, Pvt; VM; POPR 2/2/33; AWP 71

McNeil, Jacob, Pvt; VST; POPR 12/8/32; AWP 76

Paitsell, Jacob; Pvt.
Pollard, Chatlin, Pvt; VM; POPR 1/2/33; AWP 71
Prater, Jonathan, Pvt; VM; POPR 6/15/33; AWP 76
Pugh, Richard, Pvt; VCL; POPR 9/11/24; AWP 75

Ray, Benjamin, Pvt; VST; POPR 1/17/33; AWP 77
Ray, James, Pvt; VM; POPR 1/17/33; AWP 78
Richardson, Richard, Pvt; VM; POPR 12/8/32; AWP 82
Robertson, Richard, Pvt; VCL; POPR 12/24/32; AWP 75

Saunders, Philemon, Pvt; VM; POPR 9/12/33; AWP 70
Sink, Abraham, Pvt; VST; POPR 1/17/33; AWP 73
Smith, Henry, Pvt.
Smith, William, Pvt; NCL; POPR 7/9/24; AWP 75
Starkey, Jonathan, Pvt.
Stewart, William, Pvt; VM; POPR 2/15/33; AWP 73
Swepton, John, Pvt.

Thompson, Thomas, Pvt; VST; POPR 11/17/32; AWP 78
Thomasson, John

Via, John, Jr., Pvt; VM; POPR 3/22/34; AWP 76; DD 3/7/34

Walker, Elisha, Pvt; AWP 94
Webster, John, Pvt.
Webster, Reuben, Pvt.
Wingfield, William, Pvt.
Woody, Martin, Pvt; VM; POPR 9/16/33; AWP 76
Wray, Benjamin, Pvt; AWP 84
Wright, John, Pvt; VM; POPR 1/13/33; AWP 86
Wray, James

Young, James, Pvt; VM; POPR 4/23/33; AWP 79

# UNITED STATES PENSIONERS 1883

Giving the name of each pensioner, the Post Office address, and the cause for which pensioned.

William H. Gregory, Dickinson's, survivor 1812
Francis Preston, Glade Hill, survivor 1812
Mary F. Turner, Hale's Ford, survivor 1812
Martha Hatcher, Hale's Ford, widow of 1812
Elizabeth Bradley, Hale's Ford, widow of 1812
Mary Powell, Hale's Ford, widow of 1812
Jane Childress, Hale's Ford, widow of 1812
Nancy Chewning, Hale's Ford, widow of 1812
Keziah Booth, Hale's Ford, survivor of 1812
William R. Divers, Hale's Ford, survivor of 1812
Jacob Kesler, Hardy's Ford, survivor of 1812
Martha J. Allen, Long Branch, widow of 1812
Charlotte Arthur, Naff's, widow of 1812
Catherine Lumpkin, Penhook, widow of 1812
Jane Thompson, Pernello, widow of 1812
Jordon N. Peters, Pernello, survivor of 1812
Caroline Hodges, Pigg River, widow of 1812
James Keys, Pigg River, survivor of 1812
William Hale, Pigg River, survivor of 1812
Susan Stone, Prillaman's, widow of 1812
Julia Carter, Prillaman's, widow of 1812
Nancy Meador, Red Plains, widow of 1812
Patsy Payne, Red Plains, widow of 1812
Judith P. Wright, Retreat, widow of 1812
Serena Dickerson, Rocky Mount, widow of 1812
Elizabeth Hodges, Rocky Mount, widow of 1812
Elizabeth A. Hieth, Rocky Mount, widow of 1812
Lucy Cassell, Rocky Mount, widow of 1812
Sophronia Luke, Rocky Mount, survivor of 1812
Nancy Brodie, Shady Grove, widow of 1812
Annie Lester, Shady Grove, widow of 1812
Rhoda Lovell, Shady Grove, widow of 1812
Susan A. Brewer, Shady Grove, widow of 1812
Judith Dodson, Snead's Camp, widow of 1812
Mary C. Cooper, Snow Creek, widow of 1812
Caty Love, Sydnorsville, widow of 1812
John A. Mason, Sydnorsville, survivor of 1812
Lydia Divers, Taylor's Store, widow of 1812
Nancy Board, Taylor's Store, widow of 1812
Lucy Harman, Taylor's Store, widow of 1812
Mary J. Hodges, Union Hall, widow of 1812
Elizabeth Kesler, Union Hall, widow of 1812
Norma Crum, Union Hall, widow of 1812
Jordan Robertson, Union Hall, widow of 1812

# CONFEDERATE SOLDIERS

This chapter includes a complete list of Confederate Soldiers of record in the Confederate Roster Books, Archives Department of the Virginia State Library, with names spelled as there recorded, and lists furnished the writer from other reliable sources.

It has been impossible to secure a list of the large number of persons from Franklin County who enlisted in companies not organized in the County. This list does not include the name of any soldier who deserted his command, or who was dishonorably discharged from the service.

## COMPANY B, 24th VIRGINIA REGIMENT, INFANTRY

### Commissioned Officers

| | |
|---|---|
| Bernard, John A. | Captain |
| Hambrick, J. A. | Captain |
| Mansfield, William | Lieutenant |
| Smith, George A. | Lieutenant |
| Charlton, John J. | Lieutenant |

### Non-Commissioned Officers

| | |
|---|---|
| White, E. C. | Sergeant |
| Angel, Josh | Sergeant |
| Webb, Benj. B. | Corporal |

### Privates

Abshire, Isaac
Abshire, Tazwell
Abshire, E.
Adams, J(ames) L.  Wounded
Akers, M.
Abshire, R.  Died in service

Brown, James E.  Wounded
Bowles, William
Beckner, William H.  Wounded
Black, R. R.
Bernard, W. L.
Bray, D.  Died in service
Bowles, Jos.

Childress, J. D.
Clark, J. E.
Charlton, John J.  Wounded

Claiborne, W. T.  Wounded
Cooper, G. W.  Wounded
Chitwood, Esquire
Cornett, J. A.
Carter, W. D.  Wounded

Foster, Charles H.
Fralin, Jesse F.
Finch, T. R.

Guthrie, William  Wounded

Hunt, T. P.  Wounded
Harrison, Ed (J.E.)  Wounded
Hael, J. P.  Wounded
Hensley, C. C.
Hill, G. H.
Hodges, H. H.  Wounded

Hodges, W. H. Wounded

Kingory, S. O.
Kingsey, W. T.

Lynch, C. Died in service
Lynch, James
Lynch, Christopher Died in
service

Metto, J. William
Mountcastle, E. J. Wounded
Mills, M. G. Wounded
Muse, J. C. Wounded
Morgan, J. H.

McBride, C. T.

Orange, H. A.

Patterson, James Tazwell

Rakes, William Died in service

Starkey, Nathan
Smith, J. C.

Sink, William Wounded
Sink, Jesse (M)
Starchman, William H.
Shurm, Joe
Scott, Milton J.
Sink, J. Died in service
Saunders, C. J.
Siggleton, I. L. Wounded

Trent, William Wounded
Trent, Jno.

Wray, F. J.
Walker, C. T.
Wood, Henry Wounded
Walker, J. R.
Webb, Moses (G)
Willis, F. F. Wounded
Willis, S. B.
Waide, J. R.
Wray, Irvine
Webb, Jake (Jacob)

Young, G. H.

## COMPANY D, 24th VIRGINIA REGIMENT, INFANTRY

### Officers

Taylor, Thos.          Captain Died in service
Taliaferro, Tell       (Captain, later Major)
Finney, G. W.          Lieutenant
Ritterman, Geo. W.     Lieutenant

### Privates

Ashworth, John W.

Bernard, John O.
Brown, J. E.
Bowles, Joseph
Board, William
Belcher, Wm. J. Wounded
Brown, William Died in service
Byrd, D. M.
Booth, P. B.

Cooper, Lowry M.
Crum, Jas. O.
Campbell, A. J. Wounded
Cooper, J. W. Wounded
Crum, A. J.

Cassell, Larkin T. (Drummer)
Cooper, T. T.
Cooper, W. W. Died in service
Cooper, W. H.

Deane, Cornelins
Davidson, J. Wounded
Dunsford, J. F. Died in service
Denton, E. H. (Lt. dropped)

Eanes, B. H. Wounded
English, Wm. W.

Finney, G. W. Wounded
Finney, James L.
Feazell, W. M.

151

Greer, J. W.

Hodges, Giles
Houston, W. M.
Hash, J. H.

Law, W. D.
Law, J. C.
Law, Mathe G.

Metz, L. R.
Mason, Silas H.

Osbern, F. A.

Parker, George T.

Ramsey, E. N.

Smithson, A. T.

Trench, Edwin I.
Turner, W. H.

Wingfield, Lewis Franklin
Williamson, W. H.
Worsham, J. B.

Young, Jno. P.
Young, M.
Young, Harrison

## COMPANY K, 42nd VIRGINIA REGIMENT, INFANTRY

### Commissioned Officers

| | | |
|---|---|---|
| Hale, Samuel | Died in service | Captain |
| Helm, J. W. | | Captain |
| Calloway, Thomas C. | | Lieutenant |
| Metts, M. C. | | Lieutenant |
| Angle, A. R. | | Lieutenant |

### Non-Commissioned Officers

| | |
|---|---|
| Richardson, Thomas | Sergeant |
| Price, Owen H. | Sergeant |
| Wray, B. C. | Sergeant |
| Martin, J. S. | Corporal |
| Teel, M. M. | Corporal |
| Miles, I. J. | Corporal |

### Privates

Angel, A. R.

Beach, James T.
Boitnott, David H.   Died in service
Boitnott, L. D.   Wounded
Boitnott, J. W.

Clingenpeel, K. A.
Charles, L. H.   Died in service

Drivers, P. D.

Eddy, D. T.

Forbes, S. H.   Wounded
Forbes, W. T.
Faris, J. L.

Haynes, Isaih
Hodges, Harvey
Hensley, J. W.
Hutcherson, L.D.   Died in service

King, M. O.

Lumsden, Creed W.

Majors, J. F.   Died in service
Metts, Jno. H.   Wounded

Newman, A. H.   Wounded

Overfelt, Silas
Overfelt, T. R.

Scott, Jesse
Snyder, Jacob
Saul, C. T.  Died in service
Saul, G. H.  Died in service
Smith, H. T.

Thurman, Giles

Updike, J.

Wray, Fletcher

Wilkes, W. A.
Waldron, Moses
Waldron, Samuel  Wounded
Wray, R. G.
Waldron, John
Waldron, A.
Walton, J.
Woods, Joseph Y (or G)  Died in
    service
Weaver, S. W.  Wounded

## COMPANY B, 57th VIRGINIA REGIMENT, INFANTRY

      This company, the "Franklin Sharpshooters", constituted
a part of the force of Virginia Volunteers, called into service
by the Governor for one year from the first day of August, 1861,
unless sooner discharged.  Enrollment was at Young's Store, (five
miles northwest of Henry, Virginia,) on the 22nd day of July,
1861.  The Company marched 200 miles to Richmond, arriving on
the 29th day of July, 1861.  The figures following the names
indicate ages at time of enrollment.  The letter R following a
name indicates that the soldier was recruited sometime after the
company was formed.

### Commissioned Officers

Waddy T. James, Captain, 24
Allen Farmer, Lieutenant, 46
Crockett H. Prillaman, Lieutenant, 31
Richard A. Hurt, Lieutenant, 32

### Non-Commissioned Officers

John H. Smith, Sergeant, 31
John L. Ward, Sergeant, 24
Lee Allison, Sergeant
George T. Helms, Sergeant, 25
Carr P. Turner, Sergeant, 23
William D. Young, Sergeant, 22

Thomas M. Williams, Corporal, 23
Fleming M. Prillaman, Corporal, 25
Charles Smith, Corporal, 32
M. H. Slone, Corporal
John T. McGuffin, Corporal, 20
William S. Brown, Drummer, 27

### Privates

Baker, John, 55
Bowles, Daniel M., 18
Barnes, Charles A., 21
Brown, Charles H., 20
Bowles, Fountain B., 23
Bowles, Butler
Bowles, Warfield P., 19
Bowles, William L., 26
Barbour, George
Brammer, John M., 23
Bondurant, William (R)

Custer M. H.
Cannady, Norman T., 23
Custer, J. H.
Clark, Andrew J., 37

Dowdy, Robert H., 24, wounded
    in service
Dowdy, John (R)
Dickinson, Randolph (R)
Dyer, John, 28
Davis, Solomon K., 18

153

Davis, F.
Davis, Thomas
Dickinson, Washington, 28

Eggleston, Armstead, J. (R)
Eagee, George Thomas, Lt. at
    surrender

Ferguson, Lewis, 19
Fleck, John
Frith, Robert R. 33
Ferguson, William L.

Goode, Henry F., 23
Gauldin, P. J.
Goode, George M., 35
Goode, Jonas, 31
Goode, William H., 18
Goode, William Patrick
George, N., died in service
Greer, Richard, 21

Hambrick, S.
Helms, Thomas H., 37, died in
    service (R)
Hines, J. P. died in service
Hall, Preston B., 28
Hodges, Peter, died in service
Hodges, Giles E., 23
Hodges, Harrison
Huff, Austin, 23
Hackett, Philip
Heylar, W. C.
Hallan, John
Hancock, Abram B. (R)
Harris, James (R)

Jacobs, D. P. (R)

King, George C. (R)
Keys, Floyd B., 24, died in
    service

Lackey, George, 20
Lackey, James (R)
Lackey, Josiah, 21
Leseuer, J. M.
Leseuer, John G., 27
Lemon, Creed
Law, Samuel B., 66

Machenheimer, William (R)
Moore, London (R)
Mullins, William (R)

Maxey, Bruce E. (R)
Mullins, Henry (R)
Mullins, Booker, 23 (R) wounded
Mason, J. J.
Mullins, Andrew J., 21
Massey, John Q., 22
Massey, William B., 20, wounded
    in service
Massey, John L.
Martin, Daniel D., 28
Martin, William, 32
Mullins, George M., 29
Miles, R. E.
Meeks, Robert S., 34
Maxy, William W., 18
Mullins, Jonathan F., 22
Mullins, H. M. Sr.
McMullen, John W., 24, wounded
    in service
McGuffin, John T.
Mason, Joseph W., 19, died in
    service

Nunn, Thomas, 43

Otey, John M.
Oxley, Burwell, S., 21
Oxley, Joseph B.
Oxley, John M., 43

Philpot, Edward, died in service (R
Prillaman, Isaac, 26
Prilliman, George M. (R)
Prilliman, James J., 28
Prilliman, Philip (R)
Prilliman, Christian S. (R)
Philips, Henderson, died in
    service (R)
Potter, Elisha (R)
Pugh, Pleasant, wounded in service
Peters, David C., 22
Prator, J. D.  Died in service

Ray, Payton S., 22
Ray, William R., 20
Ray, John
Ray, Eusebius, 25
Ray, Abner, 18, wounded in service
Ramsey, Henry C., 19
Ramsey, B.
Ramsey, William H., 20
Ramsey, James M., 24
Robinson, W. J. (R)
Reynolds, B. T.

Ray, Daniel (R)
Ramsey, Jessie (R)

Stanley, Swinfield (R)
Stanley, Daniel P., (R)
Stone, Samuel, Jr. (R)
Shumate, Nusom (R)
Spencer, Andrew J. (20
Stanley, Dennis P., 35, wounded
    in service
Starkey, Robert, 19
Stanley, Fred, wounded in
    service
Scott, John M., 21, died in
    service
Shumate, D. T. died in service
Stone, Cosley, 31
Stone, M., died in service
Stone, John, 29
Stone, George
Smith, Charles, died in service
Scarberry, Isaac, 22
Sigmon, Joseph P., wounded in
    service
Stone, Stepehn B., 35
Stanley, Burwell, 18
Sims, J. M.
Stanley, Ferdinand, 20
Shelton, Josiah M., 20
Sink, George
Scott, Samuel H., 19
Sigmon, Peter H., 20
Sigmon, John F., 20
Simpson, J. M.

Scott, John W., died in service

Turner, Alfred H., 29
Turner, William D.
Turner, Clark (R)
Turner, C. P.
Taylor, Owen, 20
Thornton, Samuel W., 19, wounded
    in service
Thornton, Abner K., 26
Thornton, Adison H., 21
Turner, William (R)
Turner, Edward (R)
Turner, Andrew J., 55 (R)
Turner, W.
Thornton, John S., 25
Turner, M., died in service
Tinsley, R. J.
Troupt, Jacob, 21
Taylor, Oliver

Winfrey, Charles W., 19
Whitlow, James H., 22
Wray, John
Ward, John R., 23
Williams, Thomas M.
Williams, Joseph B., 20
Williams, William
Weaver, Samuel H., 19
Williams, Thomas W. (or M)

Young, George O., 21
Young, Saunders, 35
Young, William D.

## COMPANY C, 57th VIRGINIA REGIMENT, INFANTRY

### "Franklin Fire Eaters"

### Commissioned Officers

| | |
|---|---|
| Bridges, E. T. | Captain |
| Hickman, D. P. | Captain - Major |
| Ward, John L. | Captain |
| Cannaday, G. S. | 2nd Lieutenant |

### Non-Commissioned Officers

| | |
|---|---|
| Vest, Samuel | 1st Sergeant |
| Poff, W. B. | 2nd Sergeant |
| Hickman, J. B. | 3rd Sergeant |
| Vest, Willis M. | 4th Sergeant |

## Privates

Adams, Allen W.
Ailiff, James
Adkins, W. H.
Allen, D.
Adkins, R. W.

Bowles, M. G.
Bernard, W. E.
Barlow, J.J.
Berman, W. E.
Blankenship, L.
Barton, John

Call, John M.
Cannaday, A. B.
Chancellor, Glashby
Cannaday, G. S.

Dowdy, Claiborne
Delaney, John P.
Dowdy, T. Died in service
Draper, J. A.

Edwards, John Lee. Died in
    service
Edwards, James D.

Ferguson, N. F.

Guster, D. Died in
    service

Haile, Ro. Wounded
Heckman, F. J.
Hixon, Daniel
Hall, L.
Hodges, C.
Hancock, John Silas
Hullman, F. J.
Hollins, John. Wounded
Hickson, D. Wounded

Jones, William
James, William
Jones, J. Wounded
Jones, Samuel
Janney, J.

Kempleton, Edw.

Martin, John. Died in service
Miles, A. A.
Montgomery, O. S.
Miles, J. H.

Martin, Mathew
Martin, James. Died in service
Miles, J. E. Died in service

Newbill, R. T.
Nichols, Jas. W.
Nolen, Jackson
Newbill, B. T.

Oaks, Charles

Pugh, Richard K.
Poff, J. P.
Prillaman, G. A.
Peters, W.
Peters, C. R.
Poff, William B.
Pate, J. B.
Payne, W. A. Died in service

Robinson, W. J.
Radford, G. R.
Richardson, P.
Ray, D. Died in service

Smith, William. Wounded
Stump, John Wesley
Stump, E. G.
Smith, W. C.
Smith, John
Shively, W. Wounded
Saunders, Stephen P.
Shiveley, J. Died in
    service
Sink, E. Died in service

Thomas, John S.
Terry, Pete
Trail, M. V. (or W. V.)
Trail, C. J.
Turner, Geo. W.
Trail, D.
Trail, W. C.

Underwood, P. G.
Underwood, W. B. Died in
    service

Vest, Samuel
Via, Samuel

Webb, William. Died in
    service
Webb, Wm. B.

156

## COMPANY G, 57th VIRGINIA REGIMENT, INFANTRY

### "Ladies Guard"

The members of this company were enrolled by Major Abram B. Hancock.

### Commissioned Officers

| | |
|---|---|
| Patterson, William | Captain |
| Flagg, George H. | Captain |
| Wade, Benjamin H. | Captain |
| Holland, Abram F. | Lieutenant |
| Arrington, Daniel | Lieutenant |
| Boon, M. D. L. | Lieutenant |
| Cooper, William | Lieutenant |
| Hancock, A. B. | Lieutenant |

### Non-Commissioned Officers

| | |
|---|---|
| Boone, Marquis D. L. | Sergeant |
| Holland, Abram H. | Sergeant |
| Hutchinson, John D. | Sergeant |
| Oxley, Nathaniel C. | Sergeant |
| Webb, William S. | Sergeant |
| Hutchinson, Benjamin R. | Corporal |
| Amos, William F. | Corporal |
| Williams, R. H. | Corporal |
| Richards, Powhatan | Corporal |
| Whitlow, Edward H. | Corporal |
| Wade, Andrew P. | Corporal |
| Angle, John | Sergeant |
| Whitlow, E. H. | Sergeant |
| Boon, Beverly B. | Sergeant |
| Lewis, A. S. or J. S. | Sergeant |

### Privates

Ayers, E. W.
Atkinson, J. E.
Angle, Aaron
Amos, John W.
Amos, J. N.
Amos, Joseph H. (wounded in service)
Amos, W. F.
Austin, William
Angle, Daniel
Adams, James L.
Angle, Peter

Blankenship, Jesse (or Lewis J.)
Boone, N. T.
Blankenship, Lewis J. (or L.)
Bird, Obediah W.
Bird, William T.

Bird, Robert
Belcher, Joseph B.
Bennett, Franklin
Bowles, James W.
Bearer, William H.
Boothe, W. C.
Bell, T. D.
Byrd, O. H.
Bellinger, S. (died in service)

Crum, John S. (or Crumb)
Crumb, Giles (died in service)
Clingenpeel, Jacob
Custer, H. (wounded in service)
Crumb, Henry T.
Chitwood, Thomas B.
Craig, James C.

Dutton, James S.
Dearer, Henry S.

English, Stephen H.

Feasell, Joab R.
Fuller, Joseph T.
Frailin, R. H. (died in service)
Fralin, Thomas T.

Griffith, W. F.
Gentry, William
Gilbert, Wiley P.

Hamlet, Stephen B.
Horsley, Samuel H.
Horsley, Thomas
Holloway, John H.
Hutts, John W. Y.
Hutts, James P.
Harvey, Samuel G.
Hale, George W.
Hale, William S.
Hodges, Rivers
Hodges, Joel
Hodges, Campbell
Hodges, Creed
Hodges, Herbert
Hodges, Charles
Hodges, Taliaferro
Hodges, Landon
Hall, G. W. (wounded in service)
Hodges, Franklin
Hunt, R. W. (died in service)
Hall, W. B.
Hodges, Jacob
Hodges, Otey
Hall, Richard L.
Holloway, T. J.
Hollandsworth, Chest.
Hale, David
Hall, S. T.
Hodges, Armstead (wounded in
    service)
Hodges, C. (died in service)
Hodges, William R. (died in
    service)
Hodges, Andrew J. (wounded in
    service)
Holland, A. F. (wounded in
    service)
Harnsberger, J. S.

Jones, James (died in service)
Jones, W. L. (died in service)
Jones, William S.

Kirke, William H. (or Kirks)

Laprade, William
Love, William
Legwin, William A.
Law, Peter C.
Law, Amos B. (wounded in service)
Lynch, James H.
Law, C. A.
Legwin, C. H.
Law, Joseph (died in service)

Martin, Thomas J.
Martin, John C.
Matthews, John T.
Matthews, Wiley J.
Miles, William S.
Mason, John K. (died in service)
Mullens, John F.
Morgan, M. D.
Maupin, G. O.
McGhee, Elcanah T. (wounded in
    service)
Mathews, William H. (wounded in
    service)
Mason, J. W.
Meador, William E.
McDaniel, D. (wounded in service)

Pearson, John H.
Pearson, George R.
Patterson, William
Pearson, J. W.
Parcell, Benjamin
Parcell, Frank
Phelps, A. J.
Prilliman, D.
Price, John T.

Rice, L. W.
Robertson, Hezekiah
Ramsey, S. P.
Richards, Bruce W.

Stegall, William A.
Semonas, Peter H.
Shorter, James W.
Shorter, Tazewell C.
Smith, John

158

Scott, James M.

Tramel, Andrew J.

Underwood, J. M.

Wade, Zachfield
Wilke, Richard F. (or Wilkes)
Whitlow, William B.

Whitlow, Charles F.
Whitlow. Charles T.
Whitlock, Samuel H. (died in service)
Wade, C. (died in service)
White, J. W.
White, Francis M.
White, Henry P.
Willis, George C.

## COMPANY D, 58th VIRGINIA REGIMENT, INFANTRY

### "Franklin Guards"

### Commissioned Officers

| | |
|---|---|
| Boothe, Dewitt C. (surgeon) | Captain |
| Franklin, T. Henry | Captain |
| Thurman, D. L. | Lieutenant |
| Kee, James W. | Lieutenant |
| Bush, Griffin. Died in service | Lieutenant |

### Non-Commissioned Officers

| | |
|---|---|
| Woods, George W. | Sergeant |
| Martin, S. H. | Sergeant |
| Wright, W. T. | Corporal |

### Privates

Abshire, G. W. B.   Wounded

Beard, W. A.
Bradley, W. D.
Brown, B. T.   Wounded
Blakemore, George A.
Bruin, J. M.   Died in service
Burkholder, W. F.
Booth, Elisha.   Died in service
Brown, S. A.   Wounded
Booth, Silas

Crig, T. C.   Wounded
Clinginpeel, J. W.   Wounded
Cabaniss, M. D.   Wounded
Cundiff, J. W.   Died in service
Cronch, J. W.
Crute, L. S.   Died in service

Dillion, T. T.
Draper, B. H.

Ferguson, T. N.   Wounded
Fisher, C.   Wounded

Hodges, R. M.
Hodges, J.
Hodges, R.   Died in service
Horn, W. L.   Wounded
Hutts, Tilford
Hutts, Pattison
Hodges, Jos. S.
Horn, W. T.
Hutts, J. T.
Hopkins, R. H.   Died in service
Hopkins, T. C.   Wounded
Hopkins, R.

Johnson, John (D)

Kropff, W. L.
Kennett, John W.   Wounded

Lynch, J. B.

159

Meador, Andrew T.   Died in
   service
Meador, W. B.
Martin, M. D.
McGuire, S. H.   Wounded
McGuire, P.   Died in service
Meador, M.   Died in service
Martin, W. T.

Nichols, William G.

Parker, I. H.
Payne, S. P.   Wounded
Prother, James
Pate, Anthony C.
Parker, John H.   Wounded
Patsell, J. W.
Perdue, Giles
Palmer, J. W.   Died in service
Perdue, M.   Died in service
Payne, Isham T.   Died in
   service
Peters, C. S.   Wounded

Poteet, Hyram   Wounded

Robertson, Jno. T.
Robertson, Joseph W.   Wounded
Robertson, James   Wounded
Richardson, L.   Died in service
Richardson, J. D.   Died in service

Scott, W. S.
Siple, Ambrose   Died in service
Siple, Conrad   Died in service
Stearnes, O. D.   Died in service
Southall, Jno. T.

Turner, W. T.   (or Wilson)
Turner, R. A.   Wounded
Thurman, D. L.
Thurman, H.   Wounded
Turner, A. A.   Wounded
Thomason, W. J.

Wright, James.
Wills, S. C.   (or Wells)

## COMPANY E, 58th VIRGINIA REGIMENT, INFANTRY

### "Franklin Guards"

### Commissioned Officers

Holley, J. L.   Died in
   service                         Captain
Hawley, J. L.                      Captain
Brown, W. H.   Died in service     Lieutenant
   (pro. Capt.)
Brown, Patrick S.                  Captain
Turner, Samuel                     Lieutenant
   (pro. Capt.)
Dudley, Ransom                     Lieutenant

### Non-commissioned Officers

Dudley, Sparrel                    Sergeant
Holland, Thad P.                   Sergeant
Bays, Henry H.   Wounded in        Sergeant
   service
Robertson, Richard                 Sergeant
Holley, John                       Corporal
Pagans, J. G.                      Corporal

### Privates

Arthur, John                       Bays, Charles E.
Almond, Charles   Died in service  Basham, D. W.
Almond, John   Died in service     Blankenship, W. J.
Arrington, Daniel   Wounded in     Bayse, C. E.
   service                         Bowles, Thomas
Arrington, Robert E.                  (3rd Lieut. disch)
                    160

Basham, K. L.
Burnett, Jas.
Basham, Calohill
Bansman, Hy.

Cundiff, James A.
Clyborn, C. E.
Cundiff, John  Died in service
Cundiff, Giles

Delaney, S. T.
Devers, Francis
Drewry, A. P.
Dillion, R. M.  Wounded in service
Durham, David
De Song, Samuel
Dudley, Wiley  Died in service
Dudley, J. A.  Died in service
Divers, T. B.
Dillon, Silas  Wounded in service

English, J. H.  Wounded in service

Fergusson, Nash  Wounded in service
Ferguson, Stephen
Ferguson, Thomas
Ferguson, T. A.  Wounded in service

Hoal, W. H.  Wounded in service
Holland, T. P.
Holland, Jno. C.
Hudson, J. D.
Hale, Jno. L.
Holland, John
Hudson, Henry  Died in service
Hudson, James  Died in service
Henderson, C. H.  Wounded in service

Jenkins, J. A.  Wounded in service

Link, J. H.  Died in service

Marcus, John
Meador, Edward
Martin, William D.
Mitchell, Fletcher
Minter, W.
Meador, O.
McLain, M. K.

Nemo, John  Died in service
Newman, S. A.
Newman, C. F.  Wounded in service

Oyler, Owen
Oyler, V. N. (3rd Corpl)
Oyler, James F. (pro. 2 Sgt, 2 Lt)

Pagan (or Peggin), Abram  Died in service
Payne, R. H.  Wounded in service
Pagan, G. W. (or Peggins, George Washington)
Pagan, Daniel C. (or D. C.)
Peggin(s) J(es) Green
Pasley, Robert
Peggin(s) Abe
Peggin(s), Daniel
Peggin(s), David
Peggin(s), Dempsey  Died in service

Robertson, Samuel (or S. G.) (1st Lt.)
Read, James
Read, William  Died in service
Robertson, J. R.

Smith, W. H.  Wounded in service
Smith, Thomas
Scott, G. E.  Wounded in service

Thurman, Robert (or R. K.)
Thurman, Dudley (2nd Lt.)
Trent, Berry  Died in service
Tomlin, J. D.
Turpin, Paul J.  Wounded in service

Wilson, J. H.
Wright, J. K.
Winston (3rd Lt. resigned)
Wright, Abram (Drum Major)
Wright, Jas. K.
Weigh, A. O.  Died in service

## COMPANY B, 3rd BATTALION, VIRGINIA RESERVES

(1) Indicates killed or died in service.
(2) Indicates wounded in service.

### Commissioned Officers

| | |
|---|---|
| Powell, Ennis | Çaptain |
| Wheary, William H. | Captain |
| Watts, M. | Lieutenant |

### Non-Commissioned Officers

(1) Parkinson, Robt. H.      Corporal

### Privates

Anderson, J. T.

Bridgewater, Jos. C.
Boitnott, H.
Brockwell, E. G.
(1) Burton, John E.

Carroll, John W.
Collier, John W.
Chappell, Wm. E.

(1) Egerton, W. B.
Ellis, O. Q.

Guilliams, J.

Harrison, Alphens
Hawkins, J.
Hunt, A. H.
Hutts, J. T.
Hawkins, Jno. T.

(1) Judkins, Joseph G.
Jordon, J. W.

(1) Kitchen, T. W.

(1) Lockett, Jas. H.
(1) Lewis, Willard
(1) Lee, R. S.

Maitland, J.
Maitland, J. E.

Moore, Jos. M.
(2) Mail, Rinol

Perdue, Benj. J. (or C.J.)
Pinkard, W. A.
Pattison, B. L.
Presson, J. E.

Rowlett, Jno. N.
Ramsey, Haley W.

Sadler, James B.
Short, F. G.
Sigmon, J. P.
(1) Simmons, Jos.

Thurman, J. M.
Thurman, William
Traylor, John H.
Traylor, Jonesboro

Vaiden, D. D.
Vaughan, John

Wells, B. C.
Wells, D. S.
Wells, Peter
Wray, David
Wilkerson, J. R.
Watkins, J. E.

Young, R. D.

## COMPANY D, 3rd BATTALION VIRGINIA RESERVES

### Commissioned Officers

| | |
|---|---|
| Meadows, Pascal | Captain |
| Rogers, Jo. A. | Captain |
| Duval, W. M. | Lieutenant |
| Matthews, Robt. A. | Lieutenant |

### Non-Commissioned Officers

| | |
|---|---|
| Rice, Charles W. | Corporal |

### Privates

Carrall, Henry W. Died in
   service
Coloena, David (Colonna)

Davis, A. T.
Donnan, J. K.
Dunnwright, T. F.

Franklin, John T.

Hart, J. M.

Jarratt, W. J.

Mann, J. R.
Minitree, G.A.
McNeil, Jonathan P.

Nelms, M. W.

Price, R. D.
Pinkard, W. J.

Uzzell, R. T.

Wynne, Jno. W.
Whitlow, Jno.

## COMPANY G, 3rd BATTALION VIRGINIA RESERVES

### Commissioned Officers

| | |
|---|---|
| Arrington, Christopher | Captain |
| Clark, O. C. | Captain |

### Non-Commissioned Officers

| | |
|---|---|
| Faris, Jno. B. | Sergeant |

### Privates

Ayers, E. W.

Beard, R. B.

Callaghan, Richard M.

Drinkard, James

English, S. H.

Hay, S. W.
Harrison, R.H.M. (d. R.E.Lee Camp
   No. 1)

Snillings, Ryland F.

Trumbull, G.

Watson, James G.
Wray, Joseph
Wood, J. W.

Confederate Soldiers of Franklin County who served in companies from Pittsylvania and Henry Counties.

## COMPANY E, 57th VIRGINIA REGIMENT, INFANTRY, PITTSYLVANIA CO.

### "Pigg River Grays"

Custer, A. - wounded at Gettysburg

Dove, A. M. - wounded

Gregory, G. W. - served 3 years
Guthrie, J. H. - served 3 years

Hancock, C. B. - served 3 years

Miles, J. H.
Matthews, J. A.
Meyers, J. M. - served 4 years

McBride, James C. - served 2 years

Powell, W. T.
Payne, B. W.

Stump, S. R.

Young, C. C. - wounded at Gettysburg

Zeigler, W. A.
Zeigler, J. B.

## COMPANY F, 57th VIRGINIA REGIMENT INFANTRY

### "Henry and Pittsylvania Rifles"

Shoon, J. T.

Arthur, J. W. - wounded at Gettysburg

Bowlin, N. - captured, died in prison

Cook, E. J.

Jones, C. F.

2nd Sergeant

Kidd, B. F.

Martin, Jno. - died in prison

Robertson, G. - killed

Stockton, F. K.
Smith, Charles

Whitworth, Abe.

## COMPANY D, 57th VIRGINIA REGIMENT, INFANTRY, PITTSYLVANIA CO.

### "Gatveston Tigers"

Bennett, P. G.

Cooper, H.

Forbes, T. T.
Fralin, J. D. - died in hospital

Goode, H. F.

James, W. T.

McGhee, J. L.
Mullins, Edward T.

Ray, John - wounded at Gettysburg

Thornton, J. S.

Ward, J. L.
Wray, E.

# MILITARY RECORDS

## TROOP D, 2nd VIRGINIA CAVALRY

### "Franklin Rangers"

This Franklin County Company was early in the field and participated in many engagements.

### Commissioned Officers

| | |
|---|---|
| G. W. B. Hale | First Captain |
| T. B. Holland | Second Captain. Wounded |
| Marshall Wade | Third Captain |
| William A. Parker | 1st Lieutenant. Wounded |
| Moses S. Booth | 1st Lieutenant. Buried near Taylor's Store. Age 22. Killed in action. |
| Thomas B. Davis | Acting Lieutenant. Died in service |
| Samuel H. Early | First Lieutenant |
| J. R. Claiborne | First Lieutenant |
| M. D. Holland | Second Lieutenant |
| Thomas W. Craighead | 2nd Lieutenant. Died in service |
| C. H. Rush | 2nd Lieutenant. Died in service |
| Littleton T. Meador | 2nd Lieutenant |
| Callohill M. English | Brevet 2nd Lieutenant |

### Non-Commissioned Officers

| | |
|---|---|
| Benjamin G. Garrett | Orderly Sergeant |
| K. Clingenpeel | 2nd Sergeant |
| M. F. Cunningham | 2nd Sergeant. Died in service |
| James H. Meador | 3rd Sergeant. Wounded |
| Robert B. Meador | Company Quartermaster Sergeant |
| Benjamin P. Hancock | Corporal. Wounded |
| George N. Parker | Corporal |
| John C. Harper | Corporal. Wounded |
| Wm. G. Wilkinson | Sergeant |

### Privates

John Wm. Allen
James Abshire
Emory Alder
C. P. Arrington
Joshua Atkerson. Disabled by disease
Daniel W. Basham. Wounded
G. W. Basham
Joseph H. Basham
P. B. Basham. Disabled by disease

Thomas T. Basham. Died in service
William M. Basham. Disabled by disease
Daniel M. Bays
William O. Bays. Died in service
John Beuchelow (Benchelew) Wounded
William Bond
_____ Bealer

Edw. T. Byrd (Bird)
James L. Byrd
Joseph A. Byrd
Peter L. Byrd. Died in
service
Wiley A. Byrd
W.S.O. Bird (or W.J.O.)
Benjamin F. Board. Wounded
D. M. Board
Samuel H. Board
Samuel M. Board. Died in
service
J. H. Blankenship
W. P. Board
S. T. Booth. Died in service
Thomas H. Brown
John W. H. Brown. Died in
service
J. W. Burroughs. Died in
service
J. B. Burroughs. Wounded
C. F. Burroughs. Died in
service
Thomas R. Burroughs (or T.J.)
E. N. Burroughs. Wounded
Ed. P. Burroughs
William A. Burwell. Wounded
Thomas P. Bush
Charles G. Bush (or Y.) Died
in service

Walter H. Calloway
Charles H. Callaway. Died in
service
E. A. Calston
H. C. Chapman
Charles H. Couch
H. C. Chitwood
George F. Cunningham (or E.)
George L. Cunningham. Wounded
M. F. Cunningham

William B. Dewey
William H. Dillon. Wounded
Jacob Dillon
C. M. Divers
Thomas C. Divers. Wounded
T. J. Divers
William B. Dowdy
Otey Dudley
Charles D. Deyerle (or S.)
Wounded

J. S. Edwards. Wounded
Thomas A. Eanes

D. S. Ferguson. Disabled by
disease
Thomas B. Ferguson
D. W. Ferguson, D. W.

J. W. Glass, wounded

William W. Hamner
J. G. Hancock (or J. C.)
J. H. Hancock
B. P. Hancock
W. D. Hancock
D. N. Hannabass
John Hannibass
William B. Heptinstall
Marcellus Holland
M. D. Holland
Holley Harrison
James P. Harrison, died in
service
H. C. Holley
William M. Hudson. Died in
service
John G. Hurt
William H. Hurt
William M. Hurt
E. Harkey. Wounded

Marshall Jamison
Thomas T. Jones

J. W. Kempleton. Wounded

John Lord (substitute)
W. H. Lowe

William H. (or A.) Menefee. Died
in service
John H. Martin. Died in service
Samuel Martin. Wounded
Silas Martin
James L. Matthews. Wounded
William P. Mays. Died in service
E. T. McGuire
John McGhee, Sr.
John S. T. McGhee
J. E. McNeil
E. J. Meador. Wounded
J. A. Meador
W. T. Meador
S.F. Moore (or S.P.)
H. G. Morgan. Died in service
Thomas W. Morgan (or T. J.)
Wounded
J. A. Moorman

166

D. W. Parker
A. D. Pasley (or R.D.)
C.T. Pasley
J. W. Pasley
Jerome Pasley. Wounded
R. D. Paysley
Lilburn Paisley. Wounded
S. S. Pasley. Died in
service
Wythe H. Perdue
H. S. Persinger
John Pilcher
John Poindexter
John W. Poindexter
S. H. Poindexter (or S.F.)
John R. Powell
William T. Powell
H. C. Pollard

Thomas Bird Robertson
Joseph R. Rucker

John A. Saunderson
S. H. Saunderson
Charles Simmons
F. Simmons
J. Shenk
John H. Smith
John P. Smith
John O. Sowers

J. E. Sowers
Edward E. Starkey. Wounded
John Starkey. Died in service
W. W. St. Clair. Wounded
Thomas H. Stegar

James S. Taylor
William J. Toney. Wounded
R. A. Thomas

Charles W. Wade. Died in service
Edward Wade. Died in service
George W. Wade
John W. Willard. Died in service
William R. Waid
Abram Williams
Pleasant G. Williams (or P.D.)
H. C. Wood. Wounded
Silas Wood
William M. A. Wood
James A. Wray. Wounded
William H. Wray
A. S. Wright (or A.J.)
John M. Wright
O. P. Wright. Died in service
William R. Wright
M. Ward
W. G. Wilkinson

William Zoll (or Zell)

## TROOP A, 10th VIRGINIA CAVALRY

### "Caskie Rangers"

#### Commissioned Officers

| | |
|---|---|
| Caskie, Robert A. | Captain |
| Fulcher (or Hulcher) E.S. | Captain |
| Doyle, _____ | Lieutenant |
| Mott, W. V. | Lieutenant |

#### Non-Commissioned Officers

| | |
|---|---|
| Kennedy, W. F. | Sergeant |
| Burton,M. F. | Sergeant |
| Robertson, J.R. | Corporal |

#### Privates

Andrews, William from Augusta

Beecher, Bernhard
Burton, William E.

Brauer, W. H.
Bradshaw, William E.
Barry, Richard

167

Christian, A. G., from Augusta
Churchman, Jno. S., from Augusta
Cochran, Jas. C. from Augusta
Crawford, Wm. B., from Augusta
Cahill, B. M.
Chappell, Jno. T.
Christian, Robert J.
Crossmore, Oliver
Cross, C. Lewis

Frazier, L.T.
Farrell, J. P.

Gilkeson, F. M., from Augusta
Green, Nelson
Giblin, Michael
Green, M.

Hall, Clinton, from Augusta
Harnsberger, R.S., from Augusta
Hutcherson, Jas. M.
Hechler, George
Hutchison, W. R.

Johnson, Jas. C.
Jones, William W.

Katon, Aaron
Kadden, A.

Lee, John (R)
Lee, Danile
Laughborough, Jas. H.

McClure, A. W., from Augusta
Moffett, R. W., from Augusta
Moorman, Wm. H., from Augusta
Markle, T.
Meyers, B(ernard)
Martin, Thos. W.

Nelson, William J., from Augusta

Patrick, James W., from Augusta
Pelter, Joseph, from Augusta
Poindexter, W. C.
Peasy, B. C., died in service

Ramsey, J. R., from Augusta

Shirey, William H., from Augusta
Sproul, A. A., from Augusta
Sterritt, F. F., from Augusta
Swoope, G. W., from Augusta
Semonis, B. F.
Stein, Michael

Tyree, William W.
Tabb, John P.

Van Horn, J. Shelley
Van Horn, P.

Williams, C. W., from Augusta
Wagner, Charles

## TROOP C, 10th VIRGINIA CAVALRY

### Commissioned Officers

Flood, William Washington             Captain
    (or Floyd)

### Non-Commissioned Officers

White, H. F.                          Sergeant
King, R. B.                           Sergeant
Campbell, John                        Sergeant
Dorsett, J. S.                        Sergeant
Kirk, H. H.                           Corporal

### Privates

Amos, G. D.
Adams, Lewis B.
Ashworth, H. T.
Arrington, T.
Adams, J. H.

Belcher, B. F.
Barer, H. C.
Belcher, T. A.
Burch, Richard
Broadie, Wm. F.

168

Burch, J. W.
Brown, B. C.

Cousins, John W.
Craig, William G.
Campbell, P.
Cooper, M. W., wounded
Cooper, Geo. K.

Davidson, J. H.
Davidson, M. L.
Davidson, W. B.
Dix, B., died in service
Doyle, J. M.

Fuller, John, wounded

Gravely, Green S.
Goode, D. G.

Holcomb, Joseph W.
Hutchinson, J. M.
Hunt, T. D.
Haynes, Fleming

Johnson, H.

King, J. B.
Kirks, W.C., died in service

Lester, Jeremiah

Lawrence, C. A. E.
Law, W. B.

Martin, Calvin L.
Mason, Samuel G.
Moore, Reuben W.
Machenheimer, J. T.

Potter, Moses
Pinckard, Thos. W.
Potter, Ephrian
Price, A. G.

Robbins, Geo. W.
Richards, William A.

Shelton, Oscar
Sipe, J. W.
Steagall, A. J.
Shumate, T. S.
Shumate, S.

Williams, George W.
Walker, W. F.
Wingfield, Pinckney G.
Webb, J. T.

Young, S. B.

Zeigler, William

## TROOP K, 10th VIRGINIA CAVALRY

### Commissioned Officers

| | |
|---|---|
| Rosser, J. Travis | Captain |
| Grayson, D. C. | Captain |
| Graham, W. L. | Lieutenant-Captain |

### Non-Commissioned Officers

| | |
|---|---|
| Craghead, John W., wounded | Sergeant |
| Preston, S. B. | Sergeant |
| Semones, B. M. | Sergeant |
| Zeigler, Chess. | Sergeant |
| Franklin, J. L., wounded | Sergeant |

### Privates

Armstrong, Jno. R.
Ashworth, J. H.
Arrington, W. S.
Asher, Bob (Robt)

Bernard, M. H.
Burnett, J. W.
Burnett, W. C.
Bryant, Robt.

Byrd, S. W.
Brown, J. O., wounded
Berger, Pomp
Bird (or Byrd)
Brown, W. N.
Bernard, Robert C (or R),
    wounded
Brooks, D. S. K.
Burchett, H. N.
Burwell, J. H.
Bernard, W. A.
Bondurant, Jno. M.
Brooks, Robert L., wounded
Bennett, Buck
Burchett, H. H., wounded
Bowles, J. W., wounded
Bondurant, R. W.

Clements, C. J.
Craghead, J. M., wounded
Coffman, J. H.
Copeland, W. N.
Craighead, T. L., wounded
Cooper, J. D.

Dudley, J. T.
Dickerson, Henry
Davis, J. W.
Dickinson, W. H.
Dodson, E. J.

Frailin, J. F.
Frith, William
Frith, Bob (Robt.)
Ferguson, P. H., died in
    service

Grant, J. B.
Graveley, C. B.
Griffin, V. R., wounded

Holland, William
Holland, John H., wounded
Holland, P. A., wounded
Harrison, Bob (Robt.)
Holland, T. S.

Holland, E. M.
Housman, W. R.

James, B. A.

Kelser, G. P.

Law, C. W.
Law, William B.
Lancaster, L. P.
Lovell, J. P.

Mattox, H. C.
Mattox, E. O.
Mattox, G. T.
McInheimer, W. H.
Mattox, I. J.
Mattox, Jno. H., died in service
Madox, Thomas
Madox, Harmon

Powell, William
Poindexter, E. H.
Preston, Christopher P.
Poindexter, W. G.

Rives, R. B.
Rogers, B. F.

Smith, S. J.
Semones, J. F.
Seay, C. T.
Smith, Oliver
Street, John
Semones, J. E.
Smith, V. O.

Turner, J. H.
Turner, Jno. P.

Woolton, H. C., wounded
Witcher, James
Weaver, Josiah
Williams, W. P.

Zeigler, C. M.

## TROOP A, 37th VIRGINIA CAVALRY

Address given is as of September 15th, 1910.

### Commissioned Officers

Capt. James R. Claiborne
Capt. G. T. Williams, Lavinder

1st. Lt. Edward T. Bridges
1st. Lt. Nicholas C. Carper, died at Rocky Mount
2nd Lt. George T. Williams (promoted to Captain)
2nd Lt. G. O. Hambrick, Dallas, Texas
3rd Lt. William L. Bernard
3rd Lt. Beverly Carper (Disappeared after war, never again heard from)

## Non-Commissioned Officers

Serg. James Doss, died in Kansas
Serg. R. B. Beattie, Hagan, Virginia
Serg. Thomas D. Angell, Ottoway, Kansas
Orderly Serg. Chas. M. Akers, Calhoun, Missouri
Corp. John L. Hunter, Sulphur Springs, Texas
Corp. E. H. Keys, Ferrum, Virginia
Corp. Peter L. Hunter, died in Knoxville, Tennessee

## Privates

Angell, T. D.
Arrington, Spencer
Ayers, Samuel
Anglin, James P., died in Sydnorsville
Abshire, Joshua, French Lick, Ind.
Ayers, Dike, Glade Hill
Ayers, Samuel, Glade Hill
Angle, Benjamin, died near Rocky Mount
Angle, Edward, died at home, Flint Hill, Franklin County
Angell, William
Angell, W. R.

Basham, Wm. C.
Bernard, John O., Sontag
Board, Thaddeus, Wirtz
Bernard, Charles, died at Rocky Mount
Bernard, Linas, killed near Winchester
Blankenship, Tom, died in Franklin County
Bernard, Silas
Brooks, James (unknown)
Beatie, R. B.
Bell, John

Chitwood, J. W., Redwood
Chitwood, H. C., Rocky Mount
Cabiness, W. C., Sedalia, Mo.
Crook, Stephen, Redwood

Cannaday, Peter, died in Floyd County
Chambers, John, died in Camp Chase, Ohio
Chambers, Silas, died in Franklin County
Chambers, William, died in Franklin County
Cooper, Joseph, died in Franklin County
Cooper, Thomas, died in Franklin County
Creasy, Benjamin, died at Point Pleasant, Ohio
Crook, Daniel, died in Franklin County
Cundiff, George, died in Franklin County
Cooper, George
Carrico, W. F.

Davis, Moses, accidently killed at Beverly, West Virginia
Dent, Joel B., died at home in West Virginia
Dent, John Jacob, died at Sontag
Dillon, Samuel, Camden, Indiana
Dowdy, Woodson, Salem
Dowdy, William

Easter, Joel, died in Franklin County
Easter, Thomas, died at Camp Chase, Ohio

Edwards, John L.
Easter, James W., Roanoke
Easter, Bug.

Fishburne, R. H., Roanoke
Fishburne, Ferdinand Blair, died
    at Camp Chase, Ohio

Gearhart, Pearl, killed by bush-
    whackers in Tennessee
Gentry, Andrew, died at Bicknell,
    Indiana
Guilliams, J. W.
Guilliams, H. C., Callaway
Guilliams, R. G.
Geerhart, S.

Hannabas, Bob
Hensley, David, Roanoke
Howell, Abner, died in Bedford,
    near Stewartville
Howell, Jesse, died in Bedford,
    near Stewartville
Helm, T. D., died near Elliston
Handy, John, killed near Lynch-
    burg
Hatcher, Tom, died in Franklin
    County
Hutts, Patrick, Kennett
Hannibass, James
Hannabas, Octave, died in
    Southwest Virginia
Hall, John, died near Rocky
    Mount

Keeney, William, killed at
    Piedmont
Kennett, John Peter, Vinton
Keys, E. H. (Corporal)
Keeney, Tom

Lemon, George T., Salinas,
    California
Lee, Samuel E., wounded in
    Tennessee, died near Salem

Meadows, Joel, St. Albans, West
    Virginia
Meadors, Dock, Loneoak
McGuffin, Lee, died in California
McQueen, A.
Moran, Joshua, killed near
    Bunker Hill
Metts, James, Lamont, Mo.

Minix, Henry, Roanoke
Montgomery, James, Ona, West
    Virginia
McNeal, Thomas, Wirtz
McNeal, Giles H., Wirtz
Miles, John W., Sydorsville
Miles, William
Minix, Tom
Montgomery, William
Meadows, Tom

Neathawk, David, died in
    Franklin County

Overstreet, Silas, died at
    Home, Missouri
Oldham, W. L.
Oxley, John, died at Griffiths-
    ville, West Virginia
Overfelt, Thomas, Gogginsville
Overfelt, Bariah (or Bariat)

Pack, John A.
Pelter, Tom., Schuyler, Neb.
Perdue, Robert R.
Perdue, Giles, Taylors Store
Perdue, Charles W.
Prunty, William
Perdue, Jeter W., died in
    Franklin County
Perdue, Richard F., Redwood
Patterson, G. W., died near
    Salem

Reeves, Robert, died at Soldiers'
    Home, Virginia
Roseberry, George W.
Ross, Thomas, Philpott

Smith, Henry, died at home,
    Franklin County
Street, Simon
Stanley, Henry, killed at
    Piedmont
Street, William
Scott, Michael, St. Louis, Mo.
Skinnell, Samuel L., Wirtz
Street, Avery T.
Smith, Samuel
Street, Berry C.
Simms, James
Terrell, Eustace
Tanxley, James (unknown) (or
    Tameley)

172

Triplett, A.
Thomas, Pleasant, killed
  accidently in Franklin
  County

Webb, Boliver, died at home,
  North Carolina
Wingfield, William, died at
  Camp Chase, Ohio
Woody, John A., died in
  Roanoke
Weatherman, J. W.
Woody, William A., died at
  Camp Chase, Ohio
Wray, Robert G., died near
  Boone Mill
Wray, W. T.
Wright, John, died in Green-
  ville Tenn.
Walker, James A., Martinsville

Webb, Bolivar
Webb, Theodrick F., Rocky Mount
Wray, Fletcher T., Boone Mill
Wright, Lawrence M., Taylors
  Store
Wright, William, Kennett
Wright, T. M., wounded
Wright, Robert
Wright, Tazewell H., Roanoke
Walker, Mage. (Maze)
Wingfield, P. G.

Young, James A., wounded, died
  in Franklin County
Young, Isaac, died in Franklin
  County. Died in service
Young, Peter, died at Camp Chase,
  Ohio
Young, George O., died at
  Ferrum.

This Company, organized at Rocky Mount, August 4, 1862, was recruited beyond the maximum number. An order was given to organize another Company, which was done. J. R. Claiborn was promoted to regimental officer with the rank of Major. Other regimental officers were: Ambrose C. Dunn, Colonel; William Patterson, Adjutant; J. H. Greer, Surgeon; andCharles B. Duncan, Quarter Master.

## TROOP G, 37th VIRGINIA CAVALRY

### Commissioned Officers

| | |
|---|---|
| Bridges, Edward T. | Captain |
| Dyer, John | Lieutenant |
| Webb, John (F) | Lieutenant |
| Bernard, L. W. | Lieutenant |

### Non-Commissioned Officers

| | |
|---|---|
| Burwell, John S. | Sergeant |
| McFarland, S. S. | Sergeant |

### Privates

Arrington, P. E.

Burnard, S.H.
Burnett, W. L.
Bridges, E. T.

Combs, William C.
Chitwood, Joel T.
Chitwood, Shelton W.

Chambers, John, died in service

Davis, Th. J.

Ferguson, S. H.
Ferguson, S. F., wounded
Fisher, G. W.

Johnson, W., wounded
Jessey, John, died in service

173

Loyd, Thos., died in service

Peters, J. H.

Richards, Bolin, died in
   service

Smith, Mallory
Simmons, Meador
Scott, Milton J.
Sigmon, N. F. (or T.)
Sigmon, T. W.
Sigmon, L. F.

Stanley, I. P.

Thurman, Tax.
Thompson, P.

Webb, Moses G.
Woods, Jno. W.
Wilson, William
Wray, I. W.
Wade, B.

Young, Peter, died in service

# MUSTER ROLL OF WORLD WAR I SOLDIERS

Note: Address is a Virginia address unless otherwise noted. "Col." denotes Negro. "Vol." denotes a volunteer.

Date of Muster; Name; Address; Age; etc.

11/19/17; LaPrade, W.E.; Wirtz; 24
" ; Quinn, N.L.; Ferrum; 24
" ; Kidd, Jas. F.; Figsboro; 26
" ; Dudley, W.R.; Sontag; 23
" ; Turner, C.S.; Sago; 22
" ; Walker, H. A.; Pen Hook; 28
" ; Edwards, W.C.; Ferrum; 22
" ; Robertson, J.C.; Taylor's Store; 23
" ; Holcomb, S.H.; Rocky Mount; 29
" ; Divers, J.T.; Hardy; 24
" ; Hundley, P.L.; Pen Hook; 23
" ; Richards, C.T.; Rocky Mount; 28
" ; Clemons, W.L.; Boone Mill; 25
" ; Robertson, T.G.; Taylors Store; 24
" ; Woody, F.T.; Rocky Mount; 25
" ; Eames, J.L.; Sontag; 23
" ; Jamison, C.T.S.; Callaway; 22
" ; Pasley, G.; Scruggs; 21
" ; Hodges, L.A.; Rocky Mount; 21
" ; Haley, J.; Sago; 25
" ; Payne, W.H.; Hardy; 21
" ; Mitchell, R.T.; Figsboro; 29
" ; Hunt, I.J.; Glade Hill; 29
" ; Booth, H.H.; Pen Hook; 21
" ; Montgomery, J.A.; Wirtz; 21
" ; Mullins, J.A.; Callaway; 21
" ; Trent, T.W.; Sago; 22
10/8/17 ; Perdue, J.D.; Scruggs; 30
" ; Stump, G.R.; Deegans, West Va.; 39
" ; Huston, A.L.; Sontag; 22
" ; Prillaman, R.A.; Callaway; 26
" ; Skinnell, R.T.; Redwood; 23
" ; Jones, J.H.; Boone Mill; 23
" ; Foster, H.H.; Union Hall; 21
" ; Robertson, J.M.; Callaway; 25
" ; Smith, W.L.; Glade Hill; 26
" ; Smith, J.T.; Scruggs; 22
" ; Sink, W.L.; Wirtz; 21
" ; Dewitt, H.D.; Figsboro; 29
" ; Cobbler, H. J.; Figsboro; 26
" ; Thurman, H.; Wirtz; 23
" ; Fralin, G.G.; Union Hall; 25
" ; Nolen, L.S.; Endicott; 25
" ; Kidd, T.J.; Figsboro; 21
" ; Allman, E.C.; Glade Hill; 23
" ; Shiveley, I.V.; Ferrum; 22
" ; Prillaman, N.C.; Henry; 22
" ; Thompson, J.P.; Pizarro; 22
" ; Jefferson, W.E.; Pen Hook; 25

Date of Muster; Name; Address; Age; etc.
10/8/17; Spangler, H.C.; Dillons Mill; 22
  "    ; Ferguson, S.B.; Wirtz; 25
  "    ; Altice, J.; Redwood; 23
  "    ; Parcell, C.N.; Rocky Mount; 30
  "    ; Crook, L.; Boone Mill; 24
  "    ; Saul, J.F.; Dillons Mill; 30
  "    ; Bryant, W.; Ferrum; 28
  "    ; McBride, J.W.; Rocky Mount; 23
  "    ; Watson, B.P.; Leatherwood; 26
  "    ; Hunt, J.H.; Wirtz; 22
  "    ; Bowles, C.L.; Callaway; 23
  "    ; Stump, C.P.; Dillons Mill; 24
  "    ; Beckner, F.H.; Callaway; 23
  "    ; David, R.H.; Pen Hook; 24
  "    ; Brown, J.H.; Rocky Mount; 22
  "    ; Lovell, R.S.; Figsboro; 24
7/31/18; Bohon, Oscar; Boone Mill; 24
5/24/18; Perdue, James L.; Scruggs; 26
  "    ; Wright, Geo. Wm.; Ferrum; 21
  "    ; Young, Andrew H.; Ferrum; 24
7/15/18; Mason, Edward W.; Callaway; 22
8/8/18 ; Blankenship, J.T.; Scruggs; 22
5/24/18; Rogers, Asa Ross; Sago; 27
  "    ; Morris, Grady; Glade Hill; 22
  "    ; Wray, W.A.; Wirtz; 21
  "    ; Cooper, J.L.; Sago; 21
  "    ; Bowles, T.M.; Sontag; 23
  "    ; Smith, R.S.; Taylors Store; 24
  "    ; Foster, J.H.; Ferrum; 22
  "    ; Prillaman, C.E.; Callaway; 23
5/22/18; Tyree, O.S.; Figsboro; 24
5/24/18; Renick, C.M.; Callaway; 25
  "    ; Woody, W.I.; Roanoke; 25
  "    ; Mitchell, L.L.; Rocky Mount; 24
  "    ; Thornton, C.; Henry; 23
  "    ; Hartwell, C.A.; Hardy; 22
  "    ; Cooper, H.L.; Rocky Mount; 22
5/22/18; McBride, W.H.; Union Hall; 28
5/24/18; Webster, A.T.; Boone Mill; 29
  "    ; Holly, D. C.; Endicott; 22
  "    ; Gibson, W.; Boone Mill; 22
  "    ; Patterson, B.F.; Rocky Mount; 27
  "    ; Bates, W.H.; Union Hall; 22
  "    ; Robertson, J.T.; Hardy; 23
  "    ; Saul, T.B.; Callaway; 21
  "    ; Amos, R.B.; Hardy; 23
  "    ; Robertson, J.T.; Union Hall; 22
7/23/18; Wigington, H.C.; Petersburg; 24
7/21/18; Truman, N.C.; Hardy; 22
5/24/18; Hambrick, G.; Rocky Mount; 24
  "    ; Ellis, D.; Taylors Store; 23
  "    ; Montgomery, C.O.; Wirtz; 27
7/21/18; Parcell, M.C.; Sontag; 23
  "    ; Stanley, C.; Sontag; 22

<u>Date of Muster; Name; Address; Age; etc.</u>

5/25/18; Leffue, G.; Rocky Mount; 22
5/24/18; Laprade, J.; Wirtz; 21
   " ; Hodges, J.L.; Sydnorsville; 24
   " ; Doss, H.B.; Ferrum; 23
   " ; Underwood, W.; Callaway; 22
   " ; Bousman, G.W.; Glade Hill; 23
   " ; Meadors, J.W.; Henry; 29
   " ; Edwards, F.L.; Ferrum; 28
   " ; Sutherland, G.D.; Roanoke; 26
   " ; Stone, G.C.; Henry; 24
   " ; Shiviley, W.D.; Ferrum; 26
   " ; Reynolds, J.W.; Naffs; 22
   " ; Ellis, D.; Taylors Store; 22
   " ; James, T.A.; Endicott; 21
   " ; Jones, B.; Henry; 22
   " ; Luke, J.W.; Sydnorsville; 25
   " ; Lynch, J.W.; Boone Mill; 30
7/21/18; Perdue, J.D.D.; Rocky Mount; 31
5/24/18; Dillon, E.E.; Scruggs; 22
5/22/18; Mason, W.M.; Hopewell; 24
5/24/18; Mason, M.F.; Bassett; 28
   " ; Laprade, E.P., Pen Hook; 22
   " ; Dowdy, W.L.; Callaway; 21
7/21/18; Eames, J.S.; Rocky Mount; 21
5/24/18; Boitnott, I.J.; Boone Mill; 28
   " ; Burge, J.A.; Majestic, Ky.; 22
8/7/18 ; Ingram, Isaac F.; Ferrum; 31
5/24/18; Ingram, A.B.; Ferrum; 24
   " ; Prillaman, C.A.; Callaway; 23
   " ; Whitehead, B.H.; Figsboro; 23
   " ; Hunt, J.W.; Rocky Mount; 25
7/21/18; Lovell, J.C.; Sago; 23
5/27/18; Hodges, D.R.; Redwood; 24
7/21/18; Wray, J.W.; Wirtz; 22
7/15/18; Wingfield, P.P.; Sontag; 24
   " ; Jamison, C.H.; Callaway; 22
5/24/18; Bowles, T.H.; Ferrum; 30
9/21/17; Brubaker, J.H.; Callaway; 27
   " ; Truman, R.L.; Hardy; 21
   " ; Truman, J.W.; Hardy; 25
   " ; Perdue, D.J.; Union Hall; 28
   " ; Minix, J.I.; Boone Mill; 23
   " ; Richardson, W.R.; Hardy; 23
   " ; Palmer, O.E.; Kennett; 21
   " ; Mattox, J.S.; Boone Mill; 29
   " ; Bernard, J.W.; Boone Mill; 26
   " ; Oyler, P.B.; Wirtz; 28
   " ; Bowman, W.R.; Dillons Mill; 24
   " ; Moran, L. H.; Callaway; 22
   " ; Holland, H.L.; Glade Hill; 24
   " ; Peters, A.N.; Wirtz; 21
   " ; Hodges, O.W., Sontag; 25
   " ; Blankenship, C.R.; Glade Hill; 26
   " ; Dudley, W.B.; Redwood; 24
   " ; Angle, L.T.; Wirtz; 28

177

Date of Muster; Name; Address; Age; etc.

9/21/17; Anderson, C.O.; Redwood; 25
"       ; Turner, D. H.; Henry; 21
"       ; Angle, J.A.; Wirtz; 22
"       ; Williams, E.T.; Henry; 22
"       ; Martin, W.; Callaway; 26
"       ; Prillaman, J.D.; Callaway; 22
"       ; Prillaman, H.A.; Callaway; 24
"       ; Ellis, W.K.; Scruggs; 25
"       ; Arrington, J.M.; Sontag; 21
"       ; Law, L.L.; Glade Hill; 22
"       ; Hudson, W.; Boone Mill; 21
"       ; Washburn, J.C.; Sago; 23
"       ; Dudley, P.T.; Redwood; 22
"       ; Slone, N.J.; Callaway; 23
"       ; Hodges, B.; Sydnorsville; 21
"       ; Dillon, J.T.; Glade Hill; 21
"       ; Stone, C.R.; Henry; 27
"       ; Bowles, I.T.; Dillons Mill; 21
"       ; Fralin, J.T.; Rocky Mount; 26
"       ; Young, C.E.; Ferrum; 27
"       ; Stanley, C.D.; Nola; 23
"       ; Horsley, H.M.; Sago; 28
"       ; McDowell, G.E.; Pen Hook; 23
"       ; Mitchell, W. H.; Rocky Mount; 21
"       ; Allman, J.B.; Union Hall; 21
"       ; Bradner, E.L.; Glade Hill; 30
"       ; Hall, J.P.; Wadesboro; 21
"       ; Grubb, J.C.; Glade Hill; 25
"       ; Brodie, J.H.; Figsboro; 21
"       ; Newman, J.H.; Taylors Store; 25
"       ; Fisher, L.O.; Taylors Store; 23
"       ; Pasley, W.T; Scruggs; 21
"       ; Kempleton, R.S.; Rocky Mount; 21
"       ; Scruggs, J.E.; Scruggs; 22
"       ; McGuire, F.O.; Hardy; 21
"       ; Shockley, C.; Boone Mill; 26
"       ; Kesler, B.D.; Hardy; 22
"       ; Fralin, J.W.; Rocky Mount; 24
"       ; Bowman, G.; Boone Mill; 21
"       ; Quarles, L.O.; Hardy; 26
"       ; Tosh, F.; Pen Hook; 21
"       ; Bowles, A.T.; Scruggs; 22
"       ; Hodges, O.H.; Rocky Mount; 23
"       ; Scott, J.L.; Taylors Store; 27
"       ; Prillaman, G.R.; Henry; 22
"       ; Smith, S.T.; Union Hall; 23
"       ; Helms, I.W.; Henry; 23
"       ; Angle, C.M.; Wirtz; 25
"       ; Ramsey, G.E.; Henry; 25; died at Camp Lee
"       ; Newbill, T.C.; Hardy; 21
"       ; Newman, J.B.; Taylors Store; 24
"       ; Young, M.; Nola; 21
"       ; Mills, W.F.; Boone Mill; 23

Date of Muster; Name; Address; Age; etc.

11/19/17; Painter, H. E.; Rocky Mount; 24
"      ; Rigney, C.S.; Pen Hook; 26
"      ; Cooper, D. M.; Callaway; 24
"      ; Prillaman, H.B.; Callaway; 24
"      ; Lovell, G.B.; Sago; 24
"      ; Doughton, J.L.; Rocky Mount; 22
10/8/17; Coleman, H.; Henry; 23
"      ; Scott, C.S.; Hardy; 21
"      ; Starkey, E.; Wirtz; 25
7/11/18; Hopkins, Grover; Spray, N.C.; 25
6/23/18; Mason, C.H.; 234 14th St., N.W., Washington,D.C.; 28
6/26/18; Boothe, J.S.; Taylors Store; 22
7/15/18; Nichols, Rufus, Rocky Mount; 23
"      ; Johnson, R.E.; Sontag; 24
"      ; Stump, Will; Rocky Mount; 25
"      ; Noell, H.L.; Kennetts; 21
"      ; Scruggs, P.B.; Union Hall; 23
3/28/18; Young, John W.; Nola; 28
"      ; Rakes, J.B.; Endicott; 27
5/24/18; Bernard, W.F.; Pen Hook; 23
"      ; Morris,J.W.; Wirtz; 22
6/23/18; Wood, Peter D.; Wirtz; 27
9/5/18; Nunley, W.D.; Boone Mill; 21
"      ; Lovell, J.M.; Henry; 21
"      ; Craig, B.G.; Figsboro; 21
"      ; Mason, Tawstone; Sydnorsville; 21
"      ; Boitnott, H.W.; Boone Mill; 21
"      ; Davis, Wilcie J.; Redwood; 21
"      ; Lloyd, J.C.; Union Hall; 21
"      ; Wade, Seaboy; Ferrum; 21
"      ; Fowler, T.C.; Sontag; 21
"      ; Brown, Edgar; Rocky Mount; 21
"      ; Brown, A.R.; Union Hall; 21
"      ; Drewry, H.H.; Ferrum; 21
"      ; Prillaman, W.H.; Henry; 21
"      ; Brown, O.E., Union Hall; 21
"      ; Allman, Posey; Glade Hill; 21
"      ; Lovelace, W.C.; Hardy; 21
"      ; Patsel, James G.; Hardy; 21
"      ; Martin, H.H.; Endicott; 21
"      ;,Coleman, M.J.; Henry; 21
"      ; Cannaday, W.E.; Boone Mill; 21
"      ; Hale, W.L.; Hunter Hall; 21
"      ; Perdue, Chas. P.; Redwood; 21
"      ; Gusler, Noell; Henry; 21
"      ; Rice, H.C.; Sago; 21
"      ; Mills, H.E.; Naffs; 21
"      ; Chewning, S.J.; Haleford; 21
"      ; Parcell, Peter; Sontag; 21
"      ; Mills, Herbert; Naffs; 21
"      ; Belcher, L.L.; Sago; 21
"      ; Crook, G.L.; Redwood; 21
"      ; Peters, M.C.; Boone Mill; 21

Date of Muster; Name; Address; Age; etc.
9/5/18 ; Roberts, G.H.; Rocky Mount; 21
   "    ; Conner, Merriman; Dillons Mill; 21
   "    ; Robertson, Leonard; Sydnorsville; 21
   "    ; Ingram, W.L.; Henry; 21
10/18/18; East, H.C.; Henry; 21; Vol.; S.A.T.C.
9/24/18 ; Lumpkins, W.D.; Rocky Mount; 21; Col.; U.Va.
8/21/18 ; Leftwich, Wilcie; Boone Mill; 21; Col.
   "    ; Helm, Johnnie; Boone Mill; 21; Col.
   "    ; Fisher, Ed; Boone Mill; 21; Col.
   "    ; Hancock, McKinley; Glade Hill; 21; Col.
9/24/18 ; Watson, J.M.; Callaway; 21; Col.
8/21/18 ; Campbell, Floyd; Sontag; 21; Col.
   "    ; Williamson, Geo.; Sontag; 21; Col.
8/23/18 ; Turner, Alex; Callaway; 21; Col.
7/15/18 ; Angle, M.G.; Wirtz; 21
5/24/18 ; Pate, C.S.; Pizarro; 21
6/25/18 ; Bowman, C.E.; Wirtz; 23
6/23/18 ; Perdue, W.D.; Redwood; 26
   "    ; Scott, Columbus; Endicott; 23
7/15/18 ; Law, Daniel A.; Glade Hill; 22
6/23/18; Wingfield, L.A.; Sago; 23
   "    ; Kesler, Geo. B.; Ferrum; 26
   "    ; Hodges, Edw. Daniel; Rocky Mount; 29
   "    ; Boitnott, H.J.; Naffs; 28
9/5/18  ; Plunkett, H.D.; Bowdon, N.D.; 22
7/15/18 ; Mills, D.H.; Naffs; 22
6/23/18 ; Turner, E.D.; Dodson; 23
7/21/18 ; English, R.L.; Scruggs; 20
7/23/18 ; Goode, B.C.; Henry; 25; Vol.; Tr. Detachment U.Va.
6/23/18 ; Love, Hay; Sydnorsville; 27
   "    ; Frith, Clifford; Ferrum; 25
   "    ; Austin, R.L.; Waidsboro; 30
   "    ; Davis, J.M.; Wirtz; 23
   "    ; Starkey, J.N.; Wirtz; 23
   "    ; Sink, Geo. W.; Rocky Mount; 22
   "    ; Mason, W.L.; Sydnorsville; 21
7/23/18 ; Greer, T.W.; Rocky Mount; 22; Vol.; Tr. Detachment U.Va.
6/23/18 ; Mullins, Geo. K.; Henry; 24
   "    ; Whitlow, A.W.; Henry; 23
   "    ; Peters, Thos. H.; Ferrum; 26
   "    ; Sutherland, J.T.; Pen Hook; 22
7/15/18 ; Dudley, Cabbell; Rocky Mount; 25
7/23/18 ; Woody, Allen, Oat; Rocky Mount; 31
7/15/18 ; Sigmon, L.W.; Ferrum; 25
   "    ; Newman, Asa B.; Taylors Store; 23
   "    ; Prillaman, C.F.; Henry; 27
   "    ; Hodges, Boss; Rocky Mount; 23
5/5/18  ; Goddin, Harry Thos.; Pen Hook; 25
7/15/18 ; Meador, Wyatt; Hardy; 22
   "    ; Hodges, Orren, B.; Rocky Mounty; 24
   "    ; Carter, Geo. A.; Wirtz; 24
   "    ; Perkins, W.G.; Ferrum; 21
   "    ; Schnarr, C.P.; Kennetts; 23
   "    ; Wray, S.H.; Henry; 25
                                180

Date of Muster; Name; Address; Age; etc.
7/15/18; Oyler, Thos. L.; Wirtz; 27
    "    ; Brubaker, J.H.; Callaway; 21
    "    ; Underwood, W.F.; Ferrum; 22
    "    ; Jones, Amos H.; Ferrum; 21
    "    ; Young, Posey, A.; Ferrum; 24
    "    ; Nimmo, Harry G.; Hardy; 23
    "    ; Boyd, G.C.; Endicott; 26
    "    ; Shaver, I.B.; Copper Hill; 21
    "    ; Turner, Benj. L.; Waidsboro; 29
    "    ; Mize, D.J.; Henry; 23
    "    ; Drewry, P.C.; Ferrum; 26
    "    ; Stone, Thos. H.; Henry; 26
    "    ; Young, Gene D.; Rocky Mount; 22
    "    ; Perdue, Roy; Glade Hill; 23
    "    ; Smith, Fred; Rocky Mount; 24
9/5/18 ; Stump, Henry Lee; Callaway; 26
    "    ; Via, Emmett; Callaway; 22
7/15/18; Mullins, S.J.; Ferrum; 30
    "    ; Brodie, F.A.; Figsboro; 23
5/30/18; Whitlock, Thos. F.; Rocky Mount; 22
5/24/18; Hardy, Thos. L.; Boone Mill; 22
7/29/18; Young, Arsie H.; Hunter Hall; 21
7/21/18; Chitwood, George; Rocky Mount; 21
5/24/18; Angle, Geo. Wilsie; Boone Mill; 24
    "    ; Carter, E.C.; Wirtz; 22
    "    ; Nolen, C.S.; Endicott; 24
    "    ; Hall, W.A.; Rocky Mount; 31
    "    ; Harmon, James; Redwood; 22
7/15/18; Durham, John; Scruggs; 30
6/23/18; Martin, James, K.; Nowlins Mill; 29
    "    ; Perdue, Charles T.; Boone Mill; 25
    "    ; Wagner, Walter; Endicott; 25
    "    ; Stone, Emmett; Henry; 24
7/23/18; Greer, C.C.; Rocky Mount; 25
6/23/18; Wright, Pilate J.; Ferrum; 22
9/5/18 ; Horne, Geo. A.; Hardy; 25
    "    ; Dudley, R.R.; Union Hall; 26
8/21/18; Saunders, W.H.; Ferrum; 21; Col.
8/31/18; Wade, Willie; Boone Mill; 21; Col.
9/24/18; McGhee, Kelly; Sago; 21; Col.
8/31/18; Helm, Clarence; Boone Mill; 21; Col.
8/15/18; Tyree, Harry; Rocky Mount; 21; Col.; Vol.; Tr. Detachment
              Hampton, Inst.
8/23/18; Martin, Wash.; Boone Mill; 21; Col.
9/24/18; Price, Rufus; Copper Hill; 21; Col.
    "    ; Wade, Gilmore; Sontag; 21; Col.
    "    ; Harris, Phillip; Rocky Mount; 21; Col.
    "    ; Peyton, John H.; Hardy; 21; Col.
    "    ; Basham, Carlton; Hardy; 21; Col.
9/5/18 ; Hoy, L.J.; Dillons Mill; 21;
    "    ; Thornton, R.M.; Ferrum; 21
    "    ; Southall, D.R.; Scruggs; 21
    "    ; Robertson, Vernie; Union Hall; 21

181

Date of Muster; Name; Address; Age; etc.

7/15/18; Belcher, Ernest; Rocky Mount; 21; Col.
  " ; Hughes, Sam; Sontag; 22; Col.
  " ; Muse, Lemon; Vashti; 22; Col.
  " ; Finney, J.L.; Pen Hook; 23; Col.
  " ; Muse, Zach.; Naffs; 31; Col.
  " ; Ingram, Ben; Rocky Mount; 35; Col.
  " ; Webb, Jos.; Callaway; 22; Col.
  " ; Kasey, Stewart L.; Wirtz; 21; Col.
  " ; Childress, Charlie; Scruggs; 24; Col.
  " ; Brooks, James; Rocky Mount; 23; Col.
8/2/18; Holland, John; Sontag; 24; Col.
  " ; Divers; Rocky Mount; 21; Col.
  " ; Fralin, J.L.; Sontag; 24; Col.
10/26/17; Bond, C.R.; Hardy; 21; Col.
  " ; Mattox, W.T.H.; Glade Hill; 23; Col.
  " ; Saunders, Henry Grady; Rocky Mount; 21; Col.
  " ; Muse, Hobart; Rocky Mount; 21; Col.
  " ; Divers, S.W.; Union Hall; 23; Col.
  " ; Edwards, Lonnie; Pen Hook; 21; Col.
  " ; James, Other; Pen Hook; 22; Col.
  " ; Brown, Willie; Taylors Store; 21; Col.
  " ; Holland, Harvey E.; Glade Hill; 25; Col.
  " ; Young, Willie F.; Ferrum; 29; Col.
  " ; Callaway, Henry; Boone Mill; 22; Col.
  " ; Moir, Ran; Rocky Mount; 22; Col.
  " ; Holland, Elijah; Sontag; 22; Col.
  " ; Woods, Benj. H.; Rocky Mount; 24; Col.
  " ; Smith, John H.; Rocky Mount; 22; Col.
11/19/17; Bousman, Thomas; Union Hall; 24; Col.
  " ; Starkey, R.E.; Taylors Store; 23; Col.
  " ; Levasy, H. Trout; Rocky Mount; 24; Col.
  " ; Mayhan,J.D.R.; Pen Hook; 24; Col.
  " ; Arrington, Morton; Rocky Mount; 28; Col.
  " ; Webb, Jim; Sontag; 21; Col.
9/5/17; McGuffin, E.B.; Callaway; 24
  " ; Green, Andrew; Dillons Mill; 22
  " ; Robertson, Issac W.; Callaway; 22
  " ; Peters, Geo. Anthony; Pizarro; 22
  " ; Furrow, W. E.; Callaway; 22
  " ; Turner, Edgar A.; Henry; 26
  " ; Moore, W.H.; Union Hall; 21
  " ; Meador, W.E.; Hardy; 22
  " ; Harrison, B.C.; Rocky Mount; 28
3/28/18; Newman, L.A.; Taylors Store; 28
  " ; Bowles, W.B.; Wirtz; 21
  " ; Horsley, A.J.; Sago; 23
  " ; Fralin, W.F.; Rocky Mount; 30
  " ; Divers, G. E.; Taylors Store; 26
7/29/18; Angell, R.H.; Boone Mill; 2(
7/15/18; McCall, J.M.; Rocky Mount; 21
3/28/18; Saunders, W.D.; Sago; 24
  " ; Cahill, G.W.; Henry; 27
  " ; Moorman, C.S.; Hendricks Store; 24
  " ; Hodges, A.P.; Wirtz; 22
  " ; Cannaday, J.E.; Ferrum; 28

<u>Date of Muster; Name; Address; Age; etc.</u>

9/5/18; Jones, C.F.; Callaway; 21
   "   ; Gillespie, D.G.; Pizarro; 21
   "   ; Oyler, John F.; Wirtz; 21
   "   ; Bradley, J.W.; Boone Mill; 21
   "   ; Dodson, Charlie M.; Ferrum; 21
   "   ; McGhee, H.C.; Henry; 21
   "   ; Jamison, S.W.; Sago; 21
4/25/18; Smith, Dan; Sontag; 23; Col.
   "   ; Webb, Jim; Dillons Mill; 23; Col.
   "   ; Reynolds, Charlie L.; Union Hall; 31; Col.
6/18/18; Williams, Ben; Sydnorsville; 23; Col.
9/5/18 ; Beheler, Homer; Rocky Mount; 21
7/15/18; Warren, Muncie; Sydnorsville; 21; Col.
8/2/18 ; Muse, Lennie; Sago; 27; Col.
8/21/18; Ferguson, Amcie; Boone Mill; 21; Col.
   "   ; Wade, Goodwill; Ferrum; 21; Col.
9/24/18; Law, Kinney H.; Figsboro; 21; Col.
7/15/18; Cook, W.L.; Dillons Mill; 26; Col.
4/25/18; Cook, Geo. H.; Dillons Mill; 22; Col.
   "   ; Patterson, Roy; Rocky Mount; 22; Col.
9/24/18; Stovall, Tom; Rocky Mount; 24; Col.
4/25/18; Wright, J.E.; Sontag; 25; Col.
   "   ; Burger, Willie A.; Sontag; 23; Col.
   "   ; Preston, Willie T.; Glade Hill; 25; Col.
   "   ; Fisher, Tom; Boone Mill; 23; Col.
   "   ; Brown, Preston; Rocky Mount; 23; Col.
5/1/18 ; Saunders, Sam; Rocky Mount; 27; Col.
   "   ; Coles, M.N.; Rocky Mount; 22; Col.
   "   ; Board, McKinley; Scruggs; 21; Col.
   "   ; Price, Powell; Callaway; 22; Col.
6/18/18; Tyree, Jesse; Rocky Mount; 29; Col.
5/1/18 ; Edwards, Ben; Pen Hook; 23; Col.
8/2/18 ; Holland, Oscar; Sontag; 21; Col.
6/15/18; Davis, John H.; Rocky Mount; 25; Col.; Vol.
   "   ; Hopkins, M.H.; Sontag; 28; Col.; Vol.
7/15/18; Belcher, W.L.; Sontag; 28; Col.
6/15/18; Hicks, A.J.; Rocky Mount; 22; Col.; Vol.
   "   ; Phelps, Daniel; Boone Mill; 24; Col.; Vol.
6/18/18; Thomas, Raymond; Rocky Mount; 22; Col. Vol.
   "   ; Holland, Robert; Scruggs; 26; Col.
   "   ; Patterson, Stephen; Redwood; 23; Col.
   "   ; Starkey, Albert M.; Wirtz; 26; Col.
   "   ; Boyd, S.E.S.; Callaway; 22; Col.
   "   ; Hale, J.S.; Wirtz; 23; Col.
8/2/18; James, Jesse; Pen Hook; 21; Col.
   "   ; Spencer, Archer; Union Hall; 24; Col.
6/18/18; Pinkard, Jabe; Figsboro; 21; Col.
7/15/18; Lawson, Doctor T.; Boone Mill; 30; Col.
   "   ; Potter, S.W.; Pen Hook; 27; Col.
   "   ; Gravely, Nathan; Sydnorsville; 26; Col.
   "   ; Nelson, Hobart; Boone Mill; 23; Col.
   "   ; Young, Samuel D.; Rocky Mount; 29; Col.
   "   ; Hagwood, Ernest; Rocky Mount; 22; Col.
   "   ; Tyree, James; Rocky Mount; 27; Col.

Date of Muster; Name; Address; Age; etc.
5/9/18; Wagner, J.L.; Ferrum; 22
3/28/18; Robertson, J.W.; Hardy; 31
   "      ; Slone, T.D.; Ferrum; 23
   "      ; Taylor, J.L.; Rocky Mount; 25
   "      ; Metts, W.H.; Figsboro; 23
7/15/18; Tyree, J.J.; Rocky Mount; 25
3/31/18; Crook, C.R.; Taylors Store; 27
3/28/18; Jones, B.E.; Scruggs; 21
   "      ; Davis, Henry; Wirtz; 21
   "      ; Atkins, J.A.; Philpott; 23
5/9/18; Kempleton,J.W.; Callaway; 28
3/28/18; Underwood, James A.; Nowlins Mill; 26
5/9/18 ; Anderson, R.N.; Redwood; 23
   "      ; Hodges, Bill; Glade Hill; 21
7/21/18; Angle, Kent W.; Wirtz; 31
5/9/18; Davidson, L.R.; Pen Hook; 24
   "      ; Wray, Claude; Rocky Mount; 21
   "      ; Stanley, J.W.; Rocky Mount; 24
5/22/18; Minter, Toney O.; Figsboro; 22; Vol.; Tr. Detachment, U.Va.
5/25/18; Pagans, R.T.; Scruggs; 24
5/24/18; Powell, W.R.; Pen Hook; 23
   "      ; Lumsden, Clarence; Boone Mill; 23
   "      ; Barnhart, Ira Jos.; Wirtz; 26
6/23/18; Gibson, Benj.; Dillons Mill; 24
7/29/18; Waid, C.E.; Rocky Mount; 28
7/21/18; Basham, J.L.; Hardy; 21
5/24/18; Clark, F.L.; Henry; 25
   "      ; Lipscomb, S.E.; Henry; 21
5/5/18; Menefee, L.M.; Rocky Mount; 26; Vol.; Tr. Detach. Lehigh, Pa
5/24/18; Love, Robt.; Sydnorsville; 29
7/21/18; Hancock, P.E.; Rocky Mount; 29
5/24/18; Durham, J.A.; Scruggs; 23
7/21/18; Willard, J.D.; Taylors Store; 24
5/22/18; Naff, W.H.; Boone Mill; 25; Vol.; Tr. D. U.Va.
5/24/18; Helms, T.E.; Callaway; 24
5/9/18; Angle, C.S.; Wirtz; 24
5/24/18; Young, Roy G.; Sydnorsville; 21
5/24/18; Gibson, Fletcher G; Sontag; 23
   "      ; Willis, W.F.; Rocky Mount; 23
   "      ; Poindexter, R.H.; Union Hall; 21
   "      ; Akers, Archie Lee; Callaway; 21
   "      ; Hudson, Frank; Taylors Store; 22
   "      ; Ferguson, A.M.; Union Hall; 22
8/7/18; Fralin, J.F.; Glade Hill; 24
8/21/18; Montgomery, C.A.; Wirtz; 28; Field Artill., Manassas, Va.
       Webb, Posey Lee
       Angle, Buford B.; Vol.
       Angle, Lewis; Vol.
       Peak, W. D.; Vol.
       Shoaf, Ralph W.; Vol.
       Saunders, Edward W., Jr.; Vol.
       Roberts, W. Saunders; Vol.
       Greer, W.M.; Vol.
       Greer, Edwin; Vol.

Greer, Tom W.; Vol.
Joplin, Joe S.; Vol.
Montgomery, J.N., Jr.; Vol.
Cooper, Posey F.; Vol.
Morris, Bryant M.; Vol.
Menefee, Moton; Vol.
Melton, R.Y.; Vol.
Kittinger, O.T.; Vol.
Carroll, A.N.; Vol.
Dudley, G. C.; Vol.
Goggin, J.L.; Vol.
Hopkins, Walter L.; Vol.
Saunders, John I.; Vol.
Montgomery, John E.; Vol.
Davis, B.A., Jr.; Vol.
Angle, C.D.; Vol.
Divers, D.S.; Vol.
Hopkins, Clark D.; Vol.

FRANKLIN COUNTY GRANTS OR PATENTS

(From the Land Books in the Land Office, Richmond)

BOOK A

| PAGE | NAME | DATE | ACRES | LOCATION |
|---|---|---|---|---|
| 11 | William Furgason | 20 Oct. 1779 | 427 | On Nicholas's Creek, adjoining land of Alley. |
| 13 | John Doughton | 20 Oct. 1779 | 198 | On the branches of Chestnut Creek. |
| 14 | Thomas Prunty | 20 Oct. 1779 | 354 | On waters of Snow Creek adjoining land of Jeremiah Morrow. |
| 16 | Peter Gruheart (Gearhart) | 20 Oct. 1779 | 343 | On the head of Hatchett Run and Pounding Mill Branch waters of Pigg River. |
| 18 | James Standefer, Sr. | 20 Oct. 1779 | 493 | On Stony Creek, adjoining William Davis. |
| 25 | Henry Jones | 20 Oct. 1779 | 288 | On Hatchett Run and branches of Pigg River. |
| 33 | John Robinson | 26 Oct. 1779 | 78 | On the waters of Pigg River, adjoining Callaway's land. |
| 36 | Peter Gilliam | 20 Oct. 1779 | 112 | On Blackwater River, adjoining Chirtwood's land. |
| 54 | William Hurd | 2 Nov. 1779 | 335 | On Indian Branch of Snow Creek, adjoining the lands of Randolph and Morrow. |
| 55 | Thomas and Swinfield Hill, Executors and Legatees of Robert Hill, dec'd. | 20 Oct. 1779 | 468 | On Hatchett Run. |
| 65 | Israel Standefer | Oct. 20, 1779 | 600 | On Standefer's Branch. |
| 65 | Daniel Spangleg | Oct. 20, 1779 | 197 | On south side of Pigg River, adjoining William Cook. |
| 91 | John Kemp | Oct. 20, 1779 | 345 | Beginning, etc., on Camp Branch of Black water, adjoining the land of Edmondson. |
| 101 | Thomas Hill | Oct. 20, 1779 | 278 | On the south side of Pigg River and adjoining Doughton's land. |
| 115 | John Willis | Oct. 20, 1779 | 174 | On Hatchett Run, adjoining Henry Jones' land |

186

| PAGE | NAME | DATE | ACRES | LOCATION |
|------|------|------|-------|----------|
| 124 | Josaih Carter | Oct. 20, 1779 | 200 | On both sides of Blackwater River. |
| 131 | John Ramsey | Oct. 20, 1779 | 346 | On the branches of Chestnut Crk., adjoining Standefer's land. |
| 135 | John Willis | Oct. 20, 1779 | 384 | On the waters of Hatchett Run, adjoining Turnpin's land. |
| 136 | James Cooly | Oct. 20, 1779 | 154 | On the north branches of the North Fork of Chestnut Creek. |
| 141 | David Prewit | Oct. 20, 1779 | 264 | On Camp's Branch of Snow Creek, adjoining his own land. |
| 147 | Henry Willis | Oct. 20, 1779 | 62 | On a branch of Blackwater, adjoining Hilton's land. |
| 164 | William Mavity | Oct. 20, 1779 | 366 | On the north branches of Pigg River, adjoining the land of Hill, Jones, etc. |
| 258 | William Akers | 1 Feb. 1780 | 400 | On Lazy Run of Blackwater River, adjoining Thomas Miller. |
| 451 | Stephen Heard | 20 June, 1780 | 342 | On Blackwater River, adjoining John Heard. |
| 480 | John Dickenson | 26 June, 1780 | 466 | On the Cool Branch of Blackwater River, adjoining land of Cowan. |
| 545 | John Tunley | 4 July, 1780 | 145 | On the branches of the Crabtree Fork of Snow Creek. |
| 571 | Stephen Heard | 5 July, 1780 | 254 | On the branches of Blackwater River, adjoining Ward's land. |
| 604 | James Prunty | 7 July, 1780 | 232 | On the branches of Grass Fork of Snow Creek, adjoining Randolph's land, etc. |
| 552 | Edward Richards | 15 July, 1780 | 230 | On the North Fork of Chestnut Creek adjoining James Smith. |
| 656 | Michael Dunn | 14 July, 1780 | 120 | On the branches of Snow Creek, adjoining Richard Vamon. |
| 668 | Tully Choice | 14 July, 1780 | 147 | On the Fork of Guthrie's Run, adjoining his own land and the land of Heard. |
| 673 | William Ryon | 14 July, 1780 | 202 | On the branches of the Grassy Fork of Snow Creek, adjoining Bradshaw's land. |

| PAGE | NAME | DATE | ACRES | LOCATION |
|------|------|------|-------|----------|
| 675 | John Hargar | 14 July, 1780 | 152 | On the waters of the North Fork of Chestnut Creek, adjoining Richards' land. |
| 118 | Robert Mason | 20 Oct. 1779 | 236 | On both sides of the Muddy Fork of Chestnut Creek, adjoining Frazer's land. |

## BOOK B

| PAGE | NAME | DATE | ACRES | LOCATION |
|------|------|------|-------|----------|
| 1 | Thomas and Swinfield Hill, Executors and Legatees of Robert Hill, dec'd. | 8 Nov. 1779 | 468 | On the Meadow Branch, adjoining Hill's old Survey etc. |
| 3 | Daniel Spangler | 8 Nov. 1779 | 30 | On Pigg River, adjoining his own land. |
| 4 | William Mavity | 8 Nov. 1779 | 193 | On the South Fork of Pigg River, adjoining Thomas Hutchings |
| 4 | John Huff | 8 Nov. 1779 | 82 | On the South Fork of Pigg River, adjoining his own and Jame Rentfroe's land. |
| 6 | Thomas and Swinkfield Hill, Executors and Legatees of Robert Hill, dec'd. | 10 Nov. 1779 | 378 | On the Meadow Branch and McDowel's Branch |
| 6 | William Menifee | 10 Nov. 1779 | 212 | On both sides of Pigg River, adjoining Callaway's land. |
| 7 | Thomas Hail | 10 Nov. 1779 | 75 | On both sides of Pigg River. |
| 8 | John Wilson | 10 Nov. 1779 | 176 | Adjoining his own land he now lives on, on the South Fork of Blackwater River. |
| 10 | Daniel Spangler | 10 Nov. 1779 | 84 | On the branches of Blackwater, adjoining Joseph Byrd and James Rentfroe. |
| 11 | John Kemp | 10 Nov. 1779 | 172 | On the south side of Blackwater River, adjoining Grier's land. |
| 14 | William Young | 10 Nov. 1779 | 250 | On Cole's Creek and Blackwater River. |

| PAGE | NAME | DATE | ACRES | LOCATION |
|---|---|---|---|---|
| 15 | John Ramsey | 10 Nov. 1779 | 115 | On Chestnut Creek. |
| 17 | Lewis Jinkings | 10 Nov. 1779 | 335 | On Turkey Creek a north branch of Pigg River. |
| 17 | David Prewitt | 10 Nov. 1779 | 255 | On both sides of Camp Branch of Snow Creek. |
| 18 | John Willis | 10 Nov. 1779 | 391 | On the waters of Hatchett Run. |
| 20 | Joseph Bowling | 10 Nov. 1779 | 264 | On the head of Chestnut Creek a branch of Town Creek. |
| 21 | John Dickinson | 10 Nov. 1779 | 206 | On both sides of Pigg River. |
| 23 | Thomas Hail | 10 Nov. 1779 | 52 | On a branch of Pigg River, adjoining the land he now lives on. |
| 25 | James Martin | 10 Nov. 1779 | 375 | On the branches of Chestnut Creek, adjoining David Haley. |
| 28 | Amose Richardson | 12 Nov. 1779 | 292 | On the Grassy Fork of Snow Creek and on both sides thereof. |
| 29 | John Dickenson | 16 Nov. 1779 | 656 | On the South Fork of Stony Creek, adjoining Luke Standifer. |
| 31 | Thomas Hickerson | 16 Nov. 1779 | 342 | On Mountain Creek on Pigg River. |
| 35 | James Turpin | 2 Nov. 1779 | 100 | On the branches of Blackwater and Pigg Rivers, adjoining his own land and the land of Tolbot, etc. |
| 44 | Israel Standifer | 10 Nov. 1779 | 230 | On Standifer's Creek a branch of Blackwater River. |
| 45 | John Hartwell | 10 Nov. 1779 | 209 | On the north side of Pigg River on Robertson's Branch. |
| 51 | Swinkfield Hill | 10 Nov. 1779 | 186 | On Pigg River, adjoining Bates's land. |
| 69 | Thomas and Swinkfield Hill, Executors and Legatees of Robert Hill, dec'd. | 20 Nov. 1779 | 371 | On the south side of Pigg River, adjoining John Furgason. |
| 70 | Thomas and Swinkfield Hill, Executors and Legatees of Robert Hill, dec'd. | 22 Nov. 1779 | 266 | On the south side of Pigg River, adjoining Swinkfield Hill's. |
| 71 | William McVeaty | 22 Nov. 1779 | 140 | On Pigg River, adjoining Thomas Jones. |
| 341 | Peter Saunders | 22 June 1780 | 186 | On the head branches of Irven's River. |

| PAGE | NAME | DATE | ACRES | LOCATION |
|------|------|------|-------|----------|
| 341 | Peter Saunders | 22 June 1780 | 156 | On Otter Creek, adjoining Smith's land. |
| 345 | Luke Standifer | 22 June 1780 | 324 | On Blackwater River, adjoining John Kemp's land. |
| 349 | Shadrack Woodson | 22 June 1780 | 79 | Adjoining Stephen Lee's land on the waters of Blackwater River. |
| 367 | Shadrack Woodson | 22 June 1780 | 154 | On the waters of Blackwater River and adjoining Richard Doggatt. |
| 392 | William Ryon | 13 July 1780 | 242 | On the Grassy Fork of Snow Creek. |
| 412 | Philip Hutchison | 14 July 1780 | 274 | On Buck Branch of Snow Creek. |

## BOOK C

| PAGE | NAME | DATE | ACRES | LOCATION |
|------|------|------|-------|----------|
| 20 | John Dickenson | 1 Feb. 1781 | 279 | On the south side of Pigg River, adjoining Early and Callaway's land. |
| 24 | William Weaks | 1 Feb. 1781 | 447 | On the North Fork of Story Creek, adjoining Rentfroe etc. |
| 28 | William Farguson | 1 Feb. 1781 | 169 | On the branches of the South Fork of Pigg River, adjoining Robert Jones. |
| 31 | John Swilivant | 1 Feb. 1781 | 210 | On the south side of Blackwater River, adjoining Jeremiah Sowsbury. |
| 37 | James Callaway | 1 Feb. 1781 | 707 | On the branches of Chestnut Creek, adjoining Samuel Patterson. |
| 131 | Solomon Davis | 1 Feb. 1781 | 162 | On both sides of Pigg River, adjoining Patterson's land. |
| 231 | John Dickenson | 1 Feb. 1781 | 219 | On both sides of Pigg River, adjoining William Hodges' land. |
| 445 | William Young | 1 Mar. 1781 | 379 | On the Fish Fork of Snow Creek. |
| 462 | Isham Hodges | 1 Mar. 1781 | 193 | On Chestnut Creek, adjoining Robert Grimmitt. |
| 507 | John Dickenson | 1 Mar. 1781 | 420 | On Pigg River, adjoining Isham Hodges. |

| PAGE | NAME | DATE | ACRES | LOCATION |
|---|---|---|---|---|
| 514 | James Turpine | 1 Mar. 1781 | 225 | On the branches of Hatchett Run and Pigg River. |
| 450 | William Young | 1 Mar. 1781 | 330 | On the waters of Snow Creek, adjoining James Keff. |

## BOOK D

| PAGE | NAME | DATE | ACRES | LOCATION |
|---|---|---|---|---|
| 5 | Thomas Flower | 20 July 1780 | 327 | On the head of Runnett Bag Creek, a branch of Ewin River. |
| 40 | John Ward | 20 July 1780 | 327 | On Runnett Bag Creek. |
| 42 | John Ward | 20 July 1780 | 138 | On the draughts of Wagion and Joint-crack Creek. |
| 44 | Jeremiah Early & James Callaway | 20 July 1780 | 40 | It being More's Entry No. 66 by some called the Bald Knob. |
| 97 | James Standeford | 1 Sept. 1780 | 224 | On Story Creek. |
| 97 | William Davis | 1 Sept. 1780 | 327 | On Story Creek, adjoining Dillingham's line. |
| 132 | Michael Real | 1 Sept. 1780 | 178 | On Nicholas's Creek, adjoining John Jones, etc. |
| 133 | Jacob Atkins (Ferrum Training School is probably on this old tract) | 1 Sept. 1780 | 404 | On the South Branches of Pigg River near the head of the North Fork of Story Creek and a Knobb called Jones' Knobb. |
| 159 | Stepehen Heard | 1 Sept. 1780 | 170 | On Blackwater River, adjoining William Heard. |
| 160 | Robert Pruntey | 1 Sept. 1780 | 76 | On the waters of Pigg River. |
| 161 | John Forguson | 1 Sept. 1780 | 229 | On both sides of Jumping Branch of Story Creek. |
| 167 | William Ferguson | 1 Sept. 1780 | 93 | On the South Fork of Pigg River, adjoining James Rentfroe. |
| 170 | John Ferguson | 1 Sept. 1780 | 66 | On Pigg River, adjoining Cole's land. |
| 176 | John Forguson | 1 Sept. 1780 | 275 | On the branches of Pigg River, adjoining his own land. |
| 286 | William Haynes | 1 Sept. 1780 | 193 | On the North Branches of Pigg River on a branch called Dinner Creek. |
| 330 | William Evans | 11 Dec. 1780 | 130 | On both sides of the North Fork of Chestnut Creek. |

BOOK D

| PAGE | NAME | DATE | ACRES | LOCATION |
|------|------|------|-------|----------|
| 331 | John Huff | 11 Dec. 1780 | 308 | On the waters of Turner's Creek and branches of Pigg River. |
| 334 | John Farguson | 11 Dec. 1780 | 230 | On the south side of Pigg River, adjoining William Davis's land. |
| 337 | Darby Ryon | 11 Dec. 1780 | 370 | On the branches of Pigg River, adjoining Thomas Jones. |
| 339 | Darby Ryon | 11 Dec. 1780 | 268 | On Pigg River and branches thereof, adjoining Miller Doggett. |
| 372 | John Stuart | 1 Feb. 1781 | 225 | On Blackwater River, adjoining John Clay. |
| 373 | Walter Maxey | 1 Feb. 1781 | 228 | On Smith's River, adjoining the land of John Rieve. |
| 375 | William Mavity | 1 Feb. 1781 | 285 | Adjoining William Weak and Philip Sheridan. |
| 382 | Philip Sheridan | 1 Feb. 1781 | 362 | On the North Fork of Story Creek. |
| 392 | James Standefer, Sr. | 1 Feb. 1781 | 374 | On Story Creek, adjoining James Standefer, Jr. |
| 501 | Isham Hodges | 1 Feb. 1781 | 249 | On the branches of Chestnut Creek and adjoining Dickenson's land. |
| 531 | Henry Tate | 1 Feb. 1781 | 172 | On the branches of Smith's River and adjoining Randolph's land. |
| 566 | John Jones | 1 Mar. 1781 | 391 | On the branches of Turner's Creek and Nicholas's Creek, adjoining Thomas Jones. |
| 616 | Francis Kerby | 1 Mar. 1781 | 584 | On the Pole Cat Branch of Pigg River on Coon's Creek. |
| 617 | Robert Bolton | 1 Mar. 1781 | 1,319 | On both sides of Snow Creek, adjoining Copeland's Order line. |
| 717 | Josiah Hodges | 1 Mar. 1781 | 173 | On both sides of Pigg River, adjoining Richard Whitton. |
| 746 | Jesse Heard | 1 Mar. 1781 | 183 | On the north side of Pigg River, adjoining Darby Ryon. |

| PAGE | NAME | DATE | ACRES | LOCATION |
|------|------|------|-------|----------|
| 77 | Stepehn Heard | 20 July 1780 | 1,245 | On the branches of Camp Branch and Cedar Run, between Pigg River and Blackwater River. |
| 23 | John Ward | 20 July 1780 | 135 | On the North Fork of Turkey Cock Creek and the branches of Runnett Bag. |
| 35 | John Ward | 20 July 1781 | 318 | On the south side of Runnett Bag Creek of Smith's River. |
| 38 | Edward Choat,Jr. | 20 July 1780 | 253 | On the South Fork of Doe Run. |
| 41 | Edward Choat | 20 July 1780 | 485 | On Doe Run. |
| 42 | Archibald Grayham | 20 July 1780 | 900 | On Chestnut Creek, adjoining Robert Hill's land. |
| 45 | Smith Webb | 20 July 1780 | 129 | On Doe Creek, adjoining his own land. |
| 46 | Jeremiah Earley & James Callaway | 20 July 1780 | 374 | On both sides of Puping of Pigg River. |
| 49 | Edward Choat | 20 July 1780 | 295 | On the south branches of Pigg River, adjoining John Holloway. |
| 52 | Jeremiah Earley and Company. | 20 July 1780 | 1,196 | On the branches of Blackwater River and Pigg River, adjoining John Savarywood. |
| 53 | Jeremiah Earley & James Callaway. | 20 July 1780 | 1,1057 | On Pigg River and north branches thereof, adjoining Robertson, Hill, etc. |
| 54 | Jeremiah Earley & James Callaway | 20 July 1781 | 2,256 | On the branches of Pigg and Blackwater, adjoining Manifee. |
| 57 | Jeremiah Earley & James Callaway | 20 July 1781 | 533 | On the south branch of Pigg River, adjoining John Furguson. |
| 72 | Gasper Houser | 20 July 1781 | 426 | On the North Fork of Grassy Fork of Chestnut Creek, adjoining James Martin. |
| 76 | Robert Hodges | 20 July 1781 | 193 | On Chestnut Creek, adjoining Samuel Patterson. |
| 321 | Jonathan Davis | 20 July 1781 | 530 | On the waters of Chestnut Creek, adjoining Patterson, etc. |
| 432 | John Davis | 1 Sept. 1780 | 289 | On Owne's Creek of Pigg River, adjoining his own land. |
| 558 | Robert Hill | 1 Sept. 1780 | 313 | On both sides of Pigg River. |

| PAGE | NAME | DATE | ACRES | LOCATION |
|------|------|------|-------|----------|
| 561 | Capt. Thomas Jones | 1 Sept. 1780 | 393 | On Turner's Creek and Nicholas's Creek. |
| 562 | John Grimmet | 1 Sept. 1780 | 800 | On the south side of Pigg River and adjoining Robert Hill. |
| 601 | James Standifer | 1 Sept. 1780 | 411 | On the head branches of the South Fork of Story Creek, adjoining Luke Standefer. |
| 620 | John Jones | 1 Sept. 1780 | 110 | On both sides of the South Fork of Pigg River. |
| 621 | John Bibe | 1 Sept. 1780 | 82 | On both sides of Daniel Mill Creek of Blackwater River. |
| 631 | Robert Kelly | 1 Sept. 1780 | 70 | On the draughts of Nicholas's Creek. |
| 632 | Thomas and Swinkfield Hill, Executors and Legatees of Robert Hill, dec'd. | 1 Sept. 1780 | 159 | On both sides of Blackwater River, adjoining John Stephenson. |
| 633 | James Standeford | 1 Sept. 1780 | 177 | On the branches of Story Creek. |
| 634 | Jesse Clay | 1 Sept. 1780 | 142 | In the Parish of St. Patrick, on Blackwater River, adjoining Stephen Heard. |
| 647 | Thomas Hail | 1 Sept. 1780 | 200 | On Pigg River, adjoining Mavity's land. |
| 649 | Joshua Rentfroe | 1 Sept. 1780 | 110 | On the branches of Blackwater River, adjoining William Cook. |
| 844 | Joel Ragland | 11 Dec. 1780 | 160 | On a branch of Pigg River, called Turner's Creek, adjoining Mavily's land. |
| 845 | Joel Ragland | 11 Dec. 1780 | 441 | On the branches of Pigg River, adjoining William Mavily's land. |
| 846 | John Murphy | 11 Dec. 1780 | 336 | On the waters of Pigg River near the Great Mountain, adjoining Joseph Hail. |
| 851 | John Brammer | 11 Dec. 1780 | 248 | On White Oak Creek. |
| 852 | Richard Macoy | 11 Dec. 1780 | 377 | On branches of Blackwater River. |

## BOOK F

| PAGE | NAME | DATE | ACRES | LOCATION |
|---|---|---|---|---|
| 50 | Stepehn Heard | 10 April 1781 | 303 | On the branches of Blackwater River, adjoining Blankinship's land. |
| 162 | John O'Bryan | 1 June 1782 | 178 | On waters of Nicholas's Creek, adjoining Dennis O'Bryan. |
| 190 | Robert Grimmet | 1 June 1782 | 195 | On branches of Chestnut Creek. |

## BOOK G

| PAGE | NAME | DATE | ACRES | LOCATION |
|---|---|---|---|---|
| 143 | Thomas Evans | 1 Sept. 1782 | 378 | On the branches of Blackwater and Pigg Rivers. |
| 198 | Robert Hairstone | 1 Sept. 1782 | 153 | Adjoining his own lines on Running Bag Creek. |
| 204 | Samuel Patterson | 1 Sept. 1782 | 140 | On Gap Branch of Chestnut Creek. |
| 206 | William Cook | 1 June 1782 | 107 | On the North Fork of Pigg River, adjoining James Rentfroe. |
| 209 | Joseph Davis | 1 June 1782 | 566 | On the branches of Nicholas's Creek. |
| 209 | Samuel Hairstone | 1 June 1782 | 236 | On the branches of Nicholas's Creek, adjoining James Standifer. |
| 210 | Samuel Patterson | 1 June 1782 | 333 | On Hades Gap, a branch of Chestnut Creek. |
| 211 | William Cook | 1 June 1782 | 187 | On Hatchett Run, adjoining the land of Callaway. |
| 212 | John Heard | 1 June 1782 | 413 | On the Foul Ground Branch, adjoining Gilmore, Hartwell, etc. |
| 212 | Luke Thornton | 1 June 1782 | 237 | On Chestnut Creek, adjoining Walton's Order line. |
| 216 | Robert Hairstone | 1 June 1782 | 774 | On Runnett Bag Creek, adjoining Mead's land. |
| 218 | Lansford Hall | 1 June 1782 | 202 | On the north side of Pigg River, adjoining Dickenson. |

| PAGE | NAME | DATE | ACRES | LOCATION |
|---|---|---|---|---|
| 246 | William Warrain | 1 Nov. 1782 | 313 | On the branches of Chestnut Creek, adjoining Johnston. |
| 250 | Daniel Ross | 1 Nov. 1782 | 260 | On the north side of Smith's River and on Nicholas's Creek. |
| 215 | Robert Hairstone | 1 June 1782 | 132 | On the waters of Runnett Bag Creek, adjoining his own land. |
| 215 | James Edmundson | 1 June 1782 | 180 | On the south side of Blackwater River on both sides of Standefer's Creek. |

## BOOK H

| PAGE | NAME | DATE | ACRES | LOCATION |
|---|---|---|---|---|
| 9 | Stephen Heard | 7 May 1783 | 460 | On the south side of Blackwater River, adjoining Richard Bailey. |
| 10 | Stephen Heard | 7 May 1783 | 269 | On the south side of Blackwater River, adjoining Bennian's line. |
| 62 | Henry Tate | 27 May 1783 | 200 | On the north side of Smith's Creek, adjoining Randolph otherwise Hairston. |
| 230 | William Rentfroe | 30 June 1783 | 145 | On Runnett Bag Creek. |
| 243 | Daniel Prilleman | 17 June 1783 | 285 | On the waters of Nicholas's Creek, adjoining Dennis O'Brian. |
| 251 | Nathan Sellars | 3 July 1783 | 164 | On the Pine Spur on the top of the Blue Ridge. |
| 255 | Israel Standefer | 30 June 1783 | 419 | On the head branches of Bull Run and Standefer's Creek. |
| 297 | Aaron Wousley | 3 July 1783 | 286 | On the waters of Nicholas Creek. |
| 326 | Shadrack Woodson | 17 June 1783 | 134 | On the rich run of Blackwater River. |
| 369 | Robert Stogdan | 30 June 1783 | 662 | On Nicholas's Creek, adjoining the land of Dennis O'Bryan. |
| 372 | Archelaus White | 25 June 1783 | 122 | On the south branches of the North Fork of Blackwater River, adjoining his own land. |

| PAGE | NAME | DATE | ACRES | LOCATION |
|------|------|------|-------|----------|
| 411 | William Farguson | 27 Aug. 1783 | 664 | On the branches of Nicholas's Creek, adjoining William Standefer. |
| 438 | William Kelley | 1 Sept. 1783 | 158 | On the Fork of Blackwater River, adjoining Stout's land. |
| 452 | John Keile | 1 Sept. 1783 | 444 | On the branches of Nicholas's Creek, adjoining Robert Stockton. |
| 459 | Joseph Lewis | 1 Sept. 1783 | 257 | On the head branches of Pigg River, beginning where Beck's line adjoins Greer's. |
| 461 | Joseph Lewis | 1 Sept. 1783 | 174 | On the head branches of Pigg River, adjoining his new survey. |
| 507 | John Lumsden | 1 Sept. 1783 | 409 | On the branches of Blackwater River, adjoining John Nowlin. |
| 517 | John Hilton | 3 Oct. 1783 | 200 | On both sides of Blackwater River, beginning at Randolph's corner. |
| 520 | Edward Choat | 1 Sept. 1783 | 307 | On the branches of Doe Creek, adjoining Edward Choat, Jr. |
| 572 | Samuel Patterson & William Ryan | 4 Oct. 1783 | 900 | On the branches of Pigg River and Doe Creek, adjoining Holloway's line. |

## BOOK I

| PAGE | NAME | DATE | ACRES | LOCATION |
|------|------|------|-------|----------|
| 13 | Jacob Brillemon | 23 May 1783 | 250 | On the south branch of Blackwater, adjoining Daniel Donohoo. |
| 231 | Robert Jones, Sr. | 6 Dec. 1783 | 160 | On the South Fork of Pigg River, adjoining his own land. |
| 236 | Jacob Prilliman, Jr. | 6 Dec. 1783 | 65 | On the north side of the South Fork of Blackwater River. |
| 352 | William Ferguson & William Mavity | 9 Feb. 1784 | 1,450 | On Story Creek, adjoining Ryon's land. |
| 357 | James Callaway | 9 Feb. 1784 | 402 | On the branches of Blackwater and Pigg River, adjoining his own and Bird's land. |

| PAGE | NAME | DATE | ACRES | LOCATION |
|------|------|------|-------|----------|
| 370 | John Henderson | 17 Feb. 1784 | 122 | On the south branches of the North Fork of Blackwater adjoining his own line. |
| 372 | Thomas Jones | 17 Feb. 1784 | 400 | On the South Fork of Pigg River, adjoining Robert Jones, Sr. |
| 383 | Edmund Sweeny | 24 Feb. 1784 | 346 | On both sides of Nicholas' Creek, adjoining O'Brian's and Ross's land. |
| 385 | John Rentfro | 21 Feb. 1784 | 300 | On the north branches of Pigg River, adjoining Jones, Geerhart, etc. |
| 394 | Robert Stockton | 25 Feb. 1784 | 52 | On the waters of Nicholas' Creek, adjoining his own land. |
| 400 | William Harrison | 3 Feb. 1784 | 111 | On both sides of Shooting Creek. |
| 447 | Robert Stockton | 27 Feb. 1784 | 286 | On the waters of Nicholas' Creek, adjoining his own land. |

BOOK K

| PAGE | NAME | DATE | ACRES | LOCATION |
|------|------|------|-------|----------|
| 101 | Benjamin Hale | 6 Dec. 1783 | 190 | On the north side of the South Fork of Pigg River. |
| 199 | Peter Huff | 3 Feb. 1784 | 26 | On both sides of the South Fork of Blackwater River, adjoining his own line. |
| 221 | Walter McCoy | 14 Feb. 1784 | 96 | On Turner's Creek, a branch of Pigg River, adjoining Smith's land. |
| 223 | William Weeks | 12 Feb. 1784 | 208 | On both sides of Runnett Bag Creek, adjoining William Kennedy. |
| 232 | Darby Ryon | 23 Feb. 1784 | 146 | On Nicholas's Creek, adjoining his own and Robert Jones' land. |

BOOK M

| PAGE | NAME | DATE | ACRES | LOCATION |
|------|------|------|-------|----------|
| 152 | John Craghead | 1 June 1784 | 270 | On the south side of Blackwater River, adjoining Samuel Smith. |

| PAGE | NAME | DATE | ACRES | LOCATION |
|------|------|------|-------|----------|
| 225 | Samuel Patterson | 1 June 1784 | 400 | On the South Fork of Doe Run, adjoining Smith's land. |

## BOOK P

| DATE | NAME | DATE | ACRES | LOCATION |
|------|------|------|-------|----------|
| 91 | Thomas and Swinfield Hill, heirs of Robert Hill, deceased. | 10 July 1784 | 391 | On the branches of Blackwater River and adjoining Thomason's line. |

## BOOK R

| DATE | NAME | DATE | ACRES | LOCATION |
|------|------|------|-------|----------|
| 12 | John Dickenson | 11 Aug. 1785 | 396 | On both sides of Snow Creek, adjoining Joshua Brock's land. |
| 380 | Solomon Davis | 20 Sept. 1785 | 85 | On both sides of Snow Creek, adjoining Joshua Brock's land. |

## BOOK S

| PAGE | NAME | DATE | ACRES | LOCATION |
|------|------|------|-------|----------|
| 105 | Joseph Hodges | 4 Aug. 1785 | 50 | On the south side of Pigg River, adjoining Richard Wilton, etc. |

## BOOK V

| PAGE | NAME | DATE | ACRES | LOCATION |
|------|------|------|-------|----------|
| 372 | James Prunty | 2 Dec. 1785 | 400 | On both sides of Ditto's Creek of Snow Creek, adjoining Caldwell's line. |

## BOOK W

| PAGE | NAME | DATE | ACRES | LOCATION |
|------|------|------|-------|----------|
| 266 | John Lumsden | 31 Mar. 1786 | 440 | On the Maple Swamp, a branch of Blackwater River. |

199

| PAGE | NAME | DATE | ACRES | LOCATION |
|------|------|------|-------|----------|
| 270 | John Dickinson | 31 Mar. 1786 | 162 | On the north side of Pigg River, adjoining Solomon Davis, etc. |

## BOOK Y

| PAGE | NAME | DATE | ACRES | LOCATION |
|------|------|------|-------|----------|
| 23 | James Callaway | 20 Dec. 1785 | 12,800 | In the counties of Bedford and Henry on Blackwater River, adjoining James Stephens, etc. |
| 490 | Benoni Perryman | 19 July 1786 | 400 | On the branches of Blackwater River, adjoining Richard Perryman. |

## BOOK 3

| PAGE | NAME | DATE | ACRES | LOCATION |
|------|------|------|-------|----------|
| 132 | Hugh Innes | 22 June 1786 | 933 | On both sides of Snow Creek and adjoining Randolph's line. |
| 298 | Benoni Perryman | 15 July 1786 | 340 | On the branches of Blackwater River, adjoining Israel Standafer. |

## BOOK 5

| PAGE | NAME | DATE | ACRES | LOCATION |
|------|------|------|-------|----------|
| 165 | Thomas Jones | 5 July 1786 | 600 | On branches of Runnett Bag Creek, adjoining John Mead. |

## BOOK 8

| PAGE | NAME | DATE | ACRES | LOCATION |
|------|------|------|-------|----------|
| 203 | Joel Walker | 11 Jan. 1787 | 226 | On branches of the North Fork of Pigg River, adjoining Joseph Lewis. |
| 395 | Ashford Napier | 23 Jan. 1787 | 188 | Near the head of the Maple Branch of Snow Creek, adjoining the land of David Prewet. |
| 642 | John Wilson | 14 May 1787 | 36 | On the South Fork of Blackwater River. |

## BOOK 9

| PAGE | NAME | DATE | ACRES | LOCATION |
|------|------|------|-------|----------|
| 108 | William Ferguson | 14 Apr. 1787 | 112 | On branches of Nicholas's Creek, adjoining Samuel Hairston, etc. |
| 119 | William Ferguson | 15 Apr. 1787 | 276 | On the south branches of Pigg River. |
| 348 | Joseph Lewis | 15 May 1787 | 40 | On the waters of the North Fork of Pigg River, adjoining his own land. |

## BOOK 10

| PAGE | NAME | DATE | ACRES | LOCATION |
|------|------|------|-------|----------|
| 366 | William Kennady, Sr. | 21 June 1787 | 551 | On head branches of Runnett Creek, adjoining Jones' land. |
| 448 | Allen Brock | 3 Aug. 1787 | 11 | On waters of Snow Creek, adjoining Copeland, Heard, etc. |
| 453 | William Kelly | 3 Aug. 1787 | 60 | On branches of Blackwater River, adjoining Price's land. |
| 605 | Samuel Patterson | 13 Sept. 1787 | 235 | On both sides of North Fork of Chestnut Creek, adjoining Callaway's land. |
| 721 | James Callaway and John Earley | 8 Oct. 1787 | 200 | On the north side of Pigg River, adjoining Swinfield Hill. |

## BOOK 11

| PAGE | NAME | DATE | ACRES | LOCATION |
|------|------|------|-------|----------|
| 28 | Samuel Patterson | 6 Feb. 1787 | 510 | On the South Branches of Chestnut Creek. |

## BOOK 12

| PAGE | NAME | DATE | ACRES | LOCATION |
|------|------|------|-------|----------|
| 729 | Samuel Patterson | 13 Sept. 1787 | 323 | On the branch of Chestnut Creek, adjoining Ramsey's line and others. |

BOOK 13

| PAGE | NAME | DATE | ACRES | LOCATION |
|---|---|---|---|---|
| 392 | John Willis | 31 July 1787 | 628 | On Cole's Creek, a branch of Blackwater River. |

BOOK 17

| PAGE | NAME | DATE | ACRES | LOCATION |
|---|---|---|---|---|
| 414 | Abraham Ritter | 9 July 1788 | 150 | On the branches of Lic] Run of Blackwater River, adjoining Callaway, etc. |

BOOK 20

| PAGE | NAME | DATE | ACRES | LOCATION |
|---|---|---|---|---|
| 260 | Jacob Prillemon | 18 Mar. 1789 | 167 | On the branches of Blackwater and Pigg Rivers. |

BOOK 29

| PAGE | NAME | DATE | ACRES | LOCATION |
|---|---|---|---|---|
| 538 | Thomas Crutcher, Guy Smith, John Ferguson and George Ferguson | 21 Nov. 1793 | 2,922 | In the Counties of Franklin and Henry on the waters of Chestnut and Reed Creeks. |

BOOK 30

| PAGE | NAME | DATE | ACRES | LOCATION |
|---|---|---|---|---|
| 115 | Samuel Patterson | 14 Aug. 1793 | 1,300 | On the waters of Doe Creek and of Chestnu· Creek, adjoining the land of Dickerson. |
| 229 | Hugh McWilliams | 19 Aug. 1794 | 35 | On the north branches of Snow Creek. |

BOOK 31

| PAGE | NAME | DATE | ACRES | LOCATION |
|---|---|---|---|---|
| 45 | Hugh Woods | 22 Nov. 1793 | 126 | On the head branches o] Chestnut Creek, ad-joining Robert Woods. |

| PAGE | NAME | DATE | ACRES | LOCATION |
|------|------|------|-------|----------|
| | Jacob McNeal | 19 Aug. 1794 | 312 | On So. side Blackwater. |
| | Jacob McNeal | 12 Sept. 1796 | 50 | On So. side Blackwater. |
| | Thomas Miller | June 15, 1773 | 140 | On both sides the main south fork of the Blackwater River. |

N.B.  There is an old volume of land grant records in the Franklin County Clerk's Office, containing minute description of many of the tracts owned from 1795 to 1847.  There are many pen drawn maps in the book.

# THE TAX LISTS FOR 1786

The personal property and land tax lists of 1786 supply an excellent substitute for the Census Report of 1790, from which Franklin County was omitted. In the State Library at Richmond are to be found the personal property tax books of Franklin County beginning with 1786 and continuing through 1863 without a break, except for the year 1808 when Virginians paid no taxes. Beginning with 1787 and continuing through 1852 there are two books for each year. Beginning with 1853 there are three books for each year. There are 163 of these books. One of the books for 1845 is missing.

The following is a composite list made from the personal property tax book and the land tax book of 1786.

Aaron, William
Abshire, Abraham
Abshire, Christian
Abshire, Jacob
Abshire, Lodowick
Aday, Josiah
Aday, Walter
Adner, John
Agee, Joshua
Agee, Anthony
Agee, James
Agee, Matthew
Akers, William
Akin, Onecholas
Akin, James
Allen, Samuel
Altick, John
Anderson, James
Anderson, Peter
Anderson, William
Archey, Cornelius
Arthur, John
Arthur, Thomas
Atkins, David
Atkinson, Joel
Asbery, George
Austin, William

Bailey, James
Baley, Martha
Ball, James
Ball, William
Ballard, James
Ballard, Richard
Balp, Edward
Bandy, Richard
Banks, John
Banks, Samuel

Barksdill, John
Bartee, Nancy
Barnes, James
Bartee, William
Barton, David
Bates, Isaac
Bates, John
Beard, Edward
Beard, Samuel
Beaver, Christopher
Beek, Paul
Been, William
Beheler, David
Belcher, Isham
Belcher, James
Bell, William
Bennett, William
Bernan, Martain
Bernard, Nathan
Bernard, Walter
Bevers, James
Biby, John
Binnion, Isaac
Binnion, John
Binnion, Martin
Bird, James
Bird, John
Bird, Samuel
Blackburn, Jacob
Blain, John
Blair, Joseph
Blakley, Robert
Blankenship, Elisha
Blankenship, Hezekiah
Blankenship, Isham, Jr.
Blankenship, Isham, Sr.
Blankenship, Ligon
Blankenship, Peter

Blankenship, Richard
Blassingham, Philip
Bohanan, Henry
Bohanan, William
Boid, Samuel
Boon, Jacob
Boon, John
Booth, John
Booth, John Tim
Booth, Peter
Booth, Richard
Boulton, James
Boulton, Robert
Boulton, Robert Sr.
Boulton, Thomas
Bowman, John
Boyd, Ralph
Boyd, William
Bozel, John
Brock, Allen
Brook, Joshua
Brock, Moses
Brooks, William
Brower, Christian
Brower, John
Brown, Henry
Brown, Henry
Brown, Richard
Brown, William
Bryant, James
Bryant, John
Bryant, Lewis
Buckley, Samuel
Burdett, Tompkins
Burns, James
Burton, Seth

Caler, John

Callan, Samuel
Callaway, James
Campbell, John
Cantrell, Sarah
Caper, John
Carter, Bailey
Carter, John, Jr.
Carter, John, Sr.
Carter, Joseph
Carter, Robert, Jr.
Carter, Thomas
Chambus, John
Chandler, Daniel
Chandler, Thomas
Chandler, William
Charter, James
Charter, Thomas
Charter, William
Chestwood, Joel
Cheetwood, John, Sr.
Chitwood, William
Choal, Sebert
Choat, Edward, Jr.
Choat, Edward, Sr.
Choat, Isham
Choate, Augustine
Choice, Turley, Jr.
Choice, William
Christian, William
Christopher, William
Clack, Spencer
Clardy, Benjamin
Chateher, John
Claxton, David
Clay, William
Clayborn, John
Clower, Jacob
Coalman, James
Coapland, Richard
Coats, Charles
Coats, Jesse
Coats, Kinzie
Coats, Michael
Cockram, Abner
Cockram, John
Cockram, Samuel
Cockram, William
Cole, Mark
Commens, Thomas
Condee, William
Conner, William
Cook, Benjamin
Cook, Harman

Cooper, Ellis
Cooper, John
Corbin, Peter
Cornelius, George
Cowan, Robert
Cowden, James
Cowden, William
Cradler, Jacob
Craget, Peter
Cragg, Thomas
Cragg, William
Craghead, Peter
Craighead, John
Crowell, Zenus
Crump, William

Dangger, Ralph
Daniel, George
David, Absolome
David, Elizabeth
David, Isaac
Davis, John
Davis, Jonathan
Davis, Joseph
Davis, Lewis
Davis, Peter
Davis, Philip
Davis, Solomon
Davis, William
Davis, Zachariah
Delancy, Samuel
Demoss, Thomas
Demoss, William
Denoon, Hartmon
Devin, Daniel
Dickens, Jeremiah
Dickenson, John
Dickerson, John
Dickson, Nathaniel
Dillian, Samuel
Dillian, William
Dillinham, William
Dillion, Jesse
Dilmon, Daniel
Dillmon, Daniel
Dillmon, Jacob
Divers, John
Dodd, William
Doggett, Chattin
Doggett, Thomas, Jr.
Doram, Hartman
Dottson, Micajah
Drake, John

Drake, William
Dudley, Gwin
Dunn, Michel
Dunn, William
Durst, Samuel
Duvall, Benjamin
Duvall, Lewis
Duvall, Marine
Duvall, Skinner

Earley, Jeremiah
Earley, Jubel
Early, John
Earnest, George
Eddy, Woolby
Edmonds, Robert
Edmonson, Humphry
Edmonson, James
Edmonson, Richard
Edmonson, Richard, Jr.
Edwards, Abel
Edwards, Arthur
Edwards, James
Edwards, John
Elkins, Nathaniel
Ellis, John
Ellis, Joseph
Ellison, Amos
Ellison, John
Ellison, Thomas
Emmons, David
Epperson, John
Estis, Bottom
Estis, Elisha, Jr.
Estis, Elisha, Sr.
Estis, Joel
Estis, Mary
Estis, Richard
Estis, William
Eubanks, William
Evans, Thomas
Evans, William
Exceen, Daniel

Farley, Archibald
Farley, Daniel
Farley, Jeremiah
Farley, Matthew
Farley, Obediah
Farley, Stewart
Farley, Stephen
Ferguson, Alexander
Ferguson, George

Ferguson, Isham
Ferguson, John
Ferguson, John Sr.
Ferguson, John Jr.
Ferguson, William
Finney, Peter
Fitzsimmons, Patrick
Fitz, Simmons
Flory, Jacob Jr.
Flory, Jacob Sr.
Flory, Joseph
Fraser, John
French, Daniel, Jr.
French, Daniel, Sr.
French, James
French, John
Fristo, Robert
Frith, Joseph
Fuson, John

Gaskell, Enock
Geerheart, Leonard
Geerheart, Peter
Gillam, Peter
Gillaspy, Daniel
Gillaspy, John
Gisson, William
Glover, Richard
Good, Fanney
Gordon, Alexander
Gordon, Archibald
Graham, Archibald
Graham, Arthur
Graham, James
Granger, Joseph
Graveley, Joseph
Graves, William
Graves, William, Sr.
Gravit, Obediah
Greer, Ann
Greer, Aquilla
Greer, Benjamin
Greer, David
Greer, Greenberry
Greer, James
Greer, Joseph
Greer, Moses
Greer, Moses, Sr.
Greer, Nathan
Greer, Thomas (Estate)
Greer, William
Greer, Uriah
Griffith, Benjamin
Griffith, Owen

Griffith, William
Grigg, John
Grimmet, Robert
Grimmit, John
Guthrey, Henry
Guttery, David
Guttery, Henry
Guttery, John

Hairston, Robert, Esq.
Hairston, Samuel
Hale, Benjamin
Hale, Elizabeth
Hale, John
Hale, Joseph
Hale, Pearson
Hale, Thomas
Hall, Isham
Hall, Jesse
Hall, Lansford
Hall, Randolph
Hall, William
Halle, George
Hambrick, Joseph
Hammock, Ephraim
Hammock, Peter
Hammon, Richard
Hammon, Thomas
Hancock, Thomas
Handy, Isham
Handy, James
Handy, John
Hanes, John
Hardway, Stanfield
  (Dinwoody)
Hardin, Elexus
Hargar, John
Harkrider, Conrad
Harris, John
Harris, John
Harris, William
Harston, Peter
Hartwell, John
Hatcher, Archibald
Hatcher, Elijah
Hatcher, Edward
Hatcher, Farley
Haynes, George
Haynes, Henry Jr.
Haynes, Henry Sr.
Haynes, Parmenus
Haynes, William
Heard, Jesse

Heard, Stephen
Heard, William
Hedge, Enock
Henderson, Samuel
Hewlet, Martain
Hickerson, Thomas
Hickmond, Jacob
Hickly, John
Hill, Swinfield
Hill, Thomas
Hill, Violet
Hodges, Abednego
Hodges, Isaiah
Hodges, Isham
Hodges, Joseph
Hodges, Josiah
Hodges, Robert
Hodges, William
Hoff, John
Hoff, Peter
Hogan, Ann
Hogard, James
Holdman, John
Holladay, Robert
Hollan, Arah
Holland, Asa
Holland, Arah
Holland, Peter
Holland, Peter Jr.
Holland, Thomas
Holland, William
Holloway, John
Hook, John
Howser, Jasper
Hubbard, Eusabus
Hughes, Hugh
Hughton, Thomas
Hulcum, Uriah
Hunt, James
Hunt, Owen
Hunt, Thomas
Hunter, John
Hunter, Matthew
Hunter, William
Huston, Thomas
Hutcheson, Charles
Hutcheson, Paul
Hutcheson, Phillip
Hutcheson, William

Ingram, John
Ingram, William
Innes, Hugh

Jakes, John
James, Spencer James
Jamison, John Jr.
Jamison, Thomas
Jamison, William
Jenney, James
Jenny, Isaac
Jett, Daniel
Jett, Thomas
Jimmeson, William
Jimmeson, Thomas
Jinkins, William
Johnson, George
Johnson, John
Johnson, John G.
Jones, Abraham
Jones, Daniel
Jones, David
Jones, Elijah
Jones, George
Jones, Henry
Jones, John
Jones, John (Dinwoody)
Jones, Joseph
Jones, Rachel
Jones, Richard
Jones, Robert Sr.
Jones, Robert Jr.
Jones, Thomas
Jones, Zachariah

Keal, John
Kean, John
Keen, Elisha
Keen, Rachel
Keen, John
Kearby, David
Kearby, Francis
Kearby, Joseph
Keaton, William
Kelley, Andrew
Kelley, George
Kelley, John
Kelley, William
Kemp, John
Kemp, Thomas
Kensey, Jacob
Kennedy, James
Kennedy, John
Kennedy, William Jr.
Kennedy, William Sr.
Kenney, Jacob
Kennon, James
Kenney, Jacob

Kennon, James
Kenny, Jacob
Kerby, Frances
Kerby, Jessey
Kerby, Jessey Sr.
Kerby, John
King, Joseph
Kingary, Tobias
Kingrey, Jacob
Kingey, Henry

Landling, Samuel
Langdon, John
Lasswell, Moses
Laswell, Peter
Law, Henry
Law, Jesse
Law, John Jr.
Law, John Sr.
Law, Nathaniel
Law, William
Lazana, John
Lebrook, John
Lemon, Isaac
Lewis, James
Lewis, Joseph
Lewney, John
Lilley, Robert
Lister, Henry
Livsey, George
Livsey, Holliday
Livsey, John
Livsey, Peter
Livsey, Thomas
Long, Christopher Charles
Long, Thomas
Long, William
Lovell, Marcum
Lovin, Henry
Loyal, Joseph Brumsick
Lumden, John
Lumsdin, Charles
Lumsdin, Jeremiah
Lumsdin, John
Lutterell, Samuel Jr.
Lutterell, Samuel Sr.
Lyon, Edward
Lyon, Elisha

Maclary, Richard
Maddox, John
Maevey, James
Major, James
Malones, William

Mannin, Samuel
Marcum, James
Marcum, John
Marcum, Joseph
Marcum, Thomas
Marcum, William
Martin, Hugh
Martin, James
Martin, John
Martin, John Potter
Martin, William Jr.
Martin, William
Mason, James
Mason, Robert
Mattox, Michal
Maveaty, William
Maveaty, Robert
Maxcy, Jeremiah
Maxcy, Josiah
Maxcy, Walter
McCoy, James
McCoy, Samuel
McCoy, Walter
McCoy, William
McCravey, Elias
McGehee, Holdin
McGeorge, Lawrence
McGinnes, John
McGrady, Loughlin
McKenzie, James
McNeal, Jacob
McVey, James
McWilliams, Hugh
Meador, Isham
Meador, Jesse
Meador, Job
Meador, Joel Jr.
Meador, Joel Sr.
Meador, John Jr.
Meador, Jones
Meador, Joseph
Mealary, Richard
Menefee, George
Menefee, William Jr.
Menefee, William Sr.
Miles, John
Miles, Samuel
Miller, Chrisler
Miller, Daniel
Miller, George
Miller, Isaac
Miller, Jacob
Miller, Jacob Sr.
Miller, Jacob Jr.

Miller, Joseph
Miller, Samuel
Miller, Thomas
Miller, Thomas Jr.
Miller, Tobias
Miller, William
Mise, Benjamin
Moody, Thomas
Moore, Abraham
Moore, Jenny
Moore, Jesse
Moore, William
Mordica, Mosley
Morgain, David
Morgan, David
Mulling, William Jr.
Mullendore, Abram
Mullendore, Jacob
Mullins, William
Mustanuff, George

Naff, Jacob
Napier, Ashford
Napier, Robert
Nelson, William
Nichols, Floyd
Noffsinger, John
Nole, John
Nole, Joshua
Nowlin, Elizabeth
Nowlin, William

Oaks, John
Oaks, William
Obrian, Dennis
Oldakers, James
Oldakers, Jacob
Overlen (Overlee),
    Conrad

Pain, Thomas
Parberry, James
Parker, Thomas
Parrot, Nathaniel
Parrot, Thorp
Pasley, George
Pasley, Robert
Pate, Anthony
Patterson, Samuel
Patterson, William
    Ryan
Pattison, Samuel
Pedegoy, Joseph
Pedigoy, Edward

Peek, Abell
Peek, David
Peek, John
Peek, Jonathan
Peek, Samuel
Perdue, Meshack
Perrey, George
Perryman, Richard
Perryman, Robert
Peter, Stephen
Peters, Michael
Pinkard, Charles
Pinkard, Jane
Pinkard, James
Pinkard, John
Plasture, Thomas
Poteet, William
Potter, Benjamin Jr.
Potter, Benjamin Sr.
Potter, Lewis
Potter, Thomas
Powell, Robert
Pratt, John
Prewett, David
Prewett, Elisha
Prewett, John
Price, Jonathan
Price, Joseph
Prillamon, Daniel
Prillamon, Jacob
Prillamon, Jacob Jr.
Prillamon, John
Prunty, James
Prunty, Robert
Prunty, Thomas
Pugh, David
Purney, George

Radford, John
Radford, Richard
Ragland, Joel
Raines, Ambrous
Raley, Philip
Ramsey, Mary
Ramsey, Joseph
Ramsey, Thomas
Ranson, Charles
Ray, Moses
Ray, Philip
Randolph, Samuel
Read, Clemmons
Ready, Nathan
Real, Andrew
Real, George

Real, Michael
Redman, James
Redford, Richard
Redman, Stephen
Renno, John
Rentfro, Isaac
Rentfro, James
Rentfro, Jesse
Rentfro, John
Rentfro, Joshua
Rentfro, Mark
Rentfro, Moses
Rentfro, Samuel
Rentfro, William
Retter, Abraham
Retter, John
Richards, Edward
Richards, Robertson
Richards, Richard
Richards, Shadrack
Richardson, Amos Sr.
Richardson, Benjamin
Richardson, Daniel
Richardson, Edward
Richardson, John
Richardson, Jonathan
Richardson, Randolph
Richardson, Aaron
Richardson, Stanhope
Richardson, Thomas
Richardson, Turner
Richeson, Amos
Richeson, Jonathan
Rives, Frederick
Rives, Burwell
Roasin, Charles
Roberts, John
Roberts, Richard
Roberts, Thomas
Robertson, John
Robertson, Richard
Robertson, William
Robinson, John
Robinson, Richard
Robinson, Thomas
Rodgers, George
Rodgers, Henry
Rodgers, James
Rodgers, Josiah
Ross, Alexander
Ross, Daniel
Ross, David
Ross, William
Ruble, Owen

Rudy, Daniel
Ryan, Darbey
Ryan, Nathan
Ryan, William

Sandford, George
Sandford, John
Saunders, Peter
Scruggs, John
Seekman, Peter
Seerun, John
Sellers, Nathan
Shateen, William
Sheardon, Philip
Sheridan, Philip
Sherwood, Robert
Shield, John
Shrewsberry, Jeremiah
Shockley, David
Short, John
Sickmon, Peter
Simmons, Charles
Simmons, Joseph
Simmons, Peter
Simmons, William
Simpkins, William
Slone, James
Slone, Patrick
Slone, Thomas
Slone, William
Smith, Daniel
Smith, Elizabeth
Smith, Gideon
Smith, John
Smith, Peter
Smith, Phillimon
Smith, Samuel
Smith, Stephen
Smith, Thomas
Smith, William
Sneed, John
Southerland, Alexander
Southerland, Phillip
Southerland, Samuel
Spangle, Daniel
Spangle, Daniel, Jr.
Spangle, George
Spencer, Benjamin
Spencer, William Jr.
Standefer, Israel
Standefer, James Sr.
Standefer, James Jr.
Standefer, Luke
Standefer, William

Standley, Moses
Stanley, Richard
Stanley, William
Stanton, Thomas
Starkey, Joel
Starkey, John
Starkey, Jonathan
Starkey, Joshua
Staton, George
Stephens, John Sr.
Stephens, John
Stephens, William
Stevenson, William
Stewart, Barey
Stewart, Charles
Stewart, David
Stewart, Daniel
Stewart, James Jr.
Stewart, James Sr.
Stewart, John
Stewart, William
Stinnet, James
Stinnet, William
Stockton, Robert
Stokes, James
Stokley, Leavy
Stone, Eucebus
Stone, Stephen
Storm, John
Storm, Micajah
Storm, Peter
Stover, Jacob Jr.
Stover, Jacob Sr.
Strange, James
Street, Anthony
Sullivant, John
Sullivant, Samuel
Sullivant, Samuel
Swanson, Nathan
Swanson, William
Swanson, William Jr.
Swinney, Benjamin
Swinney, Edmund

Tarrant, Leonard
Taylor, John
Taylor, Robert
Taylor, Sarah
Taylor, Shelton
Teal, Adam
Teal, Nicholas
Terry, John
Terry, Thomas, Sr.
Terry, Thomas, Jr.

Terry, Thomas
Tharp, William
Thomas, David
Thomas, William
Thompson, Andrew
Thompson, Thomas
Thompson, William
Thornton, John Sr.
Thornton, Luke
Thorp, William
Throut, Mary
Tolbot, Matthew
Toney, William
Tounsend, Thomas
Trent, Bryant
Trent, Henry
Trent, John
Trent, William
Trueman, William
Tuggle, Lodowick
Turley, James
Turnbull, George
Turner, Daniel
Turner, Isaiah
Turner, James
Turpin, Margaret
Tyree, John
Twiner, John

Underwood, Samuel

Vandivender, Abraham
Vernall, Richard
Vincent, Charles
Vincent, William
Vinson, Charles
Vinson, William

Wade, Bartlet
Wade, Moses
Waggoner, Milker
Waldin, Nathan
Walker, James
Walker, Joel
Walton, William
Ward, Daniel
Ward, James
Ward, John
Warren, Drury
Warren, Henry
Warren, Thomas Sr.
Warren, William
Warren, Zacharian
Watts, Richard

Watts, Thomas
Wattson, Alexander
Webb, Jacob
Webb, James
Webb, Mary
Webb, Samuel
Webb, Smith
Webb, Theodorick
Webb, Theophalas
Webster, John
Webster, Luke
Webster, Samuel
Weeks, William
White, Jesse
White, Obediah
White, Page
White, P. Henry
Whitmore, Chearby

Whitmore, Jacob
Wilks, John
Willis, David
Willis, Isaiah
Willis, John
Willson, Edward
Willson, John
Willson, Joshua
Wimmer, Jacob
Wood, Ambrus
Wood, Peter
Wood, Stephen
Woods, Hugh
Woods, John
Woods, Robert Jr.
Woods, Robert
Woodall, David
Woodall, John

Woodcock, Henry
Woodson, Shadrack
Wray, Daniel
Wray, James
Wray, Moses Jr.
Wray, Moses Sr.
Wright, George
Wright, James
Wright, John
Wright, William Jr.
Wright, William Sr.

Young, Allen Ridley
Young, James
Young, Peter
Young, Ridley
Young, Ridley Allen
Young, William

FRANKLIN'S REPRESENTATIVES IN THE HOUSE OF REPRESENTATIVES FROM

## MARCH 3, 1793 to 1936

COL. GEORGE HANCOCK, Botetourt, born in Chesterfield County, Virginia, June 13, 1754; admitted to the bar in Chesterfield County at the June term of court, 1774; served in the Revolutionary War as Colonel of Infantry, Virginia Line, and was a member of the Staff of Count Pulaski; moved to Botetourt in 1783; and died at his home "Fotheringay", Montgomery County, July 18, 1820. Served in Congress March 4, 1793 to March 3, 1797. He was the first Representative of a District which included Franklin County.

JOHN TRIGG, Bedford County, born in what is now Bedford County in 1746; served as Major under Washington at the siege of Yorktown; and served in Congress from March 4, 1797 until his death in Bedford, June 28, 1804.

CHRISTOPHER HENDERSON CLARK, Bedford, born in Albemarle County in 1767; moved to Bedford County 1788; died Nov. 21, 1828; elected to fill vacancy caused by death of John Trigg, and took his seat Nov. 5, 1804; and served till his resignation July 1, 1806, at which time he resumed the practice of law in Bedford County.

WILLIAM ARMISTED BURWELL, Rocky Mount, born in Mecklenburg County, Nov. 11, 1780; moved to Franklin County in 1802; at one time he was private secretary to Thomas Jefferson; elected to Congress to fill the vacancy caused by the resignation of Christopher H. Clark, and took his seat Dec. 1, 1806; and served until his death in Washington, Feb. 16, 1821.

JABEZ LEFTWICH, Bedford, born Sept. 20, 1765; died near Huntsville, Ala., June 22, 1855; served from March 4, 1821, to March 3, 1825, when he was succeeded by Nathaniel H. Claiborne of Franklin County.

NATHANIEL HERBERT CLAIBORNE, Rocky Mount, elected to Congress March 4, 1825, and served to March 3, 1837.

ARCHIBALD STUART, Patrick, March 4, 1837, to March 3, 1839.

WILLIAM LEFTWICH GOGGIN, Bedford, March 4, 1839, to March 3, 1843.

WALTER COLES, Pittsylvania, (son of Isaac Coles.) He served in Congress from March 4, 1835, to March 3, 1845. Pittsylvania County was added to the Fifth District in 1843, and he represented the Fifth District, March 4, 1843 to March 3, 1845.

WILLIAM M. TREDWAY, Danville, March 4, 1845, to March 3, 1847.

THOMAS STANHOPE FLOURNOY, Halifax, March 4, 1847, to March 3, 1849.

THOMAS HAMLET AVERETT, Halifax, March 4, 1849, to March 3, 1853.

THOMAS STANHOPE BOCOCK, Appomattox, March 4, 1853, till Virginia was forced to secede from the Union, April 17, 1861.

GEORGE WILLIAM BOOKER, Martinsville, born in Patrick County, Dec. 5, 1821, Republican. Qualified under Act of July 2, 1862, and took his seat Feb. 1, 1870, and served till March 3, 1873, when he resumed the practice of law in Martinsville where he died June 4, 1883.

ALEXANDER M. DAVIS, Independence, served from March 4, 1873, to March 5, 1874, was succeeded by Christopher Yancy Thomas, who successfully contested his election.

CHRISTOPHER YANCY THOMAS, Martinsville, born in Pittsylvania County, March 24, 1818, moved to Henry County in 1844, successfully contested as a Republican, the election of Alexander M. Davis, and took his seat March 5, 1874, and served till March 3, 1875.

GEORGE CRAIGHEAD CABELL, Danville, March 4, 1875, to March 3, 1887.

JOHN ROBERT BROWN, Martinsville, March 4, 1887, to March 3, 1889.

POSEY GREEN LESTER, Floyd, March 4, 1889, to March 3, 1893.

CLAUDE AUGUSTUS SWANSON, Chatham, March 3, 1893, till his resignation Jan. 30, 1906, having been elected Governor.

EDWARD WATTS SAUNDERS, Rocky Mount, elected to fill vacancy caused by the resignation of Claude A. Swanson, and took his seat Dec. 3, 1906, and served till his resignation Feb. 29, 1920, having been elected Judge of the Supreme Court of Virginia.

RORER ABRAHAM JAMES, Danville, elected to fill vacancy caused by the resignation of Edward W. Saunders, and took his seat Dec. 6, 1920, and served until his death, Aug. 6, 1921.

JAMES MURRAY HOOKER, Stuart, elected to fill vacancy caused by the death of Rorer A. James, and took his seat Nov. 21, 1921, and served till March 3, 1925.

JOSEPH WHITEHEAD, Chatham, March 4, 1925, to March 3, 1931.

THOMAS G. BURCH, Martinsville, March 3, 1931, to 1937.

## FRANKLIN COUNTY'S REPRESENTATIVES IN THE VIRGINIA SENATE FROM THE FORMATION OF THE COUNTY IN 1786 TO 1936

### MEMBERS OF THE STATE SENATE

District composed of Franklin, Bedford, Henry, Patrick, Campbell and Pittsylvania Counties. Patrick was formed from Henry County in 1791.

| | |
|---|---|
| Charles Lynch | Oct. 16, 1786 to Dec. 19, 1789 |
| Robert Clarke | Oct. 18, 1789 to Dec. 20, 1791 |
| John Trigg | Oct. 1, 1792 to Dec. 27, 1796 |

| | |
|---|---|
| George Penn | Dec. 4, 1797 to Feb. 1, 1805 |
| John Dabney | Dec. 2, 1805 to Feb. 18, 1809 |
| Edward Watts | Dec. 4, 1809 to Feb. 22, 1817 |

District composed of Franklin, Patrick, Henry and Pittsylvania Counties.

| | |
|---|---|
| George Hairston, Jr. | Dec. 1, 1817 to Mar. 5, 1821 |
| Nathaniel H. Claiborne | Dec. 3, 1821 to Feb. 18, 1825 |
| Joseph Martin | Dec. 5, 1825 to Feb. 11, 1829 |
| George Townes | Dec. 7, 1829 to Feb. 23, 1830 |

District composed of Bedford and Franklin Counties.

| | |
|---|---|
| William Campbell | Dec. 6, 1830 to Feb. 15, 1844 |
| William T. Woods | Dec. 2, 1844 to Feb. 22, 1845 |
| Robert T. Woods | Dec. 1, 1845 to Mar. 31, 1851 |

District composed of Franklin, Henry and Patrick Counties.

| | |
|---|---|
| Archibald Stuart | Jan. 12, 1852 to Mar. 4, 1854 |
| George Hairston | Dec. 3, 1855 to Apr. 8, 1858 |
| Christopher Y. Thomas | Dec. 5, 1859 to Mar. 31, 1863 |
| Peter Saunders, Sr. | Sept. 7, 1863 to Mar. 15, 1865 |

District composed of Henry and Franklin Counties

| | |
|---|---|
| Peter Saunders | Dec. 4, 1865 to Apr. 29, 1867 |
| James Patterson | Oct. 5, 1869 to Mar. 31, 1875 |
| Peter Hairston, Jr. | Dec. 1, 1875 to Apr. 2, 1879 |

District composed of Franklin County.

| | |
|---|---|
| Waddy, T. James | Dec. 3, 1879 to Apr. 22, 1882 |
| William A. Brown | Dec. 5, 1883 to Dec. 1, 1884 |
| William B. Brown | Dec. 2, 1885 to May 24, 1887 |
| William R. Dudley | Dec. 8, 1887 to Mar. 6, 1890 |
| Benjamin N. Hatcher | Dec. 2, 1891 to Mar 8, 1894 |

District composed of Franklin and Floyd Counties

| | |
|---|---|
| W. H. Hall | Dec. 4, 1895 to Mar. 4, 1898 |
| J.A. Dinwiddie | Dec. 6, 1899 to Jan. 12, 1904 |
| S. T. Turner | Jan. 13, 1904 to Jan. 8, 1908 |
| G. O. McAlexander | Jan. 8, 1908 to Jan. 10, 1912 |
| V. M. Sowder | Jan. 10, 1912 to Jan. 12, 1916 |
| Beverly A. Davis | 1916 to 1920 |
| S. G. Proffit (resigned) | 1920 to 1922 |
| J. M. Dickerson | 1922 to 1924 |

District composed of Franklin, Roanoke, Floyd and Montgomery Counties and the Cities of Roanoke and Radford.

| | |
|---|---|
| Robert J. Noell (resigned) | 1924 to 1933 |
| Harvey B. Apperson | 1933 to 1936 |

| | |
|---|---|
| Adams, A. S. | 1916 |
| Allen, M. R. | 1859-60, (Jan.) |
| Allman, J. Bradie | 1926-32 |
| Arthur, Thomas | 1787-88 |
| Bernard, Silas G. | 1871-73 |
| Brooks, Andrew S. | 1844-45, 1847-48, 1850-51, 1852 (Jan.) 1861-62, 1862 (April) 1862 (Sept.) 1863 (Jan. |
| Brown, F. R. | 1865-67 |
| Brown, William A. | 1877-78 |
| Burwell, William A. | 1804-07 |
| Callaway, Henry T. | 1804-06 |
| Callaway, John | 1806-09 |
| Callaway, William | 1815-17, 1820-24, 1828-29 |
| Cannady I | 1857-58 |
| Carper, John C. | 1846-47 |
| Chatwood, Joseph H. | 1908 |
| Choice, Gresham | 1853-54 |
| Claiborne, Nathaniel C. | 1848-50 |
| Claiborne, Nathaniel H. | 1810-12 |
| Cooke, Benjamin | 1798-1803, 1816-19 |
| Dillard, H. D. | 1918-22 |
| Dudley, J.P. | 1901-02 |
| DuVal, Samuel | 1796 |
| Early, Joab | 1824-26 |
| Early, John | 1786-88, 1788, 1790, 1791, 1792 |
| Early, Jubal A. | 1841-42 |
| Edwards, William H. | 1848-51, 1852 (Jan.), 1855-56, 1859-60, 1861 (Jan.) |
| Ferguson, Eli | 1821-22 |
| Finney, L. Stanford | 1932-36 |
| Garrett, Silas | 1807-08, 1809-10, 1811-14 |
| Garrett, W. L. | 1904 |
| Greer, George H.T. | 1869-71 |
| Greer, Moses | 1793, 1794, 1798, 1804, 1806-07 |
| Greer, Moses T. | 1875-77 |
| Greer, Thomas B. | 1819-20, 1824-26 |
| Guerrant, John R. | 1906 |
| Hairston, Samuel | 1789 |
| Hale, John | 1795, 1797-98 |
| Hale, Sparrel | 1826-28 |
| Hale, Samuel | 1831-34, 1835-37, 1839 (Jan.) 1839-41 |
| Hancock, B. N. | 1869-71 |
| Hill, Swinfield | 1792, 1794-95 |
| Holland, John M. | 1820-21, 1822-24, 1826-31, 1834-36 |
| Hutcherson, F. S. | 1870-71 |
| Innes, Robert | 1803-04, 18-8-10, 1812-15 |
| James, Waddie T. | 1874 (Jan.) 1874-75, 1877-78 |
| Keen, Thomas S. | 1838 (Jan.) |

| | |
|---|---|
| Kinsey, Daniel A. | 1812, 1914 |
| Lee, John P. | 1910 |
| Muse, Henry Lawson | 1842-44 |
| Napier, Ashford | 1791 |
| Nicholson, D. A. | 1924-26 |
| Pasley, Solomon | 1838 (Jan.) |
| Patterson, James | 1863-67 |
| Perdue, Luke | 1879-80 |
| Powell, Charles | 1829-31 |
| Powell, William | 1871-73, 1874 (Jan.) 1874-77 |
| Rentfro, John | 1786-87 |
| Rentfro, Joshua | 1788, 1789, 1790, 1793 |
| Saunders, Edward W. | 1887-1900 |
| Saunders, Fleming | 1810-11, 1863-65 |
| Saunders, Peter | 1845-46 |
| Saunders, Peter | 1861-62, 1862 (April) 1863 (Jan.) 1883-84, 1884 (Aug.), 1885-86, 1887 (March) |
| St. Clair, Walter | 1922-24 |
| Street, William A. | 1844-47 |
| Taliaferro, Norborne | 1842-44 |
| Taliaferro, Richard M. | 1847-48 |
| Taliaferro, William T. | 1853-54 |
| Turnbull, Lewis | 1814-16, 1817-19 |
| Wade, John | 1834-35, 1839 (Jan.), 1839-40 |
| Woods, Josiah | 1796, 1797-98 |
| Woods, Robert T. | 1819-20 |
| Woods, Wyley P. | 1831-34, 1840-42 |
| Young, Thomas S. | 1881-82 |

### FRANKLIN AND FLOYD

| | |
|---|---|
| Cannaday, A. L. | 1899-1900, 1901-02 |
| Turner, S. T. | 1893-94, 1895-96, 1897-98 |

### FRANKLIN, FLOYD AND BEDFORD

| | |
|---|---|
| Chitwood, S. M. (Franklin) | 1932-36 |
| Harvey, Dr. J. Lewis (Floyd) | 1928-30 |
| Roberts, William T. (Franklin) | 1930-32 |
| Weeks, Kyle M. (Floyd) | 1924-28 |

# FRANKLIN COUNTY LAWYERS
## who have practiced in the county since 1786
### (dates, when given, show first Order Book entry)

Allen, John James, 1819.
Anthony, Christopher, Jr., 1810.

Banks, William B., 1801.
Benagh, James, 1809.
Bott, Thomas, 1800.
Bowyer, Henry, 1828.
Branch, Samuel, 1809.
Breckenridge, James, 1804.
Brown, Thomas, 1826.

Cardoza, Jacob N., 1824.
Chitwood, Joseph H.
Clark, Thomas M., 1797.
Clarke, James, 1807.
Clement, Alexander, 1812.
Clement, George W., 1845.
Clement, William C., 1848.
Cook, William, 1812.
Copeland, William, 1812.
Cralle, Richard K., 1829.
Crawford, Samuel L., 1800.

Dabney, Chiswell, 1811.
Dabney, John, 1792.
Davenport, Wilson, 1796.
Davis, Beverly A., Sr., 1895.
Davis, Beverly A., Jr., 1919.
Davis, D. Henry, 1919.
Davis, Russell L.
Davis, Samuel R., 1821.
Dennis, George.
Dibrell, Anthony, 1827.
Dillard, Archilaeus Hughes, 1850.
Dillard, George Lee.
Dillard, H. D.
Dillard, Herbert Nash.
Dillard, Hughes.
Dillard, John Lea, 1870.
Dillard, Percy.
Dillard, Peter Hairston.

Edley, David R., 1824.
Ellis, Powhatan, 1813.

Fontaine, Edmund, 1788.

Gains, John, 1817.
Garland, Maurice, 1826.
Garland, Samuel, 1820.
Gilmer, James B., 1809.
Gilmer, Peachy R., 1818.
Goggin, William L., 1828.
Gooch, Philip, 1792.
Gooch, William B., 1815.
Graham, Edward, 1801.

Hambleton, Andrew, 1804.
Hamilton, Andrew, 1815.
Hancock, G., 1788.
Harrison, Burr, 1818.
Harrison, Jesse C., 1825.
Harrison, Peyton, 1824.
Harrison, Tipton, 1820.
Harrison, Tipton B., 1821.
Henderson, Greenville, 1809.
Hendrick, James, 1819.
Holcombe, Thomas A., 1816.
Hopkins, Arthur, 1814.
Hopkins, Abram H.
Hopkins, Walter Lee.

Irvine, Edmund, 1824.

Johnston, Edward, 1828.
Jones, Marshall, 1829.

Lacy, Richard T., 1827.
Latham, Thomas A., 1826.
Lee, C. C.
Lee, George T.
Lee, John P.
Leftwich, John T., 1826.

McAlister, James S., 1813.
McCampbell, James, 1794.

Madison, John, 1797.
Marr, Daniel, 1828.
Meenan, Hugh, 1823.
Mennis, Callohill, 1818.
Mosby, Charles, 1829.
Moseley, John, 1797.

Nelson, George W., 1822.
Nelson, Hugh.

Patterson, James, 1796.
Pegram, James W., 1826.
Peters, George D.
Price, William S.

Radford, William, 1807.
Read, Nathan, Jr., 1819.
Rice, Benjamin, 1801.
Risque, Ferdinand W., 1829.
Risque, James, 1794.
Rives, Nathaniel, 1824.
Rives, William, 1815.
Roane, William R., 1814.
Robinson, Archibald, 1798.
Ronald, George, 1810.
Rucker, W.D.

Sale, Edmund N., 1820.
Sale, John F., 1821.
Scisson, Baldwin L., 1823.
Skillern, William P., 1798.
Spencer, Thomas H., 1796.
Smith, John Hill, 1814.

Stewart, Alexander, 1792.
Stewart, Archibald, 1816.
Stewart, James, 1799.

Taylor, Allen, 1815.
Townes, George, 1816.
Tucker, George, 1818.

Urquhart, John D., 1814.

Vanstarem, Nicholas, 1799.
Venable, Richard N., 1791.
Verell, James, 1792.

Walker, Peter, 1823.
Ward, Giles, 1822.
Ward, Henry C., 1829.
Ward, Henry Chiles, 1829.
Watts, Edward, 1804.
Watts, William, 1864.
Wharton, John A., 1826.
Wilson, George W., 1827.
Wingfield, Gustavus A.
Wright, George W., 1816.
Wyatt, Samuel, 1807.

## CLERKS OF FRANKLIN COURTS

### Clerks of County Court:
Stephen Smith, 1786-1791
James Callaway, 1791-1813
Caleb Tate, 1813-1838
Moses G. Carper, 1838-1852
Robert A. Scott, 1852-1871
James J. Carper, 1871-1900
O. H. Price, 1900, until the County Court was consolidated
   with the Circuit Court in 1904.

### District Court:
(Composed of Franklin, Bedford, Campbell, Pittsylvania and
Henry Counties.)
James Steptoe, 1789-1797
Ben Rice (pro tem), 1797-1800
Caleb Tate, 1800-1809

### Circuit Court:
Caleb Tate, 1809-1845
Moses G. Carper, 1845-1858
Henry E. Carper, 1858-1862

N. C. Carper, 1862-1863
James E. Greer, 1863-1864
G.H.T. Greer, 1864-1897
J. N. Carper, 1897-1902
J. B. Saunders, 1902-1903
T. W. Carper, 1903-1904
O. H. Price, 1904-1910
T. W. Carper, 1910, to date.

## SHERIFFS OF FRANKLIN COUNTY

Robert Woods   1786-August 1787
Hugh Innes   1787-89
Peter Saunders   1790-91
J. Richeson 1792-93
John Smith   1794-95
Moses Greer   1796-97
Swinfield Hill   1798-99
George Turnbull   1800-01
Thomas Hale   1802-03
John Early   October 1803-August 1804 when
Ben Cook   was appointed in his stead
Ben Cook   1805-06
John Hock   1807-08
Peter Saunders 1809
Josiah Woods   1810-11
Jonathan Richeson   1812
Stephen Smith   1813-15
Shores Price   1816-17
Thomas Thompson   1818-19
Samuel Hairston   1820-21
Moses Greer   1822
John Forbes   1823-27
J. S. Burnett   1828-29
Moses Greer Jr.   1830-31
Patrick Hix   1832-33
Henry Carper   1834-35
Peter Saunders 1836-37
Sam Saunders   1838-39
George Turner   1840-41
Samuel Helms   1842-43
Shores Price   1844-45
George W. Clements   1846-47
Robert Hairston   1848-49
Stephen Woods   1850
J. S. Burwell   1851-52
John A. Smith   1853-56
Samuel S. Turner   1857-58
W. P. Thompson   1859-62
John Wade   1863-66

T. H. Powell  1867-68
John W. Hartwell appointed in June 1870
John W. Hartwell  1871-74
William L. Hancock  1875-78
John O. Poindexter  1879-85 (died and
J. A. Bernard appointed February 1885, to serve until July, 1885
O. H. Price  part of 1885, 1886-94
B. L. Angle  1895-1903 (term expired account new constitution)
D. A. Nicholson  1904-11
J. P. Hodges  1912-26
D. Wilson Hodges (served out his father's unexpired term)
Cornelius C. Jamison  now serving

## TREASURERS OF FRANKLIN COUNTY

R. A. Scott,  1871-1873
P. D. Divers,  1874-1886
J. C. Hall,  1887-1894
P. D. Divers,  1895-1912.  Resigned November 26, 1913, and
R. L. McNeil was appointed
R. L. McNeil,  1914-1919
T. J. Dudley,  1920-1923
J. N. Montgomery, Jr.,  1924-1934

## FRANKLIN COUNTY ELECTION PRECINCTS (1863)

Courthouse
Allen's
Union Hall
Booth's Store
McVey's Tanyard
Helm's
Dickerson's
Kinsey's
Richland Grove
Bush's Store
Sydnorsville
Snow Creek
Aldridge's Store

## FRANKLIN COUNTY PHYSICIANS

Abshire, Achilles
Arthur, Thomas F.

Brammer, Frank P.
Bridges, Ned T.

Carper, John C.
Chitwood, W. T.
Cobb, W. L.

Deterly, Harry

Dickinson, D. C.
Dillard, Alfred
Dillard, George Penn
Dillard, M. P.
Dillon, Charles L.
Dudley, Morton

English, Reverdy J.

Giles, G. O.
Greer, Charlie
Greer, John Henry
Greer, Norborne
Greer, Theodric
Greer, Tom H.
Guerrant, John R.
Guerrant, Samuel S.
Guerrant, Stephen P.

Hairston, William
Hancock, W. Early
Haynes, Claude
Hickman, David
Hooker, G. W.

Jamison, E. C.

Keen, Ashford
Keen, Edmond

Lemon, Rufus M.

Moorman, J. A.
Muse, William Henry

Pedigo, Lewis G.
Peters, Henry D.
Price, Robert

Reese, William Penn

Simmons, Thomas
Stone, W. P.

Tatum, Benjamin H.
Taylor, Thomas
Tinsley, E. O.

Wade, Benjamin
Williams, Benjamin
Williams, J. M.

Younger, Robert N.

## SURVEYORS OF FRANKLIN COUNTY
(The dates of service were approximated by A. G. Fralin)

Stephen Wood
Lewis Davis  ca. 1800
_____ Payne
Samuel H. Woods  1830
Silas G. Bernard 1840-1875
Austin Wingfield
Jacob Flora  1865-1890 (went blind in later life)
Jesse Dillon  1870-1900
William H. Hutcherson  1855-1915 (lived to be a centenarian)
I. M. Menefee  1890-1910
J. S. Hale  1890-1920
N. C. Mason 1890-1915
Levi Bowman  1910-1920

## SOME FRANKLIN COUNTY TEACHERS PRIOR TO 1900

Abshire, Georgia
Angell, Biah
Angell, Lucy

Angle, Ida
Anglin, Bessie
Anglin, Lera

Anglin, Lily
Anglin, Polly
Arrington, J.T. (d. Jan. 17,1935)
Atkins, Maggie

Barnett, Mary
Barnett, Maude
Barnhart, Rev. Josephus
Bell, Maggie
Bell, Stella
Bennett, Creighton
Bennett, Eugenia
Bernard, Cordia
Boatwright, Endora
Boatwright, Prfo. Charles
Boatwright, Pattie
Board, Cora
Bowman, Jonas
Brodie, Elizabeth
Brown, Lillian
Brown, Roslyn

Callaway, Louvinia L.
Callaway, Mary
Cannaday, Georgia
Carper, Lucy
Carter, Effie
Chitwood, Cora
Chitwood, O. P.
Clingenpeel, C. J.
Cook, Alma
Cook, Ella
Cooper, Annie
Cooper, Lizzie
Cooper, Mary
Cooper, Susie
Craft, Fannie
Crumpecker, Peter S.

Dickerson, Tol
Dillard, Ella
Dillon, C. L.
Dillon, James R.
Dillon, Jesse Thomas
Dillon, John H.
Dillon, Lucy
Dillon, Sally
Divers, Alvie
Divers, Della
Divers, Lee
Drewry, Ben
Drewry, Samuel Richard

Duncan, Annie
Duncan, Asa Leland
Duncan, Erastus, Capt.
Duncan, Kate
Duncan, Laura
Duncan, Lizzie
Duncan, Lula
Duncan, Mattie
Duncan, Sallie

English, Blanche
English, Louella

Fishburn, Sue E.
Fisher, Bud

Goad, Sue M.
Griffith, Mrs. Julia Sims
Guerrant, Jennie
Guerrant, Lorlie
Guerrant, Stephen

Hairston, Mrs. Prudence
Hall, Rev. John C.
Hall, Lucy
Hall, Tempie
Hancock, Chappie
Hancock, Eula (Ula)
Hancock, Mary Vick
Hancock, William
Hannabass, Daniel
Hartsell, Louvinia
Haynes, Florence
Heckman, James W.
Hickman, James
Hill, Kate
Hodges, Nannie E.

Ikenberry, Cephas

Jamison, Alice
Jamison, Allie
Jamison, Curtis
Jamison, Frances
Jamison, Sallie
Jamison, Sue
Jeter, James
Jones, Peter P.

Kesler, Benjamin F.
Kinsey, A. T.
Kinsey, Bettie

Kinsey, Lucy
Kirk, Nannie

Law, Annie
Lee, Annie
Lee, Lula
Linthicum, Perla
Lovelace, Mattie
Lovelace, Sallie

Mackenheimer, Dora
Mansfield, Mrs. Cassie
Mansfield, Carrie
Mansfield, Mildred
Martin, Nannie
Martin, Sallie Mae
Mason, Tom
Matthews, Elliott
Matthews, Joe
Matthews, Wilson
Mills, Robert
Mitchell, Benjamin F.
Mitchell, George
Mitchell, Rev. John W.
Mitchell, Thomas A.
Moir, James C.
Montgomery, Electa
Montgomery, Thomas F.

Naff, Edith
Naff, John
Naff, Joseph A.
Newhill, Mattie
Noell, Bonus
Noell, Caleb
Noell, Charles Robert

Parker, Addoe
Parker, Alice
Pearson, Mrs. Eliza Pinkard
Peters, John B.
Phelps, Mollie
Phelps, Thomas
Powell, Cornelia
Powell, Jennie
Preston, Angie
Preston, Josie
Price, Bettie
Price, Henry Clay
Price, Kate

Price, Lura

Ramsey, Fannie
Ramsey, Lena
Richards, Eliza
Richards, Sallie
Ross, Lera

Showalter, Ella
Showalter, Stephen
Sloan, Eson
Sloan, Laura O.
Smith, Alma W.
Smith, Electra
Smith, Dr. Horace P.
Smith, Mary A.
Smith, Tippie S.
Stanley, Clayton
Stone, Chappie
Stone, Roxie
Stone, Sallie
Stone, Rev. T. J.
Strayer, Nell

Tench, Martha
Tench, Mary
Tinsley, Benjamin
Thornton, Mrs. Jemima Tate

Vickselyer, Bettie

Wade, Mrs. Lucy
Wade, Mattie
Wade, W. T.
Walker, Tom
Warren, Walter
Watkins, Delia
Webb, Boliver
Webb, Dennie
Webster, Ammon R.
Webster, Edward N.
Webster, Lizzie
White, Edna
Whitlow, Valera
Williams, Nellie
Wray, Irving
Wright, Georgie

Zeigler, Alpha
Zeigler, Mary

# FRANKLIN COUNTY MINISTERS
(Dates denote years for which marriage returns appear)

Adams, Joshua 1858
Albea, William W.
Angell, Zechariah 1858
Anthony, Abner 1831
Anthony, Albert
Arnold, Mosby
Ashworth, Henry
Ashworth, Joel
Ashworth, John
Ashworth, Thomas
Austin, Garland A.

Barnhart, Abraham 1858
Beck, Richard 1833-1835
Bennett, William W.
Bibb, Robert P.
Bird, Luke
Bowman, George
Bowman, Isaac
Bowman, John 1858
Brooks, J. A.
Brown, J. T.
Brown, Pleasant 1858
Burnett, Jeremiah 1857
Burns, Horatio 1797-00
Burns, Jeremiah 1794
Burns, Jesse
Burwell, Robert

Cabaniss, E. G. 1830
Cabaniss, Edwin A.
Class, William
Claughton (Clayton) R.A.
Cobbs, Nichols H. 1835
Comer, John
Comer, John, Sr.
Conner, J. W.
Corn, Peter
Crump, William

Darden, James M. 1835
Davis, William 1836
Doniphan, Alex
Douglass, Thomas 1787
Dyer, George

Eames, Joseph
Eanes, A. W. 1838
Eller, John

Fears, Jesse 1794-95
Floyd, John W.
Forbes, John R.
Foster, Lewis

Goggins, Thomas
Goodman, Joseph 1831
Gray, Robert
Greer, Moses 1829
Greer, Moses, Jr.

Haggard, Rice 1791
Hairston, Robert
Hall, John C.
Hall, Randolph 1787 1790-91
Hank, Jehu
Hank, John 1840
Hankins, William 1858
Harris, A. F.
Hash, W. M.
Hatchett, Joseph
Helm, Dan
Helmes, John P.
Hooker, Nathan A.
Howard, Peter
Howry (Harvey), Michael 1858
Hubbard, Stephen 1831

Jackson, M. W. 1835
Jefferson, James M.
Jefferson, J. H.
Jones, Jesse
Jones, Robert 1787-89
Jordon, William M.
Jones, Pete 1858
Kelly, George W. 1834-1858
Kelly, William W.
Kidd, Benjamin 1831
King, John
King, Samuel 1799-1801

Lacy, Thomas 1839
Lee, John R. 1858
Lewis, John W.
Lovell, William 1786
Lumsden, Jeremiah or John 1789
Lumsden, Nehemiah 1789
Luster, James

Martin, John R. 1858
Martin, Orson
Martin, William P. 1796
Matthews, William H.
Maxey, Bennet 1792
Mayo, David M. 1839
McEnally 1832
Meador, Benjamin
Meadow, Joel W. 1858
Miller, Ford 1799
Miller, Jacob 1794-96-99
Minter, Othniel 1832
Minter, Silas
Mitchell, James
Moore, Jeptha 1795
Morgan, Jubal A. 1836

Naff, Abraham 1858
Norman, Alfred

Payne, Joseph 1833
Perdue, Randolph
Plybon, S. O.
Powers, Urias

Regester, Sam
Reid, James
Rentfro, Isaac 1791
Rentfro, Jesse 1786
Rise, Samuel
Ross, C. L.

Sanderson, T. M. 1858
Saunders, John 1801
Saunders, Joseph
Sayford, Samuel
Scherer, G.
Schoolfield, William M. 1835
Shelor, Thomas G. 1848
Short, Reuben

Showalter, John
Shrewsbury, Daniel
Shrewsbury, Nathaniel 1789
Smith, William
Smith, William Ray
Southall, Daniel 1791
St. Clair, John T.
Starr, William
Stockton, Robert 1794
Sumner, Owen
Sweeny, Benjamin

Talley, Happy
Taylor, John A.
Taylor, John T.
Thompson, William
Traylor, John A. 1831
Turner, Bird S. 1858
Turner, E. B. 1858
Turner, J. 1835
Turner, William

Van Over, Henry 1791-94

Walker, A. 1837
Walker, Arnold 1850
Walker, W. M.
Weatherford, Charles
Webb, Theo. F. 1837-1858
Welch, Peyton
West, Benjamin C., Sr. 1837
Wildman, William W.
Williams, B. M. 1858
Wingfield, R. L.
Wise, Henry
Wood, Stephen 1832
Wyatt 1797-1800

Young, V. C.

## ORIGIN OF FRANKLIN COUNTY

Franklin was formed from Bedford and Henry in 1786, receiving its name from Benjamin Franklin.

| | | | |
|---|---|---|---|
| Charles City | 1634 | Original Shire | |
| Henrico | " | " | |
| James City | " | " | |
| Isle of Wight | 1637 | Formerly | Warrosquvoake |
| York | 1642 | " | Charles River |

| | | |
|---|---|---|
| Surry | 1652 | From James City |
| New Kent | 1654 | "   York |
| Prince George | 1703 | "   Charles City |
| Hanover | 1721 | "   New Kent |
| Goochland | 1728 | "   Henrico |
| Brunswick | 1732 | "   Prince George, Surry and |
| | | Isle of Wight |
| Louisa | 1742 | "   Hanover |
| Albemarle | 1744 | "   Goochland and Louisa |
| Lunenburg | 1746 | "   Brunswick |
| Halifax | 1754 | "   Lunenburg |
| Bedford | " | "   Lundenburg and Albemarle |
| Pittsylvania | 1767 | "   Halifax |
| Henry | 1777 | "   Pittsylvania |
| Franklin | 1786 | "   Bedford and Henry (part |
| | | of Patrick added later) |

## POST OFFICES OF FRANKLIN COUNTY
### (* Post Offices operating in 1935)

| Name of Post Office | Date Established | Date Discontinued | Name of First Postmaster |
|---|---|---|---|
| Alean (originally Piedmont) | Aug. 1, 1898 | Nov. 30,1906 | James E. Poteet |
| Algoma | May 31,1881 | Sept.15,1903 | William Dowdy |
| Alumine (later Henry) | June 3,1893 | Oct. 14, 1903 | Stokeley Dyer |
| | | | |
| Bonbrook | Dec. 1,1851 | July 30,1904 | Griffin Bush |
| Boone Mill* | Feb. 18,1828 | | George Wright |
| Booth's Store (later Hales Ford) | Dec. 13, 1823 | | John D. Booth |
| Bruce | Feb. 26,1889 | Feb. 8, 1890 | James G. Thompson |
| Bull Run | May 28,1842 | | John W. Powell |
| | | | |
| Calico Rock | Aug. 7, 1879 | Jan. 31,1907 | Jacob Boon |
| Callaway's Mill | May 13, 1828 | | Edwin Cabiness |
| Callaway's | July 14, 1871 | | |
| Callaway* | May 23, 1893 | | |
| Carron Furnace | Oct. 1, 1857 | | Crocket J. Saunder |
| Cassell | Feb. 4, 1886 | | John R. Dent |
| Cedar Grove Mill (later Hickman) | June 19, 1874 | | D. P. Hickman |
| Claiborn | Feb. 28, 1883 | | Chas. R. Hancock |
| Cooper's | Feb. 28, 1828 | | Lewis Cooper |
| Crawford | Feb. 1, 1890 | Sept.14,1907 | Mary S. Bondurant |
| | | | |
| Dan | Feb. 16,1885 | May 8, 1894 | Crockett Prillamon |
| Dickinson's | Dec.17, 1815 | Jan.31,1907 | Josiah W. Dickinso |
| Dillon's Mill | May 29, 1873 | June 29,1929 | Jesse B. Robertson |
| Dubuque | May 17, 1895 | Nov. 2, 1897 | Edward A. Hatchett |
| Dugwell | June 5, 1897 | Oct.14, 1903 | George W. Naff |
| | | | |
| Eddy | Dec.13, 1888 | Nov. 30,1906 | Isaac M. Young |
| Edwardsville | Jan. 9, 1878 | | William H. Edwards |
| Endicott* (originally Long Branch) | July 21,1885 | | George A. Menafee |
| English | Nov. 4, 1898 | Jan.31, 1907 | Blanche English |
| Eulalia | Jan. 2, 1889 | Nov.30, 1906 | Richard C. Shaon |
| | | | |
| Felicia | April 27,1886 | Dec.31,1904 | Silas C. Wood |
| Ferrum* (originally Sophronia) | March 29,1892 | | George W. Turner |
| Fisher | Nov. 4, 1885 | | John R. Foster |
| Fishersborough | Dec. 7, 1839 | | James Anderson |

| | | | |
|---|---|---|---|
| Hill's Creek | March 5, 1852 | | Callohill M. Pasley |
| Blade Hill* | April 1, 1837 | | John S. Brown |
| Bogginsville | May 4, 1848 | Oct.14,1903 | Samuel W. Hensley |
| Buizot | Aug. 9, 1880 | | William J. Ferguson |
| (later Redwood) | | | |
| | | | |
| Hales Ford | March 16, 1829 | | James A. Brown |
| (originally Booth's Store | | | |
| Handy | June 20,1892 | Oct.14,1903 | Solomon G. King |
| Hardy's Ford | Dec. 27,1877 | April 14,1906 | William Hopkins |
| Haste | March 23,1901 | Nov.30,1909 | James H. Holt |
| Haught | March 26,1894 | Feb.28, 1925 | Gaac W. Helms |
| Helms | Dec. 13, 1830 | Nov.30,1906 | Thomas Helm |
| Henry* | Nov. 4, 1908 | | Arennah L.Johnson |
| Hernando | May 3, 1894 | Aug.27,1909 | Robert E.L. Fralin |
| Hickman | Dec. 14,1881 | Aug.15,1902 | David P. Hickman |
| High Peake | Nov. 3, 1879 | June 15,1906 | Oscar A. Huff |
| Hunters Hall | Dec. 10,1827 | | George W.G. Brown |
| | | | |
| Joel | June 20,1892 | Dec.14, 1903 | John N. Ridgeway |
| Junta | Nov. 19,1885 | Sept.15,1903 | William L. Angel |
| | | | |
| Kennett | March 9,1885 | Aug. 31,1917 | Silas G. R. Kennett |
| Kinsey | June 1, 1895 | Nov. 22,1895 | Reubin P. Moore |
| | | | |
| Lemar | March 30,1901 | April 30,1906 | Admire W. Hutchinson |
| Lobelia | Aug. 13, 1900 | Jan. 31, 1907 | George W. Cooper, Jr. |
| Long Branch | Feb. 11, 1837 | | Isaac Canaday |
| (later Endicott) | | | |
| Lynnville Mills | Dec. 13, 1855 | | Lewis Wysong |
| | | | |
| Manila | Oct. 13, 1899 | Jan.31,1907 | George T. Parker |
| Menefee | Sept.29,1886 | | Richard Menefee |
| Mingo | Feb. 9, 1889 | June 30,1903 | Gustavus A. Giles |
| Mount Zion (later in Pittsylvania County) | May 19, 1837 | | James L. Doss |
| | | | |
| Naffs | Jan. 27,1855 | Dec. 15,1925 | Jacob Naff |
| Need | Aug. 3, 1895 | July 30,1904 | Mary L. Forbs |
| Neva (later in Pittsylvania County) | June 30,1897 | June 30,1902 | Thomas H. Morgan |
| Nola* | Oct. 13,1888 | | Abraham McGuffin |
| Novelty | July 16,1902 | Sept. 30,1907 | Christina Machenheimer |
| Nowlins Mills | June 6,1884 | Feb. 28,1918 | John P. Allen |
| | | | |
| Oneida | April 13,1880 | | Silas W. Eames |
| Otter | April 29,1879 | | John T. Canaday |

| | | | |
|---|---|---|---|
| Parsells | April 10, 1901 | Nov.30,1906 | Emma J. Jamison |
| Patti | June 7, 1892 | June 31,1907 | George T. Mitchell |
| Penhood* | March 25, 1854 | | Edward C. Murphy |
| Pernello | Nov. 8, 1877 | Jan. 14,1905 | Henry M. Turner |
| Piedmont (later Alean) | April 29,1893 | Aug. 1,1898 | James E. Poteet |
| Pigg River | Dec. 6, 1854 | Oct. 31,1904 | John R. Saunders |
| Poplar Camp | April 25,1831 | | Jonathan Williamson |
| Prillamans | Nov. 27, 1832 | June 15,1904 | Ira Hurt |
| Progress | Feb. 9, 1886 | Feb. 14,1903 | Mel. J. McDowell |
| Purity (later Alumine) | March 13, 1894 | April 22,1895 | Griffin Coleman |
| Pyramid | June 19,1895 | June 15,1900 | Pauline R. Dickinson |
| | | | |
| Ramsey | May 7, 1886 | Aug.31,1901 | John W. Wade |
| Red Plains | July 1,1875 | Aug.31,1901 | James R. Richardson |
| Redwood* (later Guizot) | May 24, 1890 | | Daniel Mitchell |
| Retreat | July 31,1833 | | Henry T. Callaway |
| Reverie | April 13,1886 | June 23,1892 | Stephen C. Kennett |
| Rivermont | Oct. 13,1894 | March 15,1907 | Fannie K. Haynes |
| Roberta | Jan. 14,1884 | Aug. 30, 1902 | William H. Hurt |
| Rocky Mount* | Dec. 19,1810 | | Peter Saunders |
| Roller | Feb. 27,1904 | | Thomas B. Thomason |
| Rosevale | May 14,1856 | | Allen Woody |
| Running Bay | Aug.29,1873 | | Mrs. Caroline Y. Semms |
| Sago* (later in Pittsylvania County) | July 11,1925 | | Tony G. Adams |
| Saranac | Sept.16,1886 | | Maria A. Lee |
| Scruggs* | April 17,1880 | | Daniel T. Saunders |
| Shady Grove | Jan.18,1820 | Sept.14,1907 | Benjamin Marshall |
| Shooting Creek | Sept.29,1886 | July 15,1910 | Gaac Lemon |
| Snead's Camp | May 8, 1876 | | William A. Pedigo |
| Snead | April 18,1898 | July 13,1907 | Charles F. Snead |
| Snow Creek | May 29, 1832 | Aug. 15,1910 | Gabriel Machenheimer |
| Sontag* | March 31,1854 | | William H. Dent |
| Sophronia (later Ferrum) | June 18, 1888 | | George W. Turner |
| Stanopher | Nov. 1, 1900 | Sept.15,1903 | William P. Dudley |
| Starry Creek | Jan. 4,1854 | | William Menefee |
| Stave | Feb. 1,1902 | Nov. 15,1904 | George E. Goode |
| Story Creek | Jan. 4,1877 | | William R. Stephens |
| Sydnorsville* | Nov. 27,1832 | | Beverly Sydnor, Jr. |
| Taccio | Feb. 5,1894 | Oct.31,1902 | Joel B. Flora |
| Tamesa | July 2,1896 | May 15,1911 | Cordillie C. Smith |
| Taylor's Store | March 11,1818 | | Sparrel Hale |
| Town Creek | Feb. 26,1834 | | Aaron Teazel |
| Ula | Sept.3,1880 | Feb. 9,1897 | George W. English |
| Union Hall* | Jan. 5,1826 | | John Dickinson |

228

| | | | |
|---|---|---|---|
| Vashti (later in Pittsylvania County) | Sept.10,1892 | | James V. Reynolds |
| Villa | Oct. 2,1854 | Sept.30,1902 | Jefferson Chitwood |
| Waidsboro* | Sept.8,1879 | | John L. Waid |
| Wirtz* | April 20,1893 | | William C. Smith |
| Woodpecker's Level | April 1,1826 | | Tarlton Brown, Jr. |
| Wyatt | May 24, 1886 | July 30,1904 | Wyatt W. Smith |
| Young's Store (later Dan) | Oct. 1, 1857 | July 7,1892 | William D. Young |

# EXTINCT FRANKLIN COUNTY SCHOOLS

Algoma
Angell

Barton Spur
Bethlehem
Black Rock
Blackwater
Boatwright
Bondbro^k
Bunker ..ill

Chestnut Level
Cook's

Dickinson's

Edgewood
Endicott

Fancy Grove
Flint Hill
Forest Hill
Fred Mason

Glade
Gogginsville
Gold Mine
Goode
Grassy Hill
Guerrant's
Guilliams

Hale's Ford Academy
Haught
High Point

Indian Ridge
Ingram

Jumper

Kemp Ford
Kennett's

Kinsey
Knob

Little Creek
Lobelia
Long Branch

Mansfield
Mason
Mayflower
Mountain
Mountain Grove
Mountain View
Mount Horeb
Muddy Fork

Neblett's Hill
Nicholas Creek
Northfield

Old Glade Hill
Old Snow Creek

Perdue
Peter's
Pigg River
Pleasant View
Poplar Grove
Prospect

Railroad
Ramsey
Retreat
Rocky Hill
Round Hill

Sandy Level
Shady Grove
Shooting Creek
Sunny View

Vinegar Ridge

# FRANKLIN OBITUARY INDEX

KEY:
CN - County News
FC - Franklin Chronicle
RT - Roanoke Times
WN - World News
TD - Times-Dispatch (Richmond)
NL - News-Leader (Richmond)
CA - Christian Advocate
CC - Chesapeake Christian
RH - Religious Herald
DR - Danville Register
HB - Henry Bulletin
BR - Bible Records
TI - Tomb Inscriptions

Abshire, Jacob. 68. 1848. BR.
Abshire, James O. 86. 2/17/1929. RT.
Abshire, John William. 72. 9/3/1925. RT.
Abshire, Mrs. Louisa. 82. 7/10/1929. RT.
Akers, Miss Hannah. 66. 5/17/1892. BR.
Akers, Mrs. Helena Crumpecker. 82. 2/6/1936. BR.
Akers, John. 40. 4/12/1862. BR.
Akers, Mrs. Lavinia Capper. 69. 8/25/1871. BR.
Akers, Robert D. 78. 7/22/1930. BT.
Akers, Samuel. 84. 4/13/1913. BR.
Akers, William. 65. 3/25/1867. BR.
Akers, William B. 78. RT.
Aldridge, Mrs. Polly Webster. 66. 10/18/1889. BR.
Aldridge, Mrs. Susan E. 74. 7/28/1930. RT.
Altice, Mrs. Mary Crook. 78. 1/16/1933. RT.
Angell, Miss Amanda. 62. 5/30/1909. FC.
Angell, J.O. 57. 1/18/1933. RT.
Angell, Robert Henderson. 65. 11/12/1933. RT.
Arthur, Mrs. Martin Tench. 54. 8/27/1911. RT.
Arthur, T.S.F. 58. 4/5/1916. RT.
Atkins, Wm. Bailey. 57. 5/4/1884. RT.

Barnhart, Mrs. Emily Webster. 38. 5/16/1895. TI.
Barnhart, Joel. 85. 2/10/1819. TI.
Barnhart, Mrs. Sallie Webster. 72. 9/18/1915. TI.
Becker, Wm. Lewis. 75. 12/5/1929. RT.
Bell, Leslie C. 80. 12/12/1920. RT.
Bell, Mrs. Mosby Reynolds. 77. 1/26/1923. RT.
Blackwell, Lewis. 84. 1/1/1913. RT.
Boitnott, George P. 82. 7/22/1933. RT.
Boitnott, Mrs. Sarah E. 82. 7/16/1928. RT.
Boone, Benjamin. 71. 2/20/1928. RT.
Boone, Benjamin D. 35. 9/15/1887. TI.

Boone, Daniel. 81. 9/4/1872. BR.
Boone, Daniel. 37. 6/20/1865. BR.
Boone, Eddie O. 67. 5/8/1927. WN.
Boone, Eva E. 7/28/1875. TI.
Boone, Gustavers. 36. 10/11/1912. TI.
Boone, Henry C. 27. 3/ /1864. TI.
Boone, Ida Estells. 7/22/1886. TI.
Boone, Isaac. 55. 5/28/1841. TI.
Boone, Isaac H. 1886. TI.
Boone, Jacob. 65. 1814. BR & TI.
Boone, John. 75. 1858. BR & TI.
Boone, John. 7/31/1887. TI.
Boone, J.Paul. 6/15/1913. TI.
Boone, Judith A. 10/28/1898. TI.
Boone, Julia F. 10/11/1874. TI.
Boone, Mrs. Lydia A. 64. 7/31/1934. BT.
Boone, Mary S. 12/8/1867. TI.
Boone, Peyton. 4/19/1918. TI.
Boone, Susan C. 12/17/1865. TI.
Boone, Mrs. Susan Fowler. 91. 12/1/1884. TI.
Boone, Thomas. 72. 7/12/1884. TI.
Boone, Washington S. 4/9/1911. TI.
Booth, McH. 74. 11/23/1934. RT.
Bowles, John H. 74. 7/30/1934. FC.
Bowling, Henry Lee. 56. 8/12/1918. RT.
Bowman, J.A. 81. 3/10/1937. RT.
Bowman, Mrs. L. D. 37. 1/2/1933. RT.
Brammer, Mrs. Florence J. 64. 3/26/1934. RT.
Brichey, Andrew J. 89. 4/18/1923. RT.
Brichey,Mrs. Elizabeth Boone. 88. 3/3/1927. BT.
Burwell, Blair B. 79. 10/15/1928. RT.
Bussey, Mrs. Eliza Jamison. 44. 7/8/1893. TI.
Bussey, Miss Minnie I. 20. 2/14/1900. TI.
Bussey, Thomas G. 34. 10/14/1918. TI.

Callaway, George E. 70. 7/30/1922. RT.
Camp, Walter P. 72. 2/23/1929. RT.
Carr, Mrs. Nannie Webster. 59. 6/27/1877. BR.
Carroll, James F. 58. 1/8/1928. RT.
Carroll, Mrs. Kate Boitnott. 29. 7/23/1905. BR.
Childress, Joseph T. 68. 1/25/1923. RT.
Correll, Mrs. Susan Toney. 81. 2/25/1900. BR.
Correll, Valentine. 79. 2/24/1900. BR.
Craig, James Edward. RT.
Crook, Mrs. Jacob. 80. 2/20/1937. RT.
Crumpecker, Gustavus Wingfield. 67. 1/4/1914. RT.

Davidson, Mrs. Amanda. 61. 12/12/1904. BR.
Deyerle, Henry S. 78. 10/2/1930. RT.
Dillon, James Robert. 51. 12/19/1908. BR.
Dillon, Jesse. 76. 8/8/1896. BR.

Dillon, Miss Martha Ann. 1 7/12/1862. BR.
Dillon, Miss Paxton. 26. 8/2/1898. BR.
Dillon, Mrs. Sarah Webster. 48. 8/2/1886. TI.
Dillon, William Samuel. 7. 2/11/1862. BR.
Drewry, Richard. 69. 6/23/1901. BR.
Drewry, Mrs. Tena Jamison. 72. 11/24/1901. BR.

Fishburn, Reuben H. 79. 4/26/1914. RT.
Fishburn, T. T. 72. 4/13/1921. RT.
Fisher, William. 57. 3/1/1872. BR.
Flora, Charles O. 50. 2/11/1924. FC.
Flora, Fleming. 73. 12/11/1929. WN.
Flora, George B. 31. 2/21/1931. BR.
Flora, James O. 70. 8/5/1934. BR.
Flora, Jonathan, 56. 9/23/1889. TSI
Flora, Mrs. Sarah Jamison. 56. 6/5/1902. TSI
Forbes, Taswell. 71. 8/19/1934. BR.

Gibson, Haden. 70. 5/8/1928. RT.
Gibson, Mrs. Mary Lute. 75. 9/7/1934. RT.
Greer, Miss Victoria A. 75. 3/11/1931. RT.
Guerrant, Dr. John R. 65. 12/19/1930. RT.
Guerrant, Mrs. Samuel S. 26. 6/4/1915. WN.
Guerrant, Mrs. Sarinda L. 89. 8/18/1929. RT.
Guerrant, Stephen P. 66. 3/18/1904. BR.
Guerrant, William G. 48. 1/11/1910. RT.

Haislip, Mrs. Elizabeth Peters. 40. 5/22/1868. TI.
Hancock, John Henry. 73. 2/26/1937. RT.
Hartzell, Miss Elizabeth. 1/20/1863. BR.
Hartzell, Mrs. Hannah. 12/26/1867. BR.
Hartzell, Jacob. 56. 4/11/1836. BR.
Hartzell, John C. 9/4/1864. BR.
Heckman, Ferd J. 76. 3/1/1920. RT.
Helm, Taswell. 85. 12/31/1928. RT.
Herringdon, George H. 77. 2/4/1933. RT.
Hill, John. 65. 6/29/1838. BR.
Hill, Martha Price. 52. 6/9/1829. BR.

Jamison, Miss Agnes. 13. 1/4/1931. RT.
Jamison, Mrs. Angeline H. 54. 1/10/1897. BR.
Jamison, Baily S.H. 82. 2/20/1927. RT.
Jamison, Carnelius T. 86. 8/24/1933. BR.
Jamison, Mrs. Catherine Boone. 81. 8/29/1866. BR.
Jamison, Mrs. Catherine Brubaker. 66. 5/5/1890. BR.
Jamison, Charles Marshall. 68. 7/11/1926. RT.
Jamison, Mrs. Christena Hartzell. 59. 5/1/1881. BR.
Jamison, Christian B. 60. 10/18/1913. BR.
Jamison, Mrs. Elizabeth Akers. 35. 1/14/1859. BR.
Jamison, Mrs. Elizabeth McWilliams. 75. 1838. BR.
Jamison, Mrs. Hannah T. 85. 1/10/1830. BR.
Jamison, Henry. 76. 9/11/1896. TI.

Jamison, Isaac. 1. 5/12/1814. BR.
Jamison, Jacob. 70. 5/7/1904. BR.
Jamison, Mrs. Jane Dickey. 22. 1763. BR.
Jamison, John. 84. 1842. BR.
Jamison, John. 81. 10/5/1864. BR.
Jamison, John. 76. 8/23/1900. RT.
Jamison, John W. 52. 4/5/1891. TI
Jamison, John William. 80. 9/14/1928. RT.
Jamison, Mrs. Lee Bryant. 35. 1/10/1919. FC.
Jamison, Louis F. 94. 1/18/1928. BR.
Jamison, Louis S. 13. 6/4/1922. TI.
Jamison, Miss Lucy A. 67. 6/26/1918. RT.
Jamison, Mrs. Martha E. 73. 7/31/1930. RT.
Jamison, Miss Mary. 4. 10/1/1815. BR.
Jamison, Riley B. 67. 4/21/1933. BR.
Jamison, Mrs. Sallie Simms. 82. 4/23/1930. RT.
Jamison, Mrs. Sallie Showalter. 88. 3/9/1906. TI.
Jamison, Mrs. Sallie Webster. 40. 7/11/1851. BR.
Jamison, Samuel. 71. 4/22/1881. BR.
Jamison, Samuel H. 62. 12/12/1924. FC.
Jamison, Samuel Henry. 68. 7/11/1926. RT.
Jamison, Mrs. Sarah Elizabeth. 80. 8/10/1930. RT.
Jamison, Mrs. Sarah Viola. 29. 7/27/1934. RT.
Jamison, Thomas. 98. 4/6/1830. BR.
Johnson, John Newton. 87. 9/27/1930. RT.

Kesler, George E. 63. 2/5/1854. TI.
Kesler, Ludowick. 90. 4/10/1854. TI.
Kesler, Mrs. Mary Boone. 82. 3/23/1853. TI.
Kinsey, Mrs. Alie Abshire. 92. 10/2/1904. BR.
Kinsey, Cornelius. 84. 8/6/1887. BR.
Kinsey, Mrs. Elizabeth Hartzell. 81. 1857. BR.
Kinsey, Jacob. 73. 2/17/1854. BR.
Kinsey, Mrs. Mariah Hill. 70. 7/9/1888. BR.
Kinsey, Otey. 64. 12/30/1872. BR.
Kinsey, Thomas A. 9/1/1935. RT.
Kinsey, William Marshall. 1915. BR.
Kinsey, William Russell. 70. 12/27/1921. BR.
Kinsey, Mrs. W. R. 83. 1/19/1935. BR.

Lemon, Joel B. 82. 1/9/1910. RT.
Lemon, Dr. Rufus M. 60. 10/28/1916. WN.

Martin, Mrs. Joseph. 70. 2/20/1925. FC.
Mills, Mrs. Sarah Maggie Saunders. 44. 9/5/1900. BR.
Mitchell, Mrs. Eugenia Akers. 77. 12/10/1930. RT.
Moorman, Kate Price. 68. 10/30/1921. BR.
Motley, John Fontaine. 48. 5/1/1898. RT.
Mullens, Edmund T. 7/9/1913. 95. FC.
Mullens, Mrs. Martha E. Hill. 39. 1/23/1863. BR.
Mullens, Mrs. Sallie Peters. 71. 9/20/1904. BR.

Naff, Abram I. 83. 12/24/1908. BR.
Naff, Mrs. Ann Turner. 77. 5/29/1917. BR.
Naff, Elder Daniel H. 76. 11/30/1924. FC.
Noftsinger, Mrs. Susan Boone. 73. 1861. BR.

Passley, J. Taylor. 56. 4/12/1933. RT.
Peters, Mrs. Christina Brubaker. 70. 7/25/1861. BR.
Peters, Daniel G. 68. 1/11/1897. TI.
Peters, David. 81. 4/28/1864. BR.
Peters, David. 68. 5/28/1891. TI.
Peters, Mrs. Elizabeth Stover. 79. 7/23/1904. TI.
Peters, Dr. Henry D. 83. 5/1/1901. BR.
Peters, Herbert Grayson. 65. 8/31/1925. RT.
Peters, James. 6. 8/20/1864. TI.
Peters, John B. 74. 12/18/1888. TI.
Peters, John W. 21. 2/19/1885. TI.
Peters, Jonathan. 89. 5/11/1914. TI.
Peters, Margaret. 26. 9/28/1876. TI.
Peters, Michael. 90. 12/26/1807. TI.
Peters, Mrs. Sallie R. 48. 12/27/1908. TI.
Peters, S. B. 82. 1/23/1935. RT.
Peters, Stephen M. 32. 11/24/1852. BR.
Peters, Thomas J. 66. 10/1/1917. TI.
Peters, Mrs. Tobitha Fralin. 69. 1/13/1891. TI.
Peters, Warren. 4. 7/19/1864. TI.
Pinkard, Rebecca Price. 62. 1/25/1857. Br.
Price, Charles Benjamin. 64. 2/19/1922. BR.
Price, Cyrus Sr. 77. 4/27/1877. BR.
Price, Cyrus S. 25. 5/16/1903. FC.
Price, Mrs. Elizabeth Boone. 82. 12/3/1896. BR.
Price, Ferdinand. 70. 12/2/1886. BR.
Price, Elizabeth Hill. 64. 12/19/1841. BR.
Price, George W. 58. 1/29/1905. BR.
Price, Henry C. 69. 9/29/1919. BR.
Price, James T. 19. 8/23/1862. BR.
Price, Jane Hancock. 30. 12/12/1858. BR.
Price, Mrs. Jennie Shaver. 80. 7/17/1934. BR.
Price, Joseph. 92. 9/30/1862. BR.
Price, Mrs. Lucinda Burroughs. 82. 1/31/1912. BR.
Price, Merit. 31. 1841. BR.
Price, Mrs. Minnie Hopkins. 49. 9/21/1913. BR.
Price, Mrs. Mollie Lemon. 38. 8/15/1906. BR.
Price, Showers. 86. 12/19/1849. BR.
Price, Taswell. 78. 12/27/1897. BR.
Price, Thomas Marshall. 43. 5/ /1898. BR.
Price, Warfield. 79. 1893. BR.
Price, William Ferdinand. 43. 4/19/1906. BR.

Renick, Capt. Calvin B. 98. 2/2/1934. RT.
Reynolds, Tommie. 96. 7/21/1914. RT.
Ross, Mrs. Laura Webster. 74. 10/30/1926. BR.

Saul, Currie. 20. 2/24/1904. RT.
Saul, Mrs. Henrietta. 74. 1/31/1931. RT.
Saul, John Peter. 75. 7/16/1930. RT.
Saul, Tazwell E. 77. 6/2/1930. WN.
Saunders, Andrew Jackson. 88. 3/30/1915. RT.
Saunders, Mrs. Ann Peters. 70. 9/5/1893. BR.
Saunders, Benjamin Franklin. 39. 1/29/1910. BR.
Saunders, Mrs. Emma Webster. 25. 7/17/1890. TI.
Saunders, James Daniel. 82. 8/8/1933. BR.
Saunders, Mrs. John Booth. 82. 9/24/1934. RT.
Saunders, John Rollins. 83. 4/13/1884. BR.
Saunders, John William. 55. 3/13/1920.
Saunders, Mrs. Nancy Webster. 64. 1/1/1903. FC.
Sigman, Ottie L. 38. 7/15/1931. RT.
Sink, Monroe T. 60. 12/31/1932. RT.
Slone, Samuel H. 91. 9/2/1934. RT.
Smith, Mrs. Callie Boone. 32. 3/10/1878. TI.
Snyder, Jacob. 79. 9/6/1911. BR.
St. Clair, Mrs. Bettie. 72. 4/18/1919. RT.

Tench, George Cabel. 64. 7/30/1936. RT.
Tench, Thomas K. 70. 8/22/1929. RT.
Terrell, Dr. J. J. 93. 11/7/1932. BR.
Terrell, Mrs. Susan Wade. 79. 10/19/1919. BR.
Tinsley, Dr. Edw. O. 68. 5/7/1936. RT.
Tinsley, Mrs. Maranda. 73. 6/1/1916. FC.
Toney, Mrs. Jane. 83. 1/24/1894. FC.
Toney, Miss Polly. 85. 1/24/1894. FC.
Trenor, Mrs. Mary Jamison. 80. 6/14/1928. RT.
Turnbull, Mrs. Sue Elizabeth. 74. 12/29/1928. RT.
Turnbull, William J. 86. 8/20/1931. RT.
Turner, Callohill M. 82. 1/31/1922. RT.

Wade, Mrs. Mary Boone. 20. 7//1844. BR.
Wade, Mrs. Susan. 26. 7/31/1844. BR.
Wade, Mrs. Susan Helen. 79. 10/19/1919. BR.
Wade, Zackfield. 26. 7//1844. BR.
Webster, Adam R. 50. 3/24/1874. BR.
Webster, Mrs. Alice Abshire. 36. 7/16/1901. RT.
Webster, Amerit. 62. 9/18/1887. BR.
Webster, Ammon R. 56. 12/9/1932. RT.
Webster, Averit. 44. 7/20/1863. BR.
Webster, Ben. w. 26. 12/10/1910. RT.
Webster, Berkley. 35. 11/20/1924. FC.
Webster, Miss Betsey. 79. 1/24/1885. BR.
Webster, C. 7/10/1831. TI.
Webster, Mrs. Catherine Jamison. 74. 9/15/1890. BR.
Webster, Mrs. Catherine Peters. 85. 6/12/1897. BR.
Webster, Charlotte. 61. 11/16/1906. TI.
Webster, Clematine. 67. 12/31/1890. BR.
Webster, Cyrus Price. 69. 1898. Br.
Webster, Daniel. 53. 5/15/1863. BR.
Webster, Daniel Silas. 47. 5/31/1897. FC.

Webster, David. 75. 2/19/1865. BR.
Webster, David. 49. 11/4/1860. Br.
Webster, Mrs. Deborah. 33. 10/15/1838. BR.
Webster, Mrs. Elizabeth Sowder. 34. 5/16/1859. BR.
Webster, Mrs. Ellen Hill. 2/4/1891. BR.
Webster, Elmira. 87. 1908. BR.
Webster, Miss Emma Lillian. 25. 12/26/1929. RT.
Webster, George. 46. 6/14/1829. TI.
Webster, Harvey Asher. 60. 12/14/1887. BR.
Webster, Herbert L. 34. 11/25/1914. FC.
Webster, Jacob R. 52. 5/2/1904. BR.
Webster, James. 56. 7/23/1862. BR.
Webster, Jesse Bigbie. 46. 1833. BR.
Webster, Joel Lee. 72. 12/2/1918. RT.
Webster, John Henry. 26. 8/6/1908. RT.
Webster, John Henry. 22. 4/20/1862. BR.
Webster, John R. 86. 6/3/1891. BR.
Webster, John William. 60. 10/15/1930. RT.
Webster, Mrs. Kate Saunders. 80. 8/30/1934. BR.
Webster, Mrs. Katherine H. 80. 9/9/1930. WN.
Webster, Louis. 59. 9/11/1872. BR.
Webster, Mrs. Lucy Dillon. 35. 3/16/1901. BR.
Webster, Lucinda Ann. 71. 1906. BR.
Webster, Luke. 73. 4/10/1898. TI.
Webster, Malery. 22. 5/9/1844. BR.
Webster, Mary. 78. 8/3/1920. TI.
Webster, Mrs. Mary A. 65. 8/2/1917. RT.
Webster, Mrs. Mary Allen. 54. 5/6/1862. BR.
Webster, Mrs. Mary Denn. 64. 3/22/1896. BR.
Webster, Norman Edward. 26. 10/20/1903. RT.
Webster, Paul R. 7. 11/19/1922. TI.
Webster, Mrs. Peggy Ricard. 94. 5/3/1876. BR.
Webster, Pollis Hillery. 71. 1897. BR.
Webster, R. B. 75. 9/6/1929. RT.
Webster, Reuben. 45. 2/22/1865. BR.
Webster, Reuben K. 78. 11/18/1920. BR.
Webster, Miss Sallie. 48. 11/3/1926. RT.
Webster, Sarah Jane. 54. 1888. BR.
Webster, Mrs. Susan Akers. 83. 7/14/1904. BR.
Webster, Susanna. 92. 11/20/1930. BR.
Webster. Mrs. Tabitha C. 79. 2/23/1923. RT.
Webster, Taswell. 79. 7/16/1930. RT.
Webster, Tyra Thompson. 73. 4/21/1905. BR.
Webster, W. H. 75. 1/3/1888. TI.
Webster, William Bird. 87. 2/10/1926. BR.
Webster, William David. 20. 9/14/1862. BR.
Webster, Walter L. 43. 3/16/1923. BR.
Webster, Yeloving Oliver. 66. 1897. BR.
Wingfield, Mrs. Lucy Dillard. 79. 10/2/1934. RT.
Wingfield, Tazewell T. 62. 5/ /1920. CC.
Wingfield, William Jasper. 79. 1/31/1930. CN.
Woodrum, Mrs. Amanda. 70. 9/15/1919. RT.

Wright, Mrs. Elizabeth Jamison.  84.  10/1/1890.  BR.
Wright, Mrs. Mary Wood Jamison.  87.  7/18/1925.  BR.
Wright, Minton M.  81.  3/8/1934.  BR.

Young, Mrs. Lucy A.  46.  8/5/1874.  TI.

## RECORDS OF FAIRMONT BAPTIST CHURCH, DILLON'S MILL, VA.

| NAMES | DEATH DATES | NAMES | DEATH DATES |
|---|---|---|---|
| Abshire, Mary | Aug.14,1890 | Hill, Louvinia A. | Jan.3,1888 |
| Akers, Eli | Dec.31.1862 | | |
| Akers, Levina | June 12,1871 | Jamison, Henry | Sept.11,1896 |
| Akers, Lucy | Aug.14,1874 | Jamison, Jane E. | Feb.22,1866 |
| Akers, William | Oct.28,1866 | | |
| Angell, Emma I. | Apr.2,1873 | Leftwich, Maranda | Oct. 6,1879 |
| Angell, Joshua H. | May 31,1864 | Livesy, Ursula | Dec. 1899 |
| | (of wound) | | |
| Angell, Looney | Feb. 14,1866 | Mitchell,James R. | June 1894 |
| Angell, Maggie | June 1895 | | |
| Angle, Caleb | Dec.7,1877 | Nunley, A. J. | Mar. 3,1889 |
| | | | |
| Beach, John B. | 1882 | Price,Ferdinand | Dec. 6, 1886 |
| Boatwright, M.E. | Feb. 1886 | Price, George W. | Jan. 29,1905 |
| Boon, Mary S. | Dec. 8,1867 | Price, J. H. | May 16,1888 |
| | (age 20) | Price, Lucinda K. | |
| Bowles, Aley A. | June 3,1882 | Price, Thomas M. | May 6, 1898 |
| | | | |
| Custer, Ruth | 1877 | Smith, John A. | July 19,1863 |
| | | Smith, Tenah | June 3, 1862 |
| Dillon, Paxie | Aug. 2,1898 | Snyder, Manerva | Feb. 1888 |
| Dobyns, V. A. | May 4,1887 | Snyder, Mariah | Aug. 22,1867 |
| | | | (wife of Geo.) |
| Gibson, Tabitha J. | 1899 | | |
| Greer, Ursula | Nov.18,1880 | Tinsley, Jannie | Feb. 1884 |
| Greer, William W. | July 4,1885 | Tinsley, John T. | Aug. 29,1887 |
| Griffith, Amanda | Feb.27,1864 | Turnbull,Elizabeth | Jan.17,1871 |
| Guilliams,Robert | (in army) | | |
| Gusler, John | Aug. 1894 | Wade, Malissa | Dec. 27,1872 |
| Gusler, Sarah | Mar.30,1874. | Wade, Octavia | Aug. 29,1855 |
| | | Webb, Creed T. | June 30,1868 |
| Heckman, Jane | Aug.19,1877 | Webb. Mahaloe F. | June 11,1863 |
| Heckman,Julia A. | 1893 | Webb, Malissa | Jan. 1893 |
| Hechman, Sally | Jan. 1877 | Webb, Seline | Mar. 4,1866 |
| Hickman, Joseph | Aug.18,1873 | Webb, T. A. | Dec. 1894 |
| | (Heckman) | Webb, Virginia | June 5, 1880 |

<u>CONFEDERATE BONDS</u>

Franklin County issued bonds to assist in providing for the families of indigent soldiers who were away from the county in the service of the State or Confederate States. The author does not know how many such bond issues there were. He has in his possession a photostatic copy of one such bond purchased by Joel Harper, in the sum of $600.00. It was issued on 5th day of January 1864, and is signed by Peter Saunders, Jr., Presiding Justice of Franklin County, and by Robert A. Scott, Clerk of the County Court. The bond reads as follows: "State of Virginia, Franklin County. Know all men by these presents, that the County of Franklin in the State of Virginia, is held and firmly bound unto Joel Harper, in the sum of Six Hundred Dollars, to be paid on or before the first day of January, in the year 1866, with interest at the rate of five per cent, per annum from the date of issue endorsed on this bond, payable on the first day of January in each year after date; but privilege is reserved to the County to pay the principal of this bond, or any part thereof, before it shall become due.

"In testimony whereof, the Presiding Justice of the Court of Franklin has hereto set his hand and caused the Seal of the County to be affixed by the Clerk, on this the 5th day of January in the year 1864."

A memorandum states: "The foregoing bond is executed in pursuance of an order of the County Court of Franklin County, made on November 2nd, 1863."

The Court Order reads as follows:

"Franklin County Court Nov. 2nd, 1863.

"It appearing to the Court by the report of Robert A. Scott agent of this County under the order made by this Court on the ___ day of June 1863, that the said agent has expended under said order for the benefit of the families of indigent soldiers the sum of Nineteen thousand two hundred and fifty five dollars of the appropriation made by said order for that purpose.

"And the Court proceeding to consider what further provision is necessary to be made for the maintenance of the families of indigent soldiers from this County who are in the military service of this State or of the Confederate States and for the maintenance of indigent soldiers who have been disabled in said service and of their families and also for the maintenance of the families of indigent soldiers who have been killed or have died in said service, it is ordered that the further sum of sixty thousand dollars be appropriated for the purposes aforesaid, and the County doth appoint Robert A. Scott, Commissioner or agent to negotiate loans to that amount and to enable him to do so the presiding justice of this Court shall cause bonds of this County to be issued signed by himself and countersigned by the Clerk of this Court and shall cause the seal of this Court to be affixed thereto but the said bonds shall not be valid or binding until issued by the said Commissioner and shall not be sold by him for less than their par value and one third of the amount so negotiated shall be payable

on the 1st day of January 1866 and one third on the first day of
January 1867 and the residue on the 1st day of January 1868 and
the right shall be reserved to pay the whole or any part of the
money so borrowed at any time before the same shall fall due.

"And it shall be the duty of the said Commissioner to pay
out and disburse the said money as he shall be from time to time
hereafter directed by this Court.

"And he shall receive for his compensation two and one
half per centum of the money so borrowed by him and shall keep
accurate accounts of his receipts and disbursements and shall
exhibit the same before this Court whenever required by the Court
to do so."

247

249

252

257

258

273

293

297

www.ingramcontent.com/pod-product-compliance
Lightning Source LLC
Chambersburg PA
CBHW060146280326
41932CB00012B/1655